$ 3.00

A READER'S GUIDE TO THE

Social Sciences

EDITED BY

BERT F. HOSELITZ

WITH CHAPTERS BY

PETER M. BLAU AND JOAN W. MOORE

HEINZ EULAU

NORTON S. GINSBURG

BERT F. HOSELITZ

GAIL KELLY

WALTER R. REITMAN

THE FREE PRESS OF GLENCOE

Copyright © 1959 by The Free Press, a corporation

Printed in the United States of America

DESIGNED BY SIDNEY SOLOMON

Library of Congress Catalog Card No.: 57-12636

Third Printing 1963

Preface

The idea for this volume on the literature of the social sciences was initially suggested by the requirements of library education. After World War II a tendency developed in library education to place less emphasis upon training in library practices as such and more upon providing the student with increased knowledge about the contents of books and the criteria of evaluating them. Among efforts to implement such objectives, a number of experiments were made with guides to the literature of the several disciplines, and one of these, dealing with the interpretation, evaluation, and use of library materials in the humanities has appeared under the title *The Humanities and the Library,* by Lester Asheim and associates (1957). That volume is based upon the content of introductory courses in the Graduate Library School of the University of Chicago and divides its attention between the literature of the humanities and the library's problems in organizing and servicing it. In the course of the experimentation with the present volume on the social sciences, the idea developed that a volume on the literature of the social sciences might be useful to a wider audience than librarians and at the same time might serve that group as well. Thus the focus finally adopted here centered on the task of presenting a general introduction to the literature of the social sciences that would deal with the differences in the literary output in the major disciplines and the nature of available tools, in the form of books, journals, pamphlets, and reference works, that are consulted and used by social scientists in their research and teaching. The present volume may serve, therefore, not only as a guide to librarians, but also as an introduction to the general reader interested in the literary output of the different social sciences, and even to social scientists in one discipline who wish to obtain a general overview of the literature of a sister discipline.

Although many books and quite a few journal articles are cited in this study, this is not a bibliography. An attempt has been made in each chapter to refer to the more important "classics" in each field, but beyond this the chief interest of each contributor has been to present a description of the type of literary output and its uses in a field of specialization, rather than a list of works. Some attention has been paid to including not only works incorporating substantive contributions, but also those discussing methodological questions, and each contributor has been free to add sections on popularized works in his fields and special items of interest in the literature of his specialty.

The books mentioned in each chapter are not necessarily selected because they are the worthiest titles in a field. In many instances, works have been cited because they present certain peculiarities worth discussion, and many of the titles are referred to mainly as examples of a type of writing or a kind of study, e.g., a "typical monograph" or a "typical textbook." Often some other titles—or, indeed, a dozen other titles—might have been put in the place of the works actually mentioned. In other words, this study is not a basic tool for the preparation of a reading list in general or specialized courses in any social science discipline. Although an effort was made to select "good" books for citation, the quality of a work has been only one of the criteria used for inclusion.

In the course of developing the successive drafts leading to the final version presented in this volume, a number of persons have made valuable suggestions. Among those who made valuable comments and suggestions, and to whom I wish to express my thanks, are Irving Kaplan, Martin Deutsch, Dorothy Stock, Bruce L. Smith, Mildred Henry, Beata Peterson, Daniel Glaser, Martin Diamond, Edward Banfield, Margaret Egan, Dorothy Kittel, Morris Janowitz, Elliot Schrero, John Armstrong, Jr., Edgar Friedenberg, Carl Kaspin, J. S. Slotkin, Elaine Bjorkland, and Donald M. Baer. It should be clearly understood, however, that only the authors of the various chapters in this book are responsible for the texts as they actually appear. I also wish to express my gratitude to my friend and colleague, Mr. Bernard Berelson, who by his constant encouragement has greatly contributed to the completion of this project. The Carnegie Corporation deserves our thanks for a grant made to the Graduate Library School of the University of Chicago out of which the research leading to this publication was supported. The first chapter of this work is an abbreviated and somewhat revised version of a paper that appeared in the *Journal of General Education,* IV, No. 2, 85-103. I am grateful to the University of Chicago Press for giving permission to reprint this material. Mrs. Lois Fern has undertaken to check the entire manuscript as to completeness and accuracy of authors and titles. (She also made the index appended to the book.) Mrs. Georgianna March and Miss Barbara Tauber typed the final draft of the manuscript. Finally, I wish to thank the authors of the various chapters for their patience and the real spirit of friendliness with which they have adjusted to a sometimes impatient and often idiosyncratic editor.

BERT F. HOSELITZ

Contents

CHAPTER I

The Social Sciences in the Last Two Hundred Years

The social sciences, of course, are more than two hundred years old. In discussing the methodological imperfections of their disciplines—primarily as compared to the exact mathematical formulations of theoretical physics—social scientists have often explained these shortcomings away by mentioning the youth of social science. This excuse, however, is shallow. Theoretical and analytical speculations about matters of social import are as old as similar speculations about the physical and biological universe. Plato's *Republic* is roughly contemporaneous with the *Hippocratic Collection,* and Aristotle's political writings appeared two generations before the works of Archimedes on mechanics.

If a case for the greater age of the physical sciences can properly be made, it rests, at best, on the relative date at which the various sciences arose as organized systems of knowledge. In antiquity and in the Middle Ages we encounter a certain amount of speculative philosophical and sometimes empirical analysis of scientific problems. However, it would be wrong to say that any of the natural sciences took shape before Kepler and Galileo. The beginnings of astronomy as a unified body of science go back to the sixteenth century, the beginnings of mechanics as an exact integrated science to the seventeenth. History, economics, and politics as unified disciplines are only a very little younger.

The historical evolution of the social sciences in the last two hundred years is of special interest, nevertheless, because the various disciplines as they are recognized today developed during this period and serious and penetrating questions were asked for the first time about the methods used in the social sciences and about their relation to each other and to other fields of scientific knowledge.

If we look back at the history of scientific endeavor since the early seventeenth century, we find during the one hundred and fifty years beginning in the second decade of the seventeenth century an imposing array of achievements and innovations in the field of biological and physical sciences, while the social sciences remain almost completely stagnant. Few contributions in the social sciences of the times can be placed beside the work of Descartes and Leibnitz, of Galileo and Newton, of Halley and Boyle, of Pascal and Huygens, of Leeuwenhoek and Harvey, of Linnaeus and Buffon. The latter half of the seventeenth and the first half of the eighteenth centuries were periods in which the interest in natural science was supreme. Paraphrasing a terse statement of Huizinga, the great new event which then was brought to light was the advance and victory of natural science as a way of looking at the world, which led to the overtaking and overshadowing of the historical point of view by the scientific point of view. (Johan Huizinga, "Naturbild und Geschichtsbild im achtzehnten Jahrhundert," in *Parerga* 1945, pp. 150 ff.)

The intellectual climate of opinion during the Middle Ages and the period of the Renaissance was predominantly humanistic and devoted to history. In part this was due to the antiempirical bias of medieval philosophy, in part to the deep interest in man and his salvation that was traditional with Christian theology and of which some features were taken up by the intellectual leaders of the Renaissance and humanism as the most significant aspect of ancient philosophy. The forms taken by the religious conflicts following the Reformation decidedly emphasized historical research. In the effort to determine the true doctrine, to assay the claims of the papacy to absolute religious authority, to defend one's own or attack opposing religious doctrine, the best and most convincing instrument was the appeal to the earliest sources of the Christian religion, to the Apostles and the Fathers of the Church. Hence we find that natural science, although not completely dormant, yet is noticeably alive only on the periphery. The greatest progress in medieval physical science and medicine was made by the Arabs and Jews. The sole "empiricist" among the Christian philosophers of the Middle Ages, Roger Bacon, deserves this designation chiefly by virtue of his methodological views rather than because of rigorous empirical scientific investigations carried on by him. With the beginning of the sixteenth century, natural science began to advance but erupted into full flowering only a century later with the work of Galileo and Descartes. Although we encounter Leonardo, Paracelsus, Copernicus, and Vesalius in the sixteenth century, the major scientific interest of the age was still lodged in the humanities. The intellectual leaders of that period were not the natural scientists but humanists like Erasmus and Thomas More and the men heading the religious movements of the time. Only Francis Bacon does not quite fit into the pattern. He, like his namesake, Roger, three centuries earlier, made his most important contribution, however, in the area of scientific methodology; in contrast to the views of Roger, his opinions met with ready acceptance. While his contemporaries Erasmus, More, and Calvin stood at the end of an era in the history of ideas, Bacon stands on the threshold of a new age.

Although the period from about 1620 to about 1760 stressed the study of natural science, it is nevertheless true that some effort was spent on the study of man and society. Hobbes's *Leviathan,* Locke's *Two Treatises on Government,* Vico's *New Science,* and Montesquieu's *Spirit of Laws* were all conceived and published in this period. In addition, there exists an abundance of economic and political tracts on questions of the day and a vast literature on religious, historical, and other humanist topics. Yet, in spite of their lasting value and their contemporary importance, Hobbes's and Locke's political works were of the nature of tracts written with an eye on the events of the day; Vico's work suffered a fate similar to that of Roger Bacon in the Middle Ages: it was neglected and forgotten for many years. Only Montesquieu stands at the threshold of that remarkable awakening of speculation about the nature and purpose of human society in France which forms one of the sources of the new concern with social science.

The revival of interest in social science occurred in the middle of the eighteenth century. Although France took the earliest leadership in this movement, it soon spread to other countries; and the roots of this renewed interest and the new attitude toward social science are to be found in the Scottish moral philosophy, in the English revolt against religious orthodoxy, and in German critical philosophy.

The main reason for this gradual increase of interest in social science and the growing intensity of intellectual labor spent on social problems is to be found in the changed pattern of the social fabric in which these movements occurred. By the middle of the eighteenth century, capitalism had begun to outgrow its early stage, and gradually it became the dominant socio-economic system in western and northern Europe. At that time the rising middle class had already won important positions in the social life of the industrially most highly developed countries, notably France, Holland, and Britain. In Germany and Italy it still lagged behind both in relative size and in social importance. But as the bourgeoisie gained in political influence and the old, established institutions began to give way under the pressures created by a rising capitalism, these very institutions, their origins and their survival values, their justification and their function, began to be questioned. The social and political structure became the objects of critical analysis, just as the orbits of the planets and the revolutions of the solar system had been subjected to critical study some two hundred years earlier.

Simultaneously with the rising influence of the bourgeoisie as a class, with the growth of industrialism, and with the ever more perfect "rationalization" of economic life, there occurred changes in the social fabric of the western European countries which were too obvious to be overlooked by their contemporaries. Outstanding among them, and in many ways the starting point of social-reform proposals, was the shift in population and the rapid development of large, squalid, overcrowded cities. The concentration of population in urban centers had started in the first part of the eighteenth century; many of the chief industrial towns of Britain—Manchester, Liverpool, Birmingham, Sheffield, Leeds, Glasgow—had grown from villages of not more than a few thousand inhabitants in 1700 to cities many times that size by 1760. In the second half of the eighteenth century, urbanization and population growth became accelerated, and it was during this period that the first symptoms of disorganization–slums, alcoholism, brutality of manners, etc.–developed, which were to become the targets of social reformers in the succeeding generations.

These conditions–the gradual transfer of political power to a new class; the increase of visible material wealth through investment in new plant and the rise of new industries; the new experiences through more frequent and more intimate contact with exotic and strange peoples; the accumulation of wealth gained in risky overseas enterprises; and the growing concentration of the "laboring poor" in the cities–were such obvious new developments as to clamor for analysis and scientific study.

Another factor which must be mentioned as setting the background for the rise of the new social science was the development of new philosophical ideas. This is not the place to give a detailed account of the history of philosophy of the time. In a very crude fashion it may be said that the decisive characteristic of the philosophy developed in Europe in the seventeenth and eighteenth centuries is its skepticism. It began with Descartes; it was apparent in the work of Locke; and it found its culmination in the philosophical writings of David Hume. Leslie Stephen says rightly of Hume that he,

> unlike Berkeley or Locke, was absolutely free from theological prepossessions. He, and he alone, amongst contemporary thinkers, followed logic wherever it led him.... From his writings we may date the definite abandonment of the philosophical conceptions of the preceding century, leading in some cases to an abandonment of the great questions as insoluble, and, in others, to an attempt to solve them by a new method. Hume did not destroy ontology or theology, but he destroyed the old ontology; and all later thinkers who have not been content with the mere dead bones of extinct philosophy, have built up their systems on entirely new lines. (Leslie Stephen, *History of English Thought in the Eighteenth Century,* 1876, I, 43.)

Hume was an exceptional man. He was more penetrating and more logically consistent than his disciples. While his philosophical views were, on the one hand, the product of his time, on the other, they impressed a new stamp on his contemporaries. The old naïve authoritarian theology was gone; dogmatic sectarianism in religion only survived in a few out-of-the-way spots, and even there its life was short. The emphasis in ethical speculation passed from the contemplation of eternal salvation to the principle of the greatest happiness of the greatest number. The dawn of utilitarianism in ethics and psychology was at hand.

When one looks from the vantage point of the twentieth century at the development of social theory around the middle of the eighteenth century, the points of departure which this theorizing took seem almost inevitable. In the absolutist state with its predominating dynastic interests that was the rule on the European continent, the social relations of all classes but the highest ranks of the aristocracy were of no interest. History consisted chiefly of disjointed and usually partisan accounts of the lives of kings and nobles, of battles and court anecdotes, of royal marriages and diplomatic feats. No unity was seen or looked for in history, no systematic investigation of sociological, economic, or political relations was attempted.

It is easy to understand that in such a situation the attention of critics of the existing social order was directed to finding the principles of a "natural" order of society as contrasted with the then existing order, which was felt to impede the full and free development of the rising middle class. But, in studying the "natural order" of society, men were driven almost unconsciously to a comparison of the legal, political, and general social systems of the European states with those of antiquity and of the newly discovered or rediscovered lands–India, China, Persia, and, most important of all, the cultures of the primitive savages in America and the South Seas. The role that the telescope had played for astronomy, that the laboratory played for natural science, was comparable to the role played by the primitive savage of America, man in the "state of nature," for the social science of the eighteenth century. Here was an ideal yardstick by which the existing political and social institutions could be measured. True, the state of nature described by Hobbes, Locke, and Rousseau is a fiction; it is not based on an attempt to describe the actual culture of the primitive peoples even as it was known then. But, although this part of their work was scarcely based on empirical research and although a careful examination of primitive cultures would probably not have enabled them to draw the conclusions which they could base on their fictions, the discovery of and interest in primitive peoples made possible the application of comparative methods in the study of politics and social psychology.

Before this interest in the children of nature became crystallized and before sufficient information about them was available, any comparison between cultures which could have been made would have had to use classical antiquity as a yardstick. But men like Socrates or Cicero could have found themselves at home in the Europe of the sixteenth and seventeenth centuries with little discomfort and only few readjustments. The constitution of the Greek city-state was not sufficiently dissimilar from that of a Swiss canton to invite extensive examination. The Persians of Montesquieu and the Hurons of Voltaire, on the contrary, were known to have a culture sufficiently different from that of eighteenth-century France to make them representative and believable critics of European society of that time.

How fruitful was the use of the comparative method in the social sciences is shown by the work of Montesquieu. His *Spirit of Laws* has sometimes been criticized as a bad book. It has been called "diffuse" and "disorganized"; a showpiece in which irrelevant and unimportant topics are frequently blown up to the size of full sections or chapters in order to provide an opportunity for the author to display his erudition; it was charged with having no central theme and with being wordy and sometimes tedious. In spite of all this, the work has two characteristics which assure it a deserved place in the list of classics of social science. It is the first attempt consciously to establish politics as a *social* science. However farfetched and wrong some of Montesquieu's hypotheses may be, they are, nevertheless, hypotheses on the relation between political organization, on the one hand, and social structure, physical environment, climate, national character, etc., on the other. Its other characteristic is that it establishes political science as a predominantly empirical, positive discipline rather than a primarily normative one. Thus the book overcomes its shortcomings and may justly be said to stand at the beginning of a new epoch in social and political science, chiefly because of its method and because of the tremendous influence of this method on later work in the social sciences.

The study of primitives together with the study of classical antiquity had yet another effect. It contributed to the gradual elaboration of a theory of history. If primitive societies and institutions could be interpreted as the simpler and more backward forms of social life, if an improvement of material culture and refinement of manners was visible in antiquity from the simplicity of the Spartans under Lycurgus to the complexity of Roman civilization under the Caesars, and if, again, a refinement of customs and learning was discernible in Europe from the Dark Ages onward, then a theory of the progress of mankind suggested itself. And in the second half of the eighteenth century we find this theory elaborated and brought to a high level of development in the work of the Abbé de St. Pierre, Turgot, and, above all, Condorcet. By that time it had passed the stage of a mere hypothesis on the course of history and had become an almost universally accepted dogma. But this rapid rise of the theory of progress was made possible by its apparent obviousness. Voltaire's arguments, presented in his *Essay on the Manners and Mind of Nations* and with more force and general appeal in his *Age of Louis XIV,* are examples of contributions containing the evidence for the theory. But, since the idea of progress was assumed in their composition, these were not idle assemblages of interesting and curious facts, but "philosophical" works consciously designed to establish the theory on the basis of empirical knowledge.

It is difficult to overestimate the importance of the theory of progress on the later development of social science. It exercised an influence on William Godwin and, through him, on Malthus and early political economy. It formed the basis of such varied philosophical systems as Hegel's philosophy of history, Auguste Comte's positivism, and Marxian historical materialism. It provided a point of departure for archeological speculations; it was taken up by Spencer, and after 1859, in combination with the stimulus provided by Darwin's *Origin of Species,* it influenced the formulation of ideas which led to the elaboration of theories of social anthropology. Although the theory of progress of the human mind is today abandoned as a scientific hypothesis, it lives on in a vulgarized form among the populace, who identify "progress" with the creation of "bigger and better" things, whether these things are houses, automobiles, battleships, or atomic bombs.

If France was the cradle of the new social science, Scotland was the place where it was brought to the highest stage of perfection in the eighteenth century. The primary tie connecting the French writers with one another was the *Encyclopédie*. This work was twice suppressed temporarily by the French crown; its publication was hampered by almost constant financial troubles; and its editors overcame these difficulties only because of the determined and sympathetic help of many independent thinkers, men of letters, and enlightened courtiers. Thus in France the fostering and communication of the new social thought was an enterprise of private individuals who were in many ways opposed to the holders of political and ecclesiastical power and who could not command the support of any officially sanctioned institutions. The Scottish "moralists," on the other hand, were connected by their common participation in academic life. With the exception of Hume, all the chief social scientists of the Scottish circle stood to each other in a teacher-student relationship or were colleagues working at universities connected by a friendly rivalry. While the polemic flavor had never been quite absent in the works of the French writers, the cool-headed Scottish professors took a more detached attitude, and, devoted to the unimpassioned logic of Hume and the rule of empiricism as the principal method, they produced works on ethics, sociology, and economics which are often surprisingly modern in attitude and outlook.

Thus, if we may say that Montesquieu and Voltaire broke a new path for politics and history, Francis Hutcheson, Adam Smith, Adam Ferguson, and Thomas Reid established the groundwork for the later development of ethics, economics, and sociology. Simultaneously, the Scottish school developed some of the basic concepts of psychology, which, although still strongly influenced by the ideas of the then prevailing theories of associationism, yet in several points go beyond this theory, notably in the analysis of instinct.

It would be wrong to assume that in the third quarter of the eighteenth century France and Scotland were two isolated islands of social-science speculation in a sea of indifference. A detailed analysis of the growth of social-science inquiry in other parts of Europe in this period would be beyond the scope of this essay, but a few words must be said about the history of social science in Germany, because this country was to take a leading role in several fields in the nineteenth century. If the underlying impetus to the new interest in social science was provided in France by the growth of rationalism and in Scotland by the evolution of skepticism and empiricism, this role was played in the Germanies by the development of a national consciousness, the accumulating attempts to define a common national heritage and to develop a common culture transcending the religious division and the political parochialism of the empire.

This development of the recognition of common national ties has been related by many German historians to the rise of Prussia under Frederick the Great. Following Heinrich von Treitschke, they maintain that, with the disintegration of Germany and the general poverty and political weakness of the small territories ruled by despotic, often corrupt, and frequently bankrupt princes, Prussia under Frederick stood out as a strong victorious power. If the awakening German national consciousness was looking for a focus of inspiration and hope, it could find it only in the unified, highly centralized, militarily strong Prussia, governed by a king who not only by his administrative and military efficiency but also by his philosophical and rationalist inclinations could serve as a model for the awakening national aspirations of the rising German middle class. This thesis meets, however, with a series of almost insurmountable difficulties. All the leading minds who deserve to be mentioned as forbears of a German national consciousness hated the Prussian despotism and deplored Frederick's preference for French letters, manners, and art. Just because Frederick paraded as a philosopher-king, just because he claimed to foster arts and sciences, his military despotism–which was, in reality, distinguished only by its greater efficiency and severity–evoked hatred and mistrust. Johann Winckelmann said that he shuddered from top to toe when he thought of Prussian despotism; Johann Herder fled his Prussian home and appealed to the emperor in Vienna rather than to Frederick to create a "new German fatherland"; Kant was silently antagonistic to the chicaneries emanating from Berlin; and Goethe talked of the "great steam-roller of Potsdam."

Heine was infinitely more perspicacious than Treitschke and the later German historians when he stated that what was common to all the Germans was to be found in the "realm of dreams," that is, in their common language, history, and culture. *(Germany: A Winter's Tale,* 1841 Cap. VII, vs. 6.) The roots of a German national consciousness that developed in the late eighteenth century have to be looked for in the rising interest in the historical origins of German culture and language. Celebrating these common origins, Friedrich Klopstock wrote odes to Arminius and the medieval emperor Henry I. Lessing worked on the development of a German theater and a German critical literature. Herder devised a plan for an all-German academy. This romantic nationalism which looked back into the historical past created a powerful impetus for historical study of legal and economic institutions, of language and folklore (conspicuously in the case of the brothers Grimm), and of education and philosophy. This romantic historical attitude, which is best exemplified by the works of Herder, was the cradle for the later schools of historical jurisprudence, producing such men as Savigny and Karl F. Eichhorn, and of historical economics, producing men like Wilhelm Roscher, Karl Knies, and Bruno Hildebrand.

The research into national languages and literatures, beginning with men like Johann G. Eichhorn (who, with Herder, treated the Bible as a fascinating national literature), also eventually led Germany into the evolutionist camp when continuing studies of the Bible, augmented by Near Eastern archeology, helped found the anti-orthodox "higher criticism" of the Old and New Testament, removing from their varied texts the authority of dogma.

At the beginning of the nineteenth century social science had attained in all the leading European countries a firm and respectable position. With few exceptions, it was not yet centered around universities, and in much of the writing the scientific core was still partly obscured by a generous admixture of philosophical, literary, and moralistic reflections. Although political economy and history were coming to be regarded as special fields of research, the disciplines had not yet become fully crystallized.

In Germany chairs of "cameral science" and even "economics" had been established at several universities. However, the evidence of textbooks and curriculums from that period shows that the subjects taught under these names embraced not only what we call today economics but also aspects of public administration, political theory, and military science. As a rule, the chairs of cameral science and economics were founded in the faculties of law. In scope and subject matter, cameralism was similar to that branch of moral philosophy on which Adam Smith had lectured at the University of Glasgow in the early 1760's; his subject was "Lectures on Justice, Police, Revenue, and Arms." In Britain most social science was still regarded as a branch of philosophy, and in many parts of the European Continent distinctions between law and social science, on the one hand, and ethics and social science, on the other, were still blurred and unprecise.

The characteristic features of the history of social science in the nineteenth century are three: the various disciplines became elaborated and more sharply defined in relation to one another; social sciences became recognized as independent branches of academic training and scholarly pursuit; and conscious attempts were made to elaborate adequate methodological procedures for the various social sciences. One does not go far wrong in assuming that there was a close interrelation between these three trends. It would, however, be wrong to assume that specialization is the only trend discernible in the history of the social sciences since about 1800. There have also been numerous attempts to provide a synthesis. Indeed, at some crucial points, when new philosophical or methodological ideas arose, they served as a basis for an attempted synthesis of the sciences of man and society. Comte, Spencer, Marx, to some extent John Stuart Mill, and (later in the century) the evolving school of German sociology attempted to produce a synthetic social science. In the twentieth century we can also observe recurrent occasions when proposals for a generalized social science were made. Among the more notable proposals of this kind are those of several members of the psychoanalytic school and the group of scholars associated with the *International Encyclopedia of Unified Science* (1938-). Among the first group should be counted works by Erich Fromm and Abram Kardiner, and among the second, some of the writings of Otto Neurath.

We are today closer than at any time since the late eighteenth century to the realization of a unification of social sciences on the basis of new principles, even though in the last hundred years the predominant trends have been toward greater specialization and division of tasks. Yet, in the last resort, these two trends are not necessarily contradictory. It is possible that the refinement and progressive specialization of tasks in the various social sciences may lead to a set of concepts and theories so basic to all social science that Comte's dream of what the science of "sociology" ought to be may become reality. There are grave dangers and pitfalls along this path, however, which must be recognized. Not the least of them is the problem of terminology; with increasing specialization, social scientists have developed specialized technical terms which have often tended to make communication between them difficult. Although they may have studied different aspects of the same phenomenon, there has been little co-operation among them, so that in many cases they appeared to be further apart than was really the case, chiefly because of difficulties of language. In spite of specialization of tasks, a high degree of unification of the social sciences could be brought about if a common conceptual apparatus could be developed which would render such unification easier rather than harder. What has been said about terminology appears to hold also for methods of inquiry and to some extent for theoretical generalizations.

But probably the greatest obstacle to an effective synthesis of social science has been the clannishness of many social scientists. Professional jealousy, rigid thinking along lines hidebound by tradition, vested interests in theories, concepts, and research procedures, have been among the major hindrances to a progressive elaboration of a synthetic social science. Frequently the gaps between the disciplines are rationalized by an appeal to fundamental differences in method or the nature of generalizations. There are, fortunately for the progress of social-science synthesis, signs that these attitudes are slowly being overcome. One step in this direction is the evolution of interdepartmental co-operation in universities and the bringing-together of specialists from different disciplines for the attack on a common scientific problem. But the final barrier to full co-operation in the social sciences will be removed only when all specialists are able to see and appraise their special field of research in its context within the whole field of the study of man and society. One approach toward this end may be provided by an examination of the historical development of the various disciplines and of the reasons which may be adduced to explain the origin of specialized fields as they existed throughout the nineteenth and twentieth centuries.

The formation of a new specialized discipline in any field of science is related to three conditions. The first is the existence and recognition of a set of new problems which attract the attention of several investigators. The second is the collection of a sufficient number of data which will permit the elaboration of generalizations wide enough in scope to point up the common features of the problems under investigation. The third condition is the attainment of official or institutional recognition of the new discipline. The first two conditions relate to the intellectual labor performed in the elaboration and independent constitution of the discipline, the third to the assurance of its permanence as a branch of independent study and research.

If we examine the course of development of the various social-science disciplines in the nineteenth century, we find that they follow, on the whole, a pattern through which the "older" natural sciences also passed. They originate with the recognition, often on the part of several men, of a set of related problems. Communication and interchange of ideas between them leads to the elaboration of a set of generalizations which, at least in first approximation, permits a satisfactory ordering of the significant data. Continuing work is done in refining these first principles and in elaborating existing generalizations and finding new ones. New and rival theories emerge, attempts are made to remove flaws and contradictions in the system, and, in some instances, theories are restated in such a form that new specialties tend to emerge. In the initial period of the formation of a discipline, so many new data are found, so much intellectual effort is expended on the working-out of basic generalizations, that little attention is paid to questions of method. The second stage in the maturing of a discipline sees the conscious attempt to lay down and perfect methods of research and investigation in the discipline. At this stage the discipline has, as a rule, become institutionalized to a high degree. While in its initial period it may have been the preoccupation of a group of semi-amateurs, philosophers, practical men in business and government, or gentlemen of leisure, it now becomes the subject of research on the part of academic specialists. University chairs are founded, schools of thought develop, specialized journals and professional societies become the chief platforms of exchange of ideas. In the third and most mature stage of a discipline the battles over method have subsided, the theoretical rivalries tend to be submerged in the efforts to elaborate propositions bridging the differences; contributions to the further progress of the discipline are primarily in straightening out, smoothing over, and further elaborating the edifice of basic theory which tends to become generally accepted. There are, of course, at this stage still some outsiders who are critical of the achievement. If this criticism does not descend to the crackpot level, it is wholesome for the progress of the discipline, lest its practitioners fall into the easy slumber of dogmatism.

Theoretical physics, which for so many purposes has been taken as the discipline coming closest to the "ideal type," may here also serve as a model. The set of related problems which gave rise to the elaboration of the first systematic theory were questions concerning the determination of the paths of the planets, the revolutions and phases of the moon, and the position of the solar system in relation to the fixed stars. This preoccupation suggested the examination of laws of movement in general; Newton's crowning achievement in this process was due to his "magnificent conception that the agent which guides the stars in their courses is the same as that which in our common experience causes apples to drop." (A. S. Eddington, *The Nature of the Physical World,* 1928, pp. 111-12.) The succeeding two centuries witnessed a refinement and elaboration of the Newtonian theory, the incorporation of the theory of electricity and thermodynamics and others. In this period significant methodological tools were worked out, partly in the field of higher mathematics, partly in the design of experimental situations. By the end of the nineteenth century theoretical physics was in the third stage of its development. The revolutionary innovations of Albert Einstein, Max Planck, Niels Bohr, and others could not disrupt the firm edifice of physical theory. Yet these new theories created the foundation for a more general and more perfect construction and systematization of theoretical physics. The question of whether the new hypotheses should be accepted or rejected—a problem so familiar in the social sciences—could not arise because consistent and well-worked-out methods of testing these hypotheses were available and commanded common recognition. In this sense the theory of relativity, the quantum theory, wave mechanics, and atomic theory are integral extensions of older physical theory.

Unfortunately, the history of the various social sciences is far more difficult to summarize and the unity of that history far more difficult to show than is the case with theoretical physics. Nevertheless, in a rough way, the succession of events is the same here. Let us look, for example, at economics, one of the most firmly established, and psychology, perhaps the "youngest," of the social sciences.

The problems which led to the elaboration of a systematic economic theory in the late eighteenth and early nineteenth centuries centered around the investigation into the final causes and determinants of the value of goods and services and the subsequent distribution of the social product. The progress in erecting a theoretical system of economic relations from the Physiocrats and Adam Smith to John Stuart Mill and Karl Marx, usually designated as "classical economics," was remarkable. But the introduction of new ideas—the first stage of the development of the discipline—did not come to an end until the principles of marginalism had been definitely stated in the 1870's. Then economics entered the second stage, the clarification of its method. The so-called *Methodenstreit* whose main representatives were Karl Menger and Gustav Schmoller is well known in the history of social-science methodology and does not require detailed comment. But the very heat of the argument and the wide publicity it gained because of the reputation of the chief antagonists make us forget that, simultaneously, less vociferous criticism of established methods was voiced. Abstract theory was criticized in England by Thorold Rogers and T. Cliffe Leslie; new inductive methods of reasoning were introduced by the growth of social statistics in the wake of the pioneering work of Adolphe Quételet; and a restatement of economic generalizations in mathematical form was attempted, notably by French and Italian economists. There was the brief episode of "institutional economics" in the United States. Since the end of World War I, problems of methodology in economics have tended to drop from the literature; and where they have persisted, they are, on the whole, repetitions of old arguments. On the other hand, the basic accepted theories have been extended and generalized. The study of imperfect competition led to the generalization of price theory; the analysis of indifference curves led to the generalization of the theory of value; and the increasing preoccupation with macro-economic problems, powerfully stimulated by the work of John Maynard Keynes, led to the generalization of the theory of employment and cyclical fluctuations. Although economic theory is far behind theoretical physics in precision of formulation, it shows greater unity, greater generality, and greater consistency than at any time in its history.

In psychology we can discern a similar historical pattern. Although theories about the human soul and mind are as old as philosophical speculation in general, a systematic science of personality originated only after a time when it could be said that "psychology first lost its soul, then its mind, and finally has lost consciousness altogether." (This anonymous quip is quoted from T. V. Smith, "The American Doctrine of Equality in the Light of Evolutionism," *International Journal of Ethics*, XXXV, No. 4 [July, 1925], 377.) The combination of ideas originating in the study of mental diseases, on one side, the physiology of the nervous system, on another, and the relative impact of hereditary and environmental factors on behavior and character formation, on a third, contributed to the development of several psychological theories in the late nineteenth and early twentieth centuries. By 1914, psychoanalysis, research on conditioned reflexes, behaviorism, the various branches of instinctual psychology, and the researches of the more traditional schools in experimental and clinical psychology and psychiatry had collected an imposing array of facts and data. After World War I, psychology entered the phase when problems of method stood in the foreground. The development of Gestalt psychology in the 1920's contained a strong methodological element; similarly, the later school of dynamic psychology of Kurt Lewin. The schools of Alfred Adler, Carl Jung, and others broke away from the Freudian stem partly on therapeutic and partly on methodological grounds. In the fields of psychological testing, psychodiagnostics, animal psychology, learning theory, and developmental and educational psychology, new methods were developed which found recognition with varying ease: factor analysis, Rorschach, thematic apperception tests, and the research of Ernst Kretschmer, William H. Sheldon, and their associates are examples. It would be tedious to go into too much detail, but from what has been said it should be clear that in the last thirty years psychological research methods have advanced at an enormous pace, commensurate with the fertility of ideas on psychological theory that characterized the period before World War I. At present it seems as if psychology were entering into the third stage of its development, the elaboration of a generalized analytical theory of dynamic psychology which draws on the findings and methods of the many men and schools that have made concrete contributions to the discipline in the past.

To the layman or the casual observer it may seem as if the picture here drawn of the present situations of economics and psychology is unwarranted and altogether too rosy. What about the conflicts between "old-fashioned" liberals and planners; what about the difference between Keynesians and anti-Keynesians in economics? What about the many schools in psychology, the strict Freudians versus the various offshoots of Freudian theory; the psychoanalysts as a group versus the other schools of psychology and psychotherapy? No doubt, these differences exist, but they are differences of applied science, not of theory. There is today little dispute about basic theory either in economics or in psychology. On the basis of the same theory different policy measures, different therapies, are advanced. The differences derive not from conflicts of theory but from conflicts of values or conflicting interpretations of theories advanced by sister-disciplines. The present-day advocates of economic planning base their program on the same theoretical fundament as the protagonists of laissez faire. They differ not in the use of economic theory but in their views on the role and pattern of motivation and the functions and limitations of government. Similarly, in psychology, differences in therapy are due to different views of biological or sociological factors rather than to conflicts over psychological theory. Such differences can be resolved only by a higher degree of interrelation between the social sciences and the development of generalized sociological theory.

The pattern of development outlined here for economics and psychology could be repeated for other social sciences. One would find, of course, many deviations from this pattern, and, above all, the duration of the various stages in different disciplines will be found to be of varying length. This last fact is, indeed, suggested by the comparison of the histories of economic and psychological theory. In economics the formation of basic principles lasted from about 1760 to 1875 and preoccupation with method from 1860 to about 1925, while in psychology the two corresponding stages cover the periods roughly from 1880 to 1920 and from 1920 to 1945. Anthropology and sociology are sciences which, from the very outset, had to deal with such a vast and bewildering array of data that methodological considerations entered at once and continued to occupy a more important place in these two disciplines than in the other social sciences. In jurisprudence and political science the normative character of many of the problems with which these disciplines deal never wholly disappeared. The character of generalizations in history and geography is at such variance with the rest of the social sciences that these two disciplines, notably history, will show considerable differences. But in outline the historical pattern of the development of all these disciplines is similar to that of the other sciences.

Two more problems in the history of the social sciences in the nineteenth century remain to be discussed. One is the examination of the situation existing at the time the various disciplines split off the main stream of social theory; the other is the description of the institutional acceptance of the disciplines as self-contained independent wholes. In the light of the general character of scientific activity since the first half of the nineteenth century, these two problems merge into one. If we can explain why a particular discipline dissociated itself at a certain time from the body of general social science, we can also observe that, contemporaneously with its formation, university chairs, scientific societies, and specialized journals were founded, which served exclusively for the advancement of study, research, and teaching of the new discipline. In fact, the establishment of chairs at the leading universities or, better still, of specialized scientific societies is the best index of the first stage of independence of a discipline. As a rule, scientific societies precede in time the establishment of specialized professorships, especially at the great old universities, because university administrators are often conservative and willing to recognize new disciplines only when they have developed a well-established system of generalizations. Among universities again, the newer ones often precede the older ones in the formal recognition of a new discipline. For example, when the University of Chicago was founded in 1891, it recognized sociology as an independent discipline from the beginning, while Harvard admitted the discipline only in the 1930's and Princeton in the 1940's. In England the pattern was similar. While Thomas Malthus was appointed in 1805 as professor of general history, commerce, and finance at the College of the East India Company at Haileybury, the first professorship in economics at Oxford was established in 1825 and at Cambridge in 1828. Similarly, the establishment of the Political Economy Club in 1821 preceded the academic recognition of economics as a separate university discipline; and, although an Ethnological Society was formed in Britain in 1843 and an Anthropological Society in 1863, anthropology gained its first recognition at a university only in 1884 with the appointment of Edward B. Tylor to a readership at Oxford. The conservatism of academic institutions in recognizing new disciplines, especially in the early part of the nineteenth century, is brought into still sharper focus if we consider that, even where chairs in a new discipline were established, co-ordinated programs of study and research in those disciplines began only many years after the establishment of the first lectureship or professorship. Moreover, the early scientific societies were often inaugurated and composed of non-academic personnel. In its early years the Political Economy Club numbered among its members many more businessmen, politicians, and public officials than academic economists. Similarly, the Ethnological Society was manned chiefly by gentlemen-ethnographers, and the same is true of similar associations in the United States. Only those scientific societies which were founded toward the close of the nineteenth century owed their origin to the initiative of academicians. Notable among these societies are the German *Verein für Sozialpolitik,* which was planned as an organization of university professors, and almost all the sociological and psychological associations, which were started and manned almost exclusively by professionals. This change in the organization and membership of scientific societies that took place in the second half of the nineteenth century is eloquent evidence of the progressive recognition of the various social-science disciplines as respectable and full-fledged academic specialties. At present the academic influence in the professional societies and journals is overwhelming. The change from the late eighteenth to the twentieth century is significant. While in the former period contributions to social science only in rare cases stemmed from professors, while almost all the most notable contributions were made by amateurs, such contributions are now very rare exceptions. The social scientist has become a specialized academic professional.

This trend has its roots in the changes which the whole society and the educational system of the advanced countries have undergone in the last hundred years. It is the fruit of an ever more refined division of labor. It has brought great progress in scientific knowledge, but it has also shown weaknesses and defects. It has enhanced the clannishness of academic specialists, of which mention was made earlier. At the same time, it has tended to make the limits between the disciplines more rigid and to perpetuate specialties which have lost much of their original reason for being. It has prevented for a long time the reshuffling of the various problem areas into new disciplines, even though the old ones have lost their former cohesion and uniform aspect. If we look at some present-day curriculums in the social sciences, we often find little justification for the assemblage of courses under a given discipline, except tradition. And yet at the time that these special disciplines originated, this composition was rational and useful.

As was mentioned earlier, a special discipline tends to emerge when a set of problems is recognized to be related and if this relationship is of such a kind as to permit a generalized treatment of these problems, or at least if it may be expected that the solutions of the several problems are interdependent. Now it appears that the origin of every social-science discipline can be traced to such a set of mutually interrelated questions. The problems leading to the establishment of economics and psychology have already been mentioned. The interest of the businessman in the behavior of prices and costs was coupled with the interest of the statesman in problems of the distribution of the social product, the sources and impact of taxation, and the conditions of material welfare and progress. Just as Eddington praised Newton's "magnificent conception" in relating the course of the stars with the fall of objects, we are justified in praising Adam Smith and his successors of the classical school of economics for discovering a relationship between these economic phenomena and co-ordinating them in a set of all-embracing generalizations. At the same time, the study of the principles of legislation, on the one hand, and the question of the mutual rights and duties of governments toward each other and toward their citizens, on the other, gave rise to political science.

The development of anthropology, psychology, and sociology as separate disciplines had to wait until after the publication of Darwin's work. The Darwinian theory, which is among the two or three most important contributions to human knowledge made in the nineteenth century, may be called without exaggeration the fundamental cornerstone of biological theory. It was, like Newton's or Smith's contribution, a "magnificent conception," combining a series of previously unconnected ideas into a systematic whole. One can but agree with Ernst Haeckel's judgment on Darwin's achievements when he says about the developments of systematic biology:

> The foundation of comparative embryology by Baer (1828), and the cell theory by Schleiden and Schwann (1838), the advance of physiology under Johannes Müller (1833), and the enormous progress of paleontology and comparative anatomy between 1820 and 1860, provided this necessary foundation. Darwin was the first to co-ordinate the ample results of these lines of research. (Quoted in Henry John Randall, *The Creative Centuries,* 1947, p. 389.)

The impact of the Darwinian theory was overwhelming. In the social sciences it gave a new lease on life to the old theory of progress, which by 1859 had lost much of its earlier appeal. Instead of "progress," the catchword now was "evolution." The concept of evolution provided a basis for empirical research in the realm of physical development of man, but it also suggested the likelihood of discovering new knowledge about human society if it was applied to cultural change. It is only a short step from the comparative study of cultures and cultural institutions separated in time to a comparative study of cultures separated in space. If we can trace historically the development of social institutions and forms of belief and can correlate each step in this development with a specific kind of material culture, we find justification in making use of our knowledge of the cultures of contemporary primitive peoples by regarding them as living representations of the historical stages through which western European society must have passed. In this light Sir Henry Maine regarded ancient law and primitive law as identical, and in this light Lewis Morgan constructed his keen hypothesis on the evolution of social institutions by means of the empirical examination of the kinship nomenclatures of the Iroquois, Hawaiians, and other native tribes of his day.

The combination of archeological and ethnographic material, combined with data gleaned by physical anthropologists on the "racial" characteristics of man, thus gave rise to anthropology as a unified body of thought. This combination was based on data collected by ethnographic and archeological research of many men, but its integration in a systematic form was made possible only by the impact exercised by the theory of evolution. Psychology, like anthropology, owes a debt to this theory. Just as modern genetics originated in the Darwin-Wallace hypothesis, so the study of transmission of "mental" characteristics has its ultimate source in the theory of evolution. The analogy between historical stages of culture and contemporary cultures on different levels led to the development of early anthropological theory. Similarly, the development of human personality from birth on was interpreted in analogy with the "progress of the human spirit" in history. The naïve, "child-like mind" of the savage which had evoked so much interest in the social philosophers of the eighteenth century proved to be translatable into meaningful and observable psychological terms. Social psychology in particular centered for a long time around the heredity versus environment controversy, and it developed in this context lines of thought which were strongly tinged by analogies with the theory of biological evolution. Examples of this trend in psychology are the theories on social psychology of William McDougall and his school and the extension of psychoanalysis from psychotherapeutic to social psychological problems.

The influence of the Darwinian theory on the development of sociology appears at first sight somewhat farfetched. But it should be remembered that even Comte's sociology was born out of his interest in the theory of progress, which later developed affinities with the theory of evolution. Similarly, Spencer was profoundly interested in, and is now commonly regarded as one of the pathbreakers of, the theory of evolution. In 1859, the year of the publication of *The Origin of Species*, the generalized study of society was in a state of severe depression. The theory of progress had been discarded as a basis for making generalizations about the pattern of social organization and social structure; historical materialism, which could have stepped into the breach, was disregarded in academic circles as the product of a cantankerous radical and was yet too little developed to serve as a central hypothesis of sociological theory; utilitarian psychology, because of its simplicity and naïveté, met with insurmountable difficulties, which even the sophisticated restatement of John Stuart Mill had been unable to overcome. The application of the principles of evolution to social phenomena seemed to offer a way out of the dilemma. And thus two branches of sociological inquiry emerged which are based on an extension of the theory of biological evolution to human society: the theories of society as an organism and the interpretation of social development as a competitive struggle for survival, an interpretation which is commonly designated by the term "social Darwinism."

Both these theories were soon found to have defects so serious that they had to be discarded. But in the process of discarding them, systems of sociological thought were developed in France by Durkheim, Tarde, and LeBon and in Germany by Gumplowicz, Weber, Simmel, and others which provided a secure basis for further development of a generalized theory of society. Although little significant progress has so far been made in sociological theory beyond the achievements of the founders of modern sociology, a large amount of empirical material has been collected and methods of research have been greatly improved. There are indications that on the basis of this new knowledge the recent *rapprochement* between sociology and social anthropology may lead to the elaboration of a set of new and fruitful hypotheses about the general principles of social action and behavior.

Our analysis of the impact of the theory of evolution on the emergence of anthropology, psychology, and sociology as independent systematic sciences leads to the conclusion that only after these disciplines discarded purely biological analogies did real progress in the disciplines themselves begin. The theory of evolution served primarily as a starter; it suggested lines of analysis which had earlier escaped the attention of social scientists. But the real theoretical and empirical contributions in these disciplines were made only when they had entered their separate paths. On the other hand, it would be wrong to deny that the greatest promise for further progress in all fields of social science lies in the mutual cross-fertilization of the various disciplines and perhaps also in a closer approach to certain branches of the humanities and natural sciences. This is not in contradiction with the earlier statement that each of the social sciences has only in the present or recent past achieved a substantially uniform and relatively unambiguous theoretical structure. Co-operation between the sciences at an earlier stage met with the serious danger of leading into blind alleys. The experience with social Darwinism and the shortcomings of the evolutionary school in anthropology are warning examples. But today the situation is different. Greater integration of the social sciences, each with a well-developed theoretical system of its own, holds out the hope that Comte's dream of a generalized science of man and society may be achieved in practice.

C H A P T E R II

History

Introduction—History occupies a special position among the social sciences. Not only is historical writing, even a "scientific" attempt at historical writing, older than other social sciences, but it also has a distinguished past as a form of literature. In fact, history occupies even today a somewhat ambiguous position between the humanities and the social sciences, and only during the last two hundred years has it gradually relinquished its primary humanistic aspects and replaced them by sociological ones. At least up to the time of Gibbon, and even beyond, history was regarded primarily as a form of literature, and today many historical works are read as contributions to world literature rather than as studies contributing to the understanding and analysis of social relations.

Since many historical works claim to present not only scientifically relevant material, but also aim to teach, amuse, or instruct, the question of the proper role and function of historical writing has often been raised. This question has been bound up with a further question concerning the method to be used in establishing historical propositions and the kinds of documents and other materials which are admissible as evidence for historical propositions. For clearly, if the purpose of history is merely to tell "what actually happened," a different method and a different group of pieces of evidence will be applicable than if history is to convert persons to a special point of view, or if it is to be employed in support of a particular political or ideological cause.

For this reason there have existed—and to some degree in the more popular literature there continue to exist—several varieties of history and varieties of historical philosophies. There appeared not long ago in a paperback edition an excellent anthology of essays on the varieties of history and historical philosophy edited by Fritz Stern, *The Varieties of History*. In this work the various approaches to history, as well as the main purposes to which historical writing have been put in more recent times, are exhibited by excerpts from the works of the outstanding representatives of each approach or method.

Philosophy of History—The problem of "philosophy of history" as such, which agitated the minds of nineteenth-century historians, above all, turned out in the end to be a consideration of the ultimate forces which determine historical developments. Though already some of the ancient philosophers thought to have discovered such general underlying forces, and though much of early medieval historiography was written with the implicit–and often explicit–assumption that the historical course of mankind was nothing but the expression in human life of the purposes of God, the direct consideration of philosophy of history may be said to have started with Georg W. F. Hegel. In his *The Philosophy of History* (rev. ed. 1899) he attempted to show that the historical course of development of mankind was a dialectical process culminating in the ultimate self-realization of the idea of freedom. Hegel's philosophy was "turned upside down" by Karl Marx, who in the Preface to his *A Contribution to The Critique of Political Economy* (tr. from 2d German ed., 1904) stated the materialist conception of history, according to which the underlying powers determining historical evolution are the dialectical conflict between the material conditions under which men live and the evolution of production relations, i.e., economic organization. The Marxian materialist conception, in turn, was contradicted by proponents of idealistic or spiritualist conceptions of history. Parallel with the Hegelian, Marxian, and anti-Marxian trends in the development of philosophies of history was one originating in France and Britain and founded on the theories of human perfectibility, which had become popular in the eighteenth century and which were brought to their most mature philosophical expression in Auguste Comte's work and that of his followers, among whom Henry Thomas Buckle was one of the most prominent. Buckle's *History of Civilization in England* (new ed., 1872) contains an exposition of a philosophy of history which is a mixture of mid-nineteenth-century rationalism, Comtean positivism, and some environmentalist conceptions which, just at that time, began to be revived again in European social science.

With the decline of the nineteenth century, the preoccupation with philosophy of history declined somewhat. To begin with, rules of historical method became worked out in greater detail, and historians in general accepted uniform standards for the evaluation and collection of evidence. In addition there developed a general reaction against relatively simple, uniform explanations of historical developments which was based to no small amount upon greater acquaintance with histories of of non-Western peoples. Finally, there developed a strong reaction against "historicism," which was identified with the attempt to find immanent historical laws which determined ultimately the course of human history.

Some secondary works discussing these trends contain excellent summaries of the various approaches and philosophies of history. Among them are Robin G. Collingwood's *The Idea of History* (1946), which summarized historical philosophies from the ancient Greeks to the modern period; Herbert Marcuse's *Reason and Revolution* (1941), which contains a sympathetic exposition of Hegelian and Marxian thought in the field of history, and Karl Popper's *The Open Society and Its Enemies* (1945), which is unsympathetic to Hegel and Marx and contains a well-reasoned indictment of historicism. The major work on the eighteenth and nineteenth century philosophies of human perfectibility is John B. Bury's *The Idea of Progress* (1921).

Historical Method—As we have seen, the difference in philosophies of history was not confined merely to disputes on approaches to historical materials, but also to their meaning and explanation. These last aspects of this question border closely on problems of historical method. Clearly historians have always been troubled with the question of when an event of which they only had indirect information could be regarded as true. Can certain actions of a person, which he is reputed or rumored to have committed, be attributed to him merely because they would fit into his pattern of behavior, even though no direct evidence is available of his having committed these actions? How appropriate for historical veracity is Thucydides' practice of attributing speeches to personalities of whom he writes, which he has composed, and which express in the historian's words the thoughts and intentions which these personages probably entertained? Is a single account of an event sufficient evidence to have us accept it as having taken place in the manner in which it is reported? How much credence can be given to witnesses, and how can we evaluate the bias of some witnesses? All these are questions which an historian has to answer if he wishes to be sure of the "historical facts" on the basis of which he is to evaluate a particular historical episode or development.

But in addition to merely making sure that the "facts" are straight, the question arises as to what incidents and events are "facts." The most frequently used sources to obtain historical data are written documents of all kinds. But for some periods such documents are either unavailable or available only in sparse and mutilated form. On the other hand, there exist monuments, or coins, or household utensils, or various other objects of bone, stone, metal, or wood. What inferences can be drawn from using these objects to provide us with "facts"? In what way can oral traditions, linguistic material, inferences about the geographical environment, or reconstruction of astronomical events, such as the appearance of comets or eclipses of the sun, be employed to provide additional factual material? These are some of the questions for which the growing body of works on historical method have tried to give answers, and in the course of time standard methods were worked out to organize the factual materials sought for not only in written documentary sources, but also in other material objects and in environmental factors impinging in some form on the events that a historian wishes to reconstruct.

Moreover, with the rapprochement of history to the realm of social science, documentary and other materials pertaining to more or less mundane affairs have become increasingly important. An old account book, which some 200 years ago would have been tossed aside as worthless, is now often considered a mine of important information on prices, or the nature of commercial contracts, or other data sought by the historian. A simple diary of an undistinguished person is now a source for patterns of living, for household chores, for attitudes towards the education of children, or for marital relations in an average family—all problems of great interest to historians concerned with the analysis of social relations in some past age. So the accumulation of data and the determination of what constitutes important and useful data hinges on the problems that historians set themselves for study. The methods by which these data are collected and evaluated are similar to those applicable to documents or other artifacts concerned with matters of high policy or statecraft.

The standardization of method has led to the production of a number of textbooks, among which the German treatise by Ernst Bernheim, *Lehrbuch der Historischen Methode* (1889), is considered outstanding. Bernheim's book has found many imitators, and some less voluminous and more modern texts on historical method have appeared at various intervals in most western languages. One of the most recent, very lucidly written works on historical method is Louis Gottschalk's *Understanding History* (1950). In addition to these works that are concerned to a considerable extent, though not exclusively, with the analysis of documents, a large literature has been brought into existence on problems of interpretation and evaluation of historical data. Some of the most important contributions in this field are Max Weber's essays edited and translated by Edward Shils and published under the title *Max Weber on the Methodology of the Social Sciences* (1949) and Maurice Mandelbaum's *The Problem of Historical Knowledge* (1938). These issues of interpretation and evaluation of data border again on the concern with the philosophy of history, and it is not surprising that much material on these points is also to be found in the work by Collingwood, which was mentioned earlier, and such other contributions to historical philosophy as Karl Löwith's *Meaning in History* (1949).

These two works approach in content and to some extent in style another recent form of evaluating historical writing and the contribution of historians to social science and human knowledge in general, and that is the history of history. The most extensive work in this field available in English is probably James W. Thompson's *A History of Historical Writing* (1942), which is an encyclopedic account of the tasks and achievements of past historians. Among works dealing with a more limited period or more limited trend of historical works are the important essay by Lord (John) Acton on "German Schools of History," which is reprinted in his *Historical Essays and Studies* (1908), and George P. Gooch's *History and Historians in the Nineteenth Century* (1913), in which are discussed the important changes in historical approach and method that took place during one of the most crucial periods of the development of history as a branch of human knowledge. Next to the nineteenth century, probably no period of historical writing has so challenged the imagination of later historians as ancient Greece. To this interest we owe two more valuable studies on Greek historiography, by John B. Bury, *The Ancient Greek Historians* (1909), and by Arnold J. Toynbee, *Greek Historical Thought from Homer to the Age of Heraclius* (1924).

Ancient and Medieval History—We shall now turn to a brief description of the major contributions to historical writing. It is clear that in this space no adequate account can be given of the rich literature that includes some of the greatest works of Western man. Anyone who is interested in the progress of the discipline of history from its beginnings in the ancient Orient, ancient China and India, and Greek antiquity will have to consult works like that of Thompson cited earlier, or some of the more specialized writings like those of Bury or Toynbee on Greek history. A most valuable source on Roman history is Wilhelm S. Teuffel's *History of Roman Literature* (tr. from 5th German ed., 1891-92), which has important sections on the Roman historians; on the historians of the early Christian period there are Charles T. Cruttwell's *A Literary History of Early Christianity* (1893) and Pierre de Labriolle's *History and Literature of Christianity from Tertullian to Boethius* (1924). Finally, there exists an abundance of works on the historical contributions of the high and late Middle Ages, among which Louis J. Paetow's *A Guide to the Study of Medieval History* (rev. ed., 1931) is perhaps the outstanding work.

What will be attempted here is, therefore, not a digest of these and other works, but rather an attempt at evaluating the extent to which the early historians were aware of the scientific significance of their contribution and the extent to which they made such a contribution. This means that we can dismiss considerations of the many chronicle-like accounts of reigns such as the one by Manetho, an Egyptian priest, or the local and tribal histories, of which the historical books of the Bible are a good example. These works contain, of course, important materials for the scientific study of history, especially since they are filled not only with accounts of what occurred but also with rules of law, morals, and behavior; but they do not form contributions to scientific history in themselves.

If Herodotus is usually referred to as the "father of history," this designation is true in the sense that in his work a conscious effort is made to write history not as did his forbears the logographers, who wove fable and fact into a single account, but to describe factual relations and to recount events which seemed to him important in the explanation of the development of the Greek communities.

Although Herodotus utilizes various documentary sources, his *History* is based primarily upon information obtained through the questioning of various individuals in the course of his travels. This method of obtaining evidence becomes characteristic of Greek historiography. Not a small measure of his fame rests on the fact that he did not credulously accept all the tales which were related to him, but assumed a critical attitude, attempting to ascertain the truth to the extent that it was in his power to do so.

With Thucydides, the link between logographer and historian is completely severed. He had little sympathy for either tellers of tales or their credulous audience. His objective in his book, the *Peloponnesian War* (written during the war, ca. 431-404 B.C.), was the presentation of the facts as rigorously, as scrupulously as possible—an ideal very similar to that of Leopold von Ranke, many centuries later.

Thucydides' work was concerned with a contemporary event, one in which he participated. His method of arriving at the facts was similar to that of Herodotus, that of direct inquiry, but his limited vision made his task much easier than that of his predecessor. Thucydides also makes an attempt to cope with the problem of causation in history, differentiating between immediate and remote causes. He manifests an appreciation of psychological factors in history, presenting admirable character studies as well as an analysis of public opinion.

Until Greece came under the sway of Roman power, Greek historiography did not again rise to the heights attained in the writings of Herodotus and Thucydides. Although the works of Xenophon (ca. 430-354 B.C.) were highly esteemed by the ancient world, the merits from the standpoint of modern historiography are essentially of a literary nature. His *Anabasis,* a memoir in which he depicts the retreat of the ten thousand Greek mercenaries in the service of the Persian king Cyrus back to their homeland, is undoubtedly the most successful of his works. In his *Hellenica,* Xenophon attempts to continue the work of Thucydides but proves to be superficial and incapable of profundity in analysis or insight.

The conquests of Alexander the Great, the rise of a Greek empire, failed to produce a great historian capable of giving lasting expression to those achievements. It was only when Rome began to extend its sway over the Mediterranean world that a Greek historian emerged capable of describing this process.

Polybius (ca. 198-117 B.C.), a Greek who spent most of his adult life in Rome, described the expansion and constitutional development of Rome to 146 B.C. His *History* represents a marked departure from the course of Greek historiography. The subject of his work was so broad in scope that it entailed a new technique in the collecting of historical evidence. Direct inquiry was impossible. Polybius, in constructing his narrative, had to utilize the narratives of other writers as his sources.

In his scrupulous regard for accuracy of fact, Polybius was the equal of Thucydides; in his conception of the scope of history, he was far superior to him. Polybius grasped the continuity of historical development, the interdependence of events, the inter-relation of the various peoples constituting the ancient world.

The writings of Polybius never achieved the popularity of those of Herodotus or Thucydides, for in matters of style, he was their inferior. But the canons of historical writing set forth by Polybius, his insistence upon objectivity in the writing of historical narrative, his close scrutiny of sources and his denunciation of mere rhetoric—all bear the impress of modern historiography.

Throughout the course of succeeding generations, the popularity of Plutarch's (ca. A.D. 50-125) *Parallel Lives* has remained undimmed. This work, in which the lives of eminent Greeks and Romans are set forth, possesses limited historical value, for Plutarch was a moralist more concerned with ethical principles than with historical fact. His work, however, did much to fix the reputation of many historical characters for subsequent ages.

The contribution of Rome to historiography, or history-as-record, in no way compares to their unique contribution to history-as-actuality. In this sphere, as in almost every other phase of cultural and intellectual life, they merely copied Greek models without ever approximating the loftiest creations of their teachers.

The first major Roman historian certainly possessed those qualifications that Polybius insisted were essential for the writing of history. Julius Caesar's (100-44 B.C.) *Commentaries on the Gallic Wars* are outstanding examples of historical memoirs. Reliable in their factual presentation, they are written in a vigorous style of such clarity as to have gained for the *Commentaries* the role of textbook for beginners in Latin. Caesar's writings, by their apparent candor and restrained style, give the impression of complete objectivity. It does not require a very close examination, however, to realize that they constitute a subtle apology and attempted vindication of his career.

The works of Sallust (Caius Sallustius Crispus) (ca. 86-34 B.C.) represent historical writings of a more formal character. In common with most Greek and Roman historians, Sallust had participated in political life, but retired to the luxury of his villa during the tumultuous period following upon Caesar's death in order to occupy himself with historical composition. It is evident that Sallust had certain misgivings about substituting a passive life of scholarship for an active political career, for a certain apologetic strain is discernible in his writings. As a historian, Sallust chose Thucydides as his model. Although his major work, a history of Rome from 78 to 67 B.C., has been lost, his monographs on the *Conspiracy of Catiline* and the *Jugurthine War* are sufficiently indicative of his skill as a historian and writer.

Livy (Titus Livius) (59 B.C.-A.D. 17) depicted, in his *Roman History,* the growth and development of Rome from the founding of the city to the establishment of the Empire. His work possesses an epic quality that won for Livy the admiration not only of his contemporaries, but also of succeeding generations. From the standpoint of history, however, it is not comparable to the writings of Thucydides or Polybius. Livy was a disciple of the Greek rhetorical school; hence, for him, perfection of style was more important than accuracy of historical data. His purpose in writing history was avowedly propagandistic. His aim was to extol Rome's greatness and to infuse the youth of his day with an intense patriotism. In Livy's history, the Gods and supernatural forces loom large; both the fabulous and the real enter indiscriminately into his tale, not because he was himself a credulous person, but because these possessed literary and propagandistic merits.

The contribution of Publius Cornelius Tacitus (ca. A.D. 55-120) to Roman historiography was in many respects unique. Greek and Roman historiography was not, on the whole, a product of disinterested scholarship. It was admittedly pragmatic and moralistic in nature. Nonetheless, its great historians–Herodotus, Thucydides, Polybius, even Sallust–attempted to present an unbiased, impartial point of view. Such objectivity was completely lacking in Tacitus. He was a bitter opponent of the Empire, unalterably convinced of the moral depravity of his time, and these two themes completely dominated his perspective.

In the *Annals,* Tacitus dealt with the period from the death of Augustus to the year A.D. 69. The *Histories* begin with the political crises of A.D. 69 and cover the Flavian period.

Of the voluminous writings of Suetonius Tranquillus (ca. A.D. 75-160), only his *Lives of the Twelve Emperors* is still extant. It is a significant if not a highly meritorious historical narrative, for it became a model of historical biography imitated by succeeding generations of writers. Suetonius was not concerned with political or military affairs, but rather with the presentation of a literary portrait of the Roman emperors from Augustus to the Flavians. It is a highly diffuse work, replete with anecdotes and richly descriptive. Although Suetonius' presentation of the events of the period is reliable, he introduces details which are not in the best taste, diminishing thereby the scholarly merit of the work, but assuring it subsequent popularity.

In the third century A.D. a new element was carried into historiography that stemmed from the growing spread of Christianity. Since Christianity had been elevated to the state religion under the later Roman emperors, bishops and other learned men of the church attempted to re-interpret the history of the world from the viewpoint of the Christian religion.

The Christian thinkers in formulating their historical concepts attempted to re-channel the stream of history, assigning to the Jews, who had played a relatively minor role in the process, the position of primacy. The great empires of antiquity were merely assigned supporting roles in the drama of world history. All the events of the past were interrelated; they were rungs in a ladder leading to the coming of Christ. These various elements were expressed in the Christian chronologies that provided a background, a genealogy, for the Christian religion. Of all the early chronologies, the *Chronicle* of Eusebius Pamphilius (ca. A.D. 260-340) was by far the most significant. Eusebius, Bishop of Caesaria, was the outstanding Christian historian of the period. His *Chronicle* was designed to provide a framework for his *Ecclesiastical History* which he wrote at a later date. Eusebius' work begins with the Creation, but does not become detailed until the alleged date of the birth of Abraham (2016 B.C.), and extends to the reign of the Emperor Constantine.

The *Chronicle* of Eusebius was written in Greek and consequently found few readers in the Latin West. In 379 Jerome dictated a Latin translation of this work. Jerome made certain revisions and additions, including more facts pertaining to Roman history and literature. He also extended the chronology to the year A.D. 378. This translation of the

Chronicle of Eusebius served as the authoritative chronology of the Christian West up until almost the seventeenth century.

A systematic and official Christian exposition of the course of world history is to be found in the *Seven Books of History Against the Pagans* of Orosius (ca. A.D. 380-ca. 420). The difficulties that beset the later Roman Empire brought forth pagan charges that its decline was due to Christianity. Orosius was the pupil and lieutenant of St. Augustine and at the latter's suggestion undertook the refutation of these charges. The providential theory of history contained in St. Augustine's *City of God* constituted the philosophical framework of the work of Orosius. It is a sketchy and incomplete treatment of the history of the ancient world in that it omitted certain nations from its purview as well as significant events in the history of the nations it mentioned. In all probability, Orosius was only interested in those historical events that were germane to his purpose. Above all, the history of the pagan past was represented as one long series of crimes and calamities. The great achievements of antiquity were completely ignored. The work is also deficient from the standpoint of scholarship, for Orosius failed to consult the great pagan historians but was content with second-hand abstracts. *The Seven Books of History Against the Pagans* possessed one redeeming feature, in that Orosius did suggest that the common people merited more consideration in a study of history than they theretofore had received. This work was the accepted manual of pagan history during the Middle Ages.

Eusebius' pre-eminence as the historian of early Christianity is confirmed by his *Ecclesiastical History*. Every pioneering venture is beset with difficulties, and this was especially true of the task which confronted Eusebius, for he undertook to write a history of an institution which in its early days was altogether un-historically minded. It required, therefore, the widest and most painstaking research work in order to gather the necessary material. Eusebius investigated documents of diverse character, inserting significant extracts from these documents in his work. It is, consequently, an important source book on early Christian history.

Subsequent centuries saw further and further elaborations of the themes first broached by Eusebius and Orosius. The Patristic literature is a mixture of moral, historical, philosophical, and religious works, and it is often difficult to disentangle the various strands in some wrtings.

But the establishment of the so-called barbarian kingdoms on the soil of the former West-Roman empire and the final rise of the Frankish monarchy tempted contemporary historians to relate the events which led to this great change in the political balance of Europe. We see, therefore, beginning in the sixth century, the increasing production of histories of the worldly powers.

Two works of this period tower above all others in historical significance. Dissimilar in character, they are both creations of men unusually gifted in their different ways. In his *History of the Franks,* Gregory, Bishop of Tours (538-594), deals with the emergence of the Merovingian culture. Although this work is much wider in scope in that it includes a history of the world from antiquity to the fifth century A.D., its importance rests upon a description of the events of Gregory's lifetime. Gregory was not essentially a scholar, but a man of affairs. As an important Churchman, he was an intimate of many of the important figures of his time. He traveled extensively, and much of the information he relates was received by him first hand. What was to become the key factor in Medieval civilization, the dominant position of the Church, is most adequately reflected in Gregory's *History*. The credulity of the age finds expression in the miracles and marvels with which this work abounds. Though this work does not conform to the canons of modern historical scholarship, its great importance stems from the vivid, dramatic way in which it reflects the age in which it was written.

The *Ecclesiastical History of the English Nation* by the Venerable Bede (672-735) does not possess the dramatic, earthy quality of Gregory's *History of the Franks,* but it is vastly superior from the standpoint of scholarship. This work is more than a description of the triumph of Christianity and the organization of the Church in England; it describes the English culture which stemmed from the fusion of the Anglo-Saxon and native elements as well as the resulting political system. Its author, after exhausting the available source material in England, sent to the continent for pertinent domuments. Although Bede's *History* contains the miraculous elements so characteristic of the writings of the time, he is less credulous than Gregory and is on a higher intellectual plane and more reliable as a historian.

But these works, though they stand at the threshold of Medieval historiography, represent, in a sense, the very peak of historical writing which was attained in that age. The consolidation of peace, the greater regularity of political relations, and the re-ordering of political boundaries led to a gradual establishment of a stable social order, in which property and other rights again became secure and in which the codification of laws and norms of behavior, of duties and rights were significant instruments in the exercise of power. These trends also had their effect on historical writing, and the characteristic productions of the high middle ages are annals and chronicles. They are mainly accounts of various noteworthy events, and they are, like the works of the Greek logographers, or the tribal histories of antiquity, valuable chiefly as source materials rather than as attempts at synthetic historical writing. Nevertheless, some of these annals and chronicles were written by gifted and wise men, and it behooves us therefore to mention the most outstanding among them.

In his *Chronicle* or *Book of Two Cities,* Bishop Otto of Freising (ca. 1114-1158) leaves the role of mere chronicler far behind and produces the first important medieval philosophy of history. In its philosophical outlook, it is based upon St. Augustine's *City of God;* in its method it follows the historical writing of Orosius. Otto illustrates the antithesis of the *City of God* and the *City of the Devil* throughout the course of history from creation to his own time. As a philosophy of history, it suffers from the weaknesses often associated with this type of historical writing. Otto's primary concern was to fit the historical process into a preconceived mold; hence accuracy of historical fact was not of too great import. Furthermore, his ecclesiastical outlook prevented an adequate appreciation of secular and pagan affairs. Otto's *Chronicle* is, however, notable in its treating of the problem of cause and effect in the historical process and in its attempt to understand the present by reference to the past.

Two French medieval historians exemplify the highest achievements of medieval historiography. The *Chronicles of England, France, Spain and the Adjoining Countries* of Jean Froissart (1337-1410), although episodical in character, is a literary masterpiece. It is unique in its description of stirring scenes and in character portraiture. But its merit is not only stylistic, for Froissart was concerned with manners, customs, and institutions, as well as with the highly pertinent problem of historical cause and effect. Froissart may be termed the spokesman for chivalry in the period of the decline of feudalism.

The *Memoirs* of Philippe de Comines (1445-1509) represents historical narrative far removed in form from the characteristic works of the Middle Ages. If the annals and chronicles merely record certain historical events, the *Memoirs* are a penetrating example of historical analysis. Comines was concerned with the meaning of history, the underlying motives which determined the trend of events, the relationship of cause and effect, and the influence of the cultural environment upon the process of history. Comines' attitude toward historical analysis was akin to the attitude of the classical historians, for he too regarded it in an entirely pragmatic light. A study of history furnishes a key to the understanding of politics, hence its special significance for statesmen.

But the highest achievement in historical writing during the Middle Ages was reached not in the Christian West, but in Islamic Africa. The Muslims had been the continuators of Greek science and philosophy, they had developed further the mathematical, chemical, and biological theories developed in antiquity, and they excelled in music, poetry, and art. In this atmosphere, their most gifted representative in history also attained a level of historical writing and historical insight which was not re-attained again until the 18th century.

The superiority of Muslim culture during the Middle Ages over that of its Christian contemporaries is vividly exemplified in the historical writings of Ibn Khaldun (1332-1406). His understanding of the historical process far surpassed that of any Christian historian of the Middle Ages. Ibn Khaldun conceived the study of history as a science treating of the origin and development of society. He grasped the element of unity and continuity in the historical process in a manner which was not approximated by Western thought for a number of centuries. His appreciation of the time element in history, its relation to growth and change, and the interplay of subjective and environmental factors in the process stamps Ibn Khaldun as a social scientist. The *Prolegomena to Universal History* is a presentation of Ibn Khaldun's theoretical views; in his *Universal His-*

tory (translated into French in 1925 under the title *Histoire des Berbères*) these theories are applied to the actual historical process of Muslim civilization, mainly in North Africa and Spain.

From the Renaissance to the Nineteenth Century—The conception of history of the Ibn Khaldun ushers in a period of historical writing in which greater emphasis is placed upon human events than upon divine providence and in which the role of the supernatural in historical development is increasingly disregarded. In Western Europe this trend is usually associated with the rise of humanism, but the complete secularization of historical writing in Europe did not occur in reality until the age of the enlightenment in the eighteenth century. The period from the Renaissance to the French Revolution thus constitutes a period of gradual change, of emancipation of history from religious and ideological doctrines, and it was in this period that the basis for the new scientific history of the nineteenth century was laid.

The first main impact of humanism upon historical writing was the return to the interests in history of the Greeks and Romans. As we have seen, the historians of antiquity were chiefly interested in the analysis of political changes. If history was to serve any other branch of human practice or knowledge it was to serve above all politics, apart perhaps only from morals. And so the historiography of the Renaissance returned, under the impact of humanist teaching, to the close relation which existed between history and politics. This is already discernible in Petrarch's (1304-1374) *History of Rome,* in which the author expresses his concern with Italian unity visualized in the form of a revived Roman empire. It became even clearer in the writings of Niccolo Machiavelli (1469-1527) and Francesco Guicciardini (1483-1540), in whose works are to be found the beginnings of modern political and national historical writing. Machiavelli was more a political philosopher than a historian. His *History of Florence* is not distinguished stylistically, nor is it as accurate factually as are other works of this period. The value of this work lies in Machiavelli's grasp of the process of political development, in his understanding of the relation between military activities and the political process. This work is also significant in that Machiavelli discards the annalistic organization of his material and introduces the topical method.

Guicciardini was to a greater extent than Machiavelli a formal historian. He also was primarily concerned with contemporary political history. His *History of Florence* is a vigorous presentation of events and a criticism of the political personalities and their policies. There is little indication of a political philosophy in this work. Guicciardini's *History of Italy* is a historical canvas much broader in scope than any of the characteristic products of medieval historiography. The latter were primarily concerned with particular dynasties; with a single state. Guicciardini's *History of Italy* analyzes the interaction between states. It treats of the rise and fall of states, of the process of political development in its broadest sense. It constitutes an analysis of world history.

But Machiavelli and Guicciardini were by no means scientific historians. They were concerned primarily with political analysis; factual accuracy, evaluation of documents, and source material were definitely of subordinate import in their historical works.

The affinity between history and politics was preserved in the subsequent decades. The German writer Samuel Pufendorf (1632-1694) wrote a large number of historical works, but also works on juridical and political problems. He was preceded in this by Jean Bodin (1530-1596), who wrote not only an important treatise on politics, but also a textbook on historical method, his *Method for the Easy Comprehension of History* (translated into English in 1945 by Beatrice Reynolds). This work is concerned more with interpretation than with evaluation and criticism of sources and thus comes close to that branch of methodological literature in history which borders on the philosophy of history. In fact, Bodin's importance lies in his pointing to a series of factors and relationships which were taken up by later writers again in sometimes essentially unchanged form and sometimes modified. For example, Bodin places great emphasis on the influence which geographical factors exert upon historical development. This point was raised again later by Montesquieu, by Buckle, by the "environmentalist" school, among whose contributions Ellen Churchill Semple's *American History and its Geographic Conditions* (1903) may be mentioned, and by Lucien Febvre in his *A Geographical Introduction to History* (1925).

Thus the work of Bodin presents theories which have continued to occupy historians to our day. He also expounds an as yet rather crude and simplistic theory of progress, which was to dominate much of the historical thinking and writing of later centuries. In this he controverted an old belief which is still discernible in some of the ancient and medieval historiography, i.e., that mankind has travelled in its historical development a road leading on a declining path from an initial golden age (or paradise). The view of progressive improvement of human institutions, as well as the insistence on man's environment as a factor in his historical development, thus form two of the main pillars on which the historical works of the age of enlightenment are based.

In distinguishing the various facets of this movement of intellectual expansion, it is possible to point to a direct link between its indivdual phases and the development of historiography. The discoveries of the period and the ensuing contacts of Europeans with other cultures spelled the doom of a provincial historical outlook and brought into the historians' focus the consideration of cultural problems. It is not far-fetched to assume that the remarkable progress of science in this period reacted upon historiography by furthering the development of new techniques of historical analysis. Above all, the scientific progress gave man an altogether new view of the universe and of himself. It gave rise to new philosophic concepts which in turn influenced historical thought. Copernicus, Galileo and Newton, Descartes and Locke were not historians, but their theories were of utmost significance to the development of historical thought. The economic developments of the period had significant political repercussions, and whatever influences politics always influences history.

The development of scientific method in historiography was of a twofold process. It involved both the rise of auxiliary sciences such as diplomatics, chronology, paleography, epigraphy, and lexicography, by means of which the historical researcher could determine reliability of documents, and the development of techniques of internal criticism which could determine the credibility of authors.

The science of diplomatics, concerned with determining the authenticity of documents, was created by Jean Mabillon in collaboration with Luc D'Achery. Mabillon's *De Re Diplomatica* (1681-1704) remained the authoritative treatise on the subject for many years. Bernard de Montfaucon, in his *Palaeographia Graeca* (1708) and in his *L'Antiquité expliquée et représentée en figures* (2d ed., 1722), gave rise to modern paleography and archeology. Historical lexicography had its origin in the *Glossarium Mediae et Infimae Latinitatis* (1678) of Charles du Fresne du Cange. Chronology was placed upon a scientific basis in the cooperative work begun in 1743 by Maur François Dantine, published in 1750 by Charles Clémencet and Ursin Durand, and revised in 1770 by François Clement. *L'Art de vérifier les dates* (2d ed., 1770) finally disposed of the works of Eusebius and Jerome.

Contributions to the process of source evaluation and analysis came from many directions. The Benedictine monks of the congregation of Saint-Maur, who were very active in the collection of the sources of French history, made significant contributions to the methodology of modern history. The Jansenist, Louis Sebastian de Tillemont, (*Histoire des empereurs . . .*, 1700-02) was the first to base a historical work on an attempted reconciliation of sources. It included a critical discussion of the source material for each period. Pierre Bayle, in his *Dictionaire historique et critique* (2d ed., 1702), pointed to the serious discrepancies between the views of authorities describing similar contemporary events. His criticism applied to "sacred" as well as profane texts. Bayle did away completely with the concept of sacred history.

Special reference must be made to the contribution to historical method and interpretation of Giovanni Battista Vico. Vico pointed to the study of linguistics and mythology and to the analysis of tradition as avenues for the re-creation of the past.

The scientific discoveries of Copernicus, Galileo, and Newton pointed to a universe guided by immutable law. This concept of law was eagerly seized upon by the philosophers of the enlightenment and applied to the field of social and historical development. If mechanistic principles could apply to the universe, they could also apply to society. Such a concept was particularly congenial to the formulation of a philosophy of history.

Most of the historians of the enlightenment were concerned, to some degree, with the element of law in social development. Vico, however, propounded a closely knit theory of historical development based upon a definite pattern. In his *Principii d'una Scienza Nuova* (1725, 2d ed. 1730), Vico postulated three premises. The first was that certain definite periods of history, similar in character, are to be found in the development of all nations. These periods he characterized as the heroic, the classical, and the period of a new barbarism. The second was that these periods followed each other in similar succession in the history of all nations. Third, this cyclical movement is not a continual reversion to the same starting point, but a spiral movement in which each cycle is differentiated from the preceding one. Since in Vico's work principles of social development are formulated, it may be considered as much a sociological treatise as a historical study.

Closely akin to the concept of continuity and pattern in the process of social development is the idea of progress associated with the enlightenment. Jean Bodin had in an earlier period rejected the concept universally held at the time that the history of mankind is a retrogression from a primeval golden age. His belief in the steady advance of mankind became one of the fundamental assumptions of the thought of the enlightenment. This is expressed in such works as *Digression sur les Anciens et les Modernes (Oeuvres,* Vol. IV, 1825) by Bernard de Fontenelle, *Outlines of an Historical View of the Progress of the Human Mind* (Eng. ed. 1802) by the Marquis de Condorcet, and *Paralelle des Anciens et des Modernes* (1690) by Charles Perrault.

For many writers of the Enlightenment, the golden age of mankind must be sought in the future rather than in a mythical past. The underlying assumption upon which the idea of progress was predicated was the perfectibility of human nature. Given the proper institutional background, man's development was almost unlimited. This trend of the philosophy of history is well summarized in John B. Bury's *The Idea of Progress* (1921).

A supreme confidence in the powers of human reason was, perhaps, the characteristic attribute of enlightened thought. The new discoveries, the progress of scientific knowledge undermined all views based solely on faith and tradition. Institutions, customs, and beliefs had to justify themselves at the bar of reason; only those interpretations of natural and social phenomena which met the requirements of rationality were tolerated. The philosophers of the Enlightenment contended that the human mind is essentially the same the world over and that the manifested differences are due to differences in social environment. These differences were attributed by the various philosophers to a number of causes. Montesquieu and his school stressed the geographic factor. Voltaire contended that the three factors which determine the cast of man's mind are climate, government, and religion. Although these thinkers acknowledged that the human mind is essentially the same everywhere, they held that it was not at all times free to express itself; the emancipation of human reason from the bonds of superstition and religion was the achievement of their age. This concept led to a view unhistorical in the extreme, for the rationalist historians maintained that those periods of mental bondage were altogether arid, of no historical import. They identified the Middle Ages as the period of cultural aridity.

The works of François Marie Arouet de Voltaire, the founder of the rationalist school of historians, exemplifies in vivid manner the achievements as well as the shortcomings of this school. His writings exhibit stylistic brilliance, a genius for character portrayal, and an unmatched critical ability. Voltaire's *The Age of Louis XIV* (Everyman's Library ed., 1926) has been termed the first modern historical work. The organization of this work is completely topical; both the annalistic and chronological method are discarded. It is a description of the state of Europe in its totality. The one shortcoming of the work lies in Voltaire's failure to link his subject with the general historical development of Europe.

Voltaire's *Essai sur les Moeurs et L'Esprit des Nations* (1769) is much more significant in purpose than in achievement. It was conceived as a cultural history of all mankind, but Voltaire was not adequately prepared to cope with this task. In the scope of this work, however, lies its importance, for it was the first work to exhibit an appreciation of non-European civilization. Its scope was further enlarged by a treatment of the newly discovered primitive peoples. Voltaire's *Essai* constitutes a landmark in the development of modern historiography; in a sense it set the task for future historians.

In his campaign against superstition and bigotry, Voltaire performed an invaluable service to humanity. His opposition to the Church, however, distorted his historical perspective. This attitude, as has been indicated, was characterstic of the rationalist historical school. They tended to regard religion as the creation of the priestly caste rather than as a social product and the Church as possessing no real historical import. The Middle Ages became the special target of their scorn. It was the age of unreason; it represented a void in the process of historical development. Neither the age nor its institutions fulfilled any positive function. Similarly, the term "barbarism," which was associated with the downfall of the Roman Empire, had for these historians an emotional rather than a historical meaning: it was simply a term of abuse. Viewing their own period as one in which the spirit and mind of man were emancipated, they were unable to grasp its relations with the epoch of "unreason," with the age of "cultural and historical aridity."

This point of view is also expressed in the historical works of the eighteenth-century English philosopher and historian David Hume. His most notable work, *The History of England from the Invasion of Julius Caesar to the Revolution of 1688* (new ed., 1763) is a poorly organized narrative, defective in scholarship. Hume was far more concerned with the presentation of a historical outlook than with the consideration of historical fact. His attitude toward orthodox Christianity and toward the Middle Ages was similar to that of Voltaire.

Hume's *History,* however, is not without merit. It was the first attempt at a relatively complete "natural" history of England. In its treatment of the English constitutional and religious struggles, Hume displayed an objectivity which contributed to a realistic appraisal of the period and of its problems. Its excellence of style made it a widely read and highly influential work.

From the standpoint of scholarship and of historical techniques, the Scotsman William Robertson ranks high among rationalist historians. He exhibited a discrimination in the handling of source material, an ability to organize his material, and a passionate concern for factual accuracy. He was of the opinion that history should be concerned with matters possessing dignity, the activities of dignified individuals. This attitude prevented an adequate appreciation of the facts of economic, cultural, or social history. These factors, although frequently mentioned in his works, were never considered of basic importance. Robertson's treatment of the Middle Ages was superior to that of Voltaire or Hume. He was not as harsh in his judgment and was one of the first historians to grasp the political and institutional development of the period as well as the leading cultural and economic influences.

The History of Scotland (16th ed., 1802), *The History of the Reign of the Emperor Charles V* (1769), *The History of America* (2d American ed., 1821), and *An Historical Disquisition concerning the Knowledge which the Ancients Had of India* (3d ed., 1799) constitute Robertson's four major works.

It may be said, with considerable justification, that Edward Gibbon in his *The History of the Decline and Fall of the Roman Empire* (1776-81) composed the masterpiece of rationalist historiography. Its stylistic brilliance has won the extravagant praise of critics, and it is still useful and reliable from the standpoint of factual presentation.

Gibbon's *History* is a detailed study of the period from A.D. 180 to the year A.D. 641. From 641 to 1453, it presents a sketch of historical developments.

Gibbon's admiration for the Roman Empire was unbounded, and he regarded its downfall as a world disaster. Although he regarded Christianity in part responsible for this downfall, he recognized the important role played by Christianity and the Church following the disintegration of the Empire, as well as the cultural achievements of the latter in the Middle Ages. As a rationalist, however, he did not hold the Middle Ages in too great esteem.

Gibbon's account of the rise of Christianity was most significant, treating it in a fully objective manner. He approached the problem historically, not from the theological approach, which regarded it of supernatural origin, nor from the philosophical position of those rationalist historians who regarded it as the creation of priests.

The all-important problem of the cause or causes of the downfall of the Roman Empire did not receive adequate treatment in Gibbon's *History*. He listed various causes tending toward a geographic explanation that the Empire had become too large, which theory he perhaps derived from Montesquieu. But he failed to explain the precise relationship between the factor of largeness and the eventual downfall of the Empire.

August Ludwig von Schlözer's *Weltgeschichte* (2d ed., 1792-1801) represents an attempt by a German historian to follow in the footsteps of Voltaire. Possessing limited critical powers as well as an undistinguished literary style, this work is not of notable significance. Schlözer was, however, an outstanding philologist and in his political outlook was an apologist for enlightened despotism.

The *Geschichte der Deutschen* (1785-88) of Michael Ignaz Schmidt is a far more significant contribution to historical literature. It exemplifies the best tendencies of rationalist historiography. It is well written, accurate in its factual presentation, and truly a history of civilization in scope.

Montesquieu's influence upon the development of historiography is essentially methodological, for he contributed little either to historical criticism or investigation. Certain significant historical factors which were merely touched upon by Voltaire and other rationalist historians received much fuller treatment in the works of Montesquieu. He attempted to synthesize the various elements of historical development; he stressed the importance of commercial and fiscal activities in the life of the state; and, whereas other historians referred to the particular genius of a people, Montesquieu attempted to explain these individual differences, attributing them to the influence of geographical factors. In his appraisal of social institutions, he expressed a relativistic attitude, insisting that these institutions must not be judged by absolute or arbitrary standards, but by the manner in which they conform to the spirit of the people they serve.

In his *Considerations on the Causes of the Grandeur and Decadence of the Romans* (transl. in 1894), Montesquieu exhibits his ability to analyze the trends and underlying factors in the development and decline of the Roman power, anticipating many explanations current among modern historians. From the standpoint of historical criticism or scholarship, however, it is not of too great significance.

Chronologically, Rousseau belongs to the period of the Enlightenment. In his philosophy, however, he represents a reaction against some of its fundamental postulates. Rousseau rejected the omnipotence of reason, manifested little enthusiasm for scientific progress, and expressed little sympathy for the cultural attainments of his age. As a progenitor of the romantic movement, Rousseau's influences upon the development of historiography must be sought primarily in the historical works of the nineteenth century. A number of German writers of the late eighteenth century, however, may be regarded as disciples of Rousseau. Isaak Iselin, author of the two volume *Uber die Geschichte der Menschheit* (1791), reflected Rousseau's sympathy for primitive man in his extended treatment of primitive society. This work is notable in its comparative analysis of the civilization, manners, and customs of the major peoples of history. Rousseau's influence is also discernible in the works of the poet-dramatist-historian, Johann Christophe Friedrich von Schiller. His major works, *The History of the Revolt of the Netherlands* (tr. E. B. Eastwick, 1901), and *The History of the Thirty Years' War* (tr. A. J. W. Morrison, 1901), while exhibiting certain powers of political analysis, are more important as a contribution to literature than to scientific history.

Romanticism in History—With the beginning of the nineteenth century the writing of history enters a new phase. Not only is the output of historical writing much increased, both absolutely and relatively over previous centuries, but the over-all approach to historical writing changes. The most significant aspect of this change may be described by saying that whereas up to the early nineteenth century, historical works were considered almost exclusively parts of general literature and read as such, history tends to be regarded more and more as a science, and the standards of evaluation applied to historical writing cease to be those of general literary criticism and become increasingly more rigorous standards of scientific appraisal. To be sure, the change never was complete, and much historical writing today falls in the class of general literature rather than social science. This is especially true of biographical works and some "popular" histories. But the approach of writers of history has changed sufficiently so that even those works which have enjoyed great popular success—as for example H. G. Wells's *The Outline of History* (1921), or Arnold Toynbee's *A Study of History* (1934), or to cite an example of a more specialized historical book, Cecil Woodham Smith's *The Reason Why* (1953)—conform throughout to standards of scholarly history.

Historical writing of the nineteenth and twentieth century has often been classified in different separate groups. For example, the distinction was made between didactic, romantic, and scientific history, or between a nationalist and a liberalist trend in historical writing. The first of these distinctions relates to the purposes to which a historical work is to be put, the second classifies historical works in accordance with the underlying political trend which it exhibits.

Didactic history is history written with the purpose of teaching a lesson for the present. Modern historians are, on the whole, averse to this trend of historical writing. They tend to believe that the one lesson which can be learned from history is that no lesson can be learned from it. Romantic historical writing—which had its high point in the early part of the nineteenth century—derives its name from the then prevailing tendency in literature. Among the most notable romantic literary writers are such figures as Sir Walter Scott, Lord Byron, the poet Hoelderlin, as well as Herder in Germany and François A. R. de Chateaubriand and Alexandre Dumas in France. Perhaps the best examples of truly romantic literature are Scott's *Waverly Novels* (1877-79) and Dumas' *The Three Musketeers* (1888). It is not suggested that romantic history conforms in all detail to the type of writing represented by these works of fiction. It has been called romantic history rather because it tends to be concerned with subject matter similar to that treated in romantic fiction. Romantic history, following in the footsteps of the researches of Herder and Macpherson, who unearthed ancient legends, seeks to reinterpret the semi-legendary origins of peoples and communities. It created great interest in knighthood and the exploits of chivalrous warriors, it tended to concentrate on the glorification of the great deeds of national—and sometimes semi-legendary—heroes of old, and it found its greatest inspiration in the re-evaluation of the "dark ages" that had been so completely and roundly damned by such rationalists of the eighteenth century as Gibbon and Voltaire. In opposing these trends which had emerged during the domination of rationalist thought in history, the romantic historians fulfilled a much needed task. They attempted to revise the views held about medieval institutions, and they furthered historical research in general in bringing into the orbit of historical writing the concern with legendary and quasi-legendary periods. In this way they extended the horizon of historians and the general scope of history. It is not surprising that in so doing they somewhat overshot the mark, that they found beauty and validity in many institutions simply because they were ancient, and that their interpretations of many aspects of earlier ages were colored by their bias in favor of the legendary, the chivalrous, and the long-established.

Among the most notable works of romantic history may be listed one of Chateaubriand's own works, *Les Martyrs* (1830), which is a history of early Christianity not only in Rome, but also in the outlying provinces of the Empire. The mystery of the forests of Gaul is given equal emphasis with that of the laws and administrative decrees, the political and military needs of the provincial governors. Among other romantic historians of note was the disciple of Chateaubriand, Augustin Thierry, whose *History of the Conquest of England by the Normans* (1825) is an even better example of romantic history than the writings of Chateaubriand, because Thierry was primarily a historian, whereas Chateaubriand was a poet. Also imbued by a scientific spirit, but essentially romantic in execution, are the historical works of Jean C. L. Simonde de Sismondi. Sismondi, a citizen of Geneva, wrote a lengthy *History of the Italian Republics* (new ed., 1870) and an even longer *Histoire des Français* (1821-44) in 30 volumes. The essentially romantic character of his work is well characterized by a statement of the Duchesse de Broglie who said that "his hatred of priests is wearisome, and he judges Hugh Capet as he would judge a Geneva syndic of the nineteenth century." His biases are, however, in part also political, and the French romantic historian Barrante could say of his work that "in his virtuous indignation Sismondi becomes the personal enemy of all the kings, nobles, and bishops of the past."

Romantic history was, however, by no means confined to France. In Germany, Karl Eichhorn, who revived the historical study of law, is often cited as the foremost representative of romantic history. Eichhorn grew up in an age in which German nationalist feeling was at its height. The first volume of his *Deutsche Staats- und Rechtsgeschichte* appeared in 1808 (2d ed. 1818-23). He had been aroused by the spirit that permeated Europe in consequence of the French Revolution, and he was deeply stirred by the Prussian defeat of 1806. He wished to dedicate his life to the redemption of Germany by fostering the patriotism of his students, and it was in this spirit that his first work was written. Eichhorn was by no means the only German romantic historian. His co-patriot, Henrich Leo, who wrote a *Geschichte der Italienischen Staaten* (1829-37), was, like Eichhorn, inspired by a fierce German nationalism, which was the stronger in the younger Leo, who witnessed the French occupation of his fatherland as a boy and who came under the strong influence of the very nationalistic Friedrich L. Jahn. But even Leo could not quite escape the scientism which tended to make itself strongly felt in Germany under the impact of the teaching of Ranke, and though essentially romantic in conception his works are more discriminating and "scientific" in execution than those of the French historians, or of some English romantics, notably Carlyle.

Romanticism spread far and wide in the third decade of the nineteenth century, and the works of writers not only in France and Germany but even in Russia and Poland came under its influence. In the latter country the national historian Joachim Lelewel composed a history of Poland in the Middle Ages (*Histoire de Pologne,* 1844) which shows strong romantic trends, and in Russia Nicholai Karamzin wrote his *Histoire de l'Empire de Russie* (1819-26), which explained the historical development of that country by the special genius of the Russian people derived from their partly oriental heritage and the influence of the Eastern Church. He was anti-Western and anti-liberal and became a popular hero of the anti-liberalistic and anti-Western wing of the later pan-Slavists.

In Britain romanticism is best represented in the work of Thomas Carlyle. Carlyle's romanticism–in contrast to that of many other romantic historians who adulated the masses as the bearers of a mysterious national genius–is manifest in his emphasis on the role of outstanding heroes. More than any other writer on historical subjects, Carlyle is responsible for stressing the function of heroes in history. In a sense this bias makes caricatures of some of his historical works. For example, in spite of its literary qualities, Carlyle's *The French Revolution* (1837) accepts the thesis that the French Revolution was from the beginning the product of a savage, bloodthirsty, nationalistic mob. There is no understanding of the underlying causes of the origin of the revolution and no true appreciation of its political significance. Carlyle's sketches of Frederick the Great (in his *History of Friedrich the Second, Called, Frederick the Great,* 1858) and others are better, but far from reliable biographical studies.

Carlyle's disciples James A. Froude and the American John L. Motley were both abler historians but less exciting writers than the master. Froude selected his sources with some bias, and hence his major work, *The History of England from the Fall of Wolsey to the Death of Elizabeth* (1856-70), is not so much a historical account of the reigns of Henry VIII and his children, but rather an often poetic epic of the "deliverance of Britain from the slavery of Rome." Motley's *Rise of the Dutch Republic* (1856) follows closely in the footsteps of his two masters. From Carlyle and Froude he derives a romantic inspiration, from his

American master, George Bancroft, the inspiration to write didactic history. Hence his life work was devoted to an account of the rise of liberty and the struggle against slavery among the Dutch. His work is primarily a polemic for liberty and republicanism and a diatribe against absolutism and religious intolerance. Parallels between Dutch and American heroes are often obvious, and William the Silent is compared explicitly with George Washington.

This account of some of the main works of the "romantic" movement in historical writing shows that it became tied up with the nationalistic trends on the one hand and the liberalistic trends of historical writing on the other. Eichhorn, Karamzin, and Thierry are forerunners of nationalistic history, which attained its full flowering in the works composed around the middle and the third quarter of the nineteenth century. Sismondi, Motley, Froude, and Lelewel are representatives of the liberalist school which reached its high point, especially in Britain and the United States, at about the same time. The reaction against romanticism in historical writing also began to emerge very early in the nineteenth century. This reaction is usually associated with the emergence of Leopold von Ranke, one of the greatest historians of all times. Ranke's influence on German history and more generally on historical writings in other countries was tremendous. But with the gradual victory of the scientific approach in history over the romantic approach, political coloration of historical writing was not entirely eliminated. The German historians Treitschke and Hans Delbrück both applied the methods of Ranke, but though they were scientific historians in their approach, they were fierce nationalists. The English historian Lord Acton, on the other hand, was also a thoroughly scientific historian, but a convinced and even fanatic liberal.

Political History—For a time, before the scientific approach in history became universally victorious, political opinions were strongly affecting historical writing. It would be wrong to call some of the work which appeared in the middle of the nineteenth century as belonging to the romantic school; the ultimate purpose of much of that historical work is based on political predilections. It is in this sense that we may speak of nationalistic conservative, liberalistic, and even revolutionary historical works. It is not surprising that this should be the case. The period from about 1775 to 1850 was a period of violent political change. Revolutions and reaction alternated. New nations were being fashioned, and the frontiers of Europe were altered several times in the course of a few years. The principle of royal and imperial legitimacy was questioned. The claims of dynasticism were measured against those of the nation. The role and power of the aristocracy was pushed in the background by the rising middle-class, and the function of this class in turn was challenged, although as yet unsuccessfully, by the workers and poor peasants. It is not surprising that in an age of such vehement and fundamental political change, when old established political values and social arrangements were questioned, writers representing the different factions should look for justification of their party position in the historical background of their countries. It is in this light that we must understand much of the "political" history of the nineteenth century.

The outstanding representative of political historical writing in France was Jules Michelet, who is regarded by some as the greatest French historian of the nineteenth century. Michelet's *History of France* (1845-47) is not only a work of historical writing but also—like the works of Carlyle and Froude—a work of outstanding literary merit. Though he started out as a conservative, Michelet became interested in rationalism and science and was inspired by the spirit of the French Revolution. He conceived of his work as an account of "the drama of human liberty," and became in this way the outstanding representative of the liberalist wing of French history. Though it is probably not advisable to read Michelet today for the historical narrative in his works, it would be difficult to select a historian who more accurately represents in his work the general spirit and national genius of his people that Michelet. He is rationalistic and a lover of freedom; he has a sense for the dramatic and for the *grande geste;* he is eloquent, and a well-turned phrase is as important to him as a new insight into historical relations; he has a sense of logic and tends to work in a way so as to leave no loose ends; above all, he has a passionate love for France, his country, and her people. More can be learned about France and the French by reading a volume of Michelet's than almost any other French book of the last 150 years.

Another liberal writer among French historians was the poet Alphonse de Lamartine, whose *History of the Girondists* (1848) is a glorification of the moderate group among the men of the great Revolution. More to the left than Michelet and Lamartine was the socialist Louis Blanc, who also wrote a *History of the French Revolution of 1789* (1848) and *The History of Ten Years, 1830-1840* (1844-45), in which he defended the principle of equality and fraternity. More conservative were Alexis de Tocqueville, who wrote *The Old Regime and the Revolution* (1856), in which he defended the principle of aristocracy, and Adolphe Thiers, whose *History of the Consulate and the Empire of France under Napoleon* (1845-62) is a glorification of Napoleon I and his work. This work gains its political touch not so much in that it describes the struggle between democracy and absolutism, but rather because of its partisanship in the conflict between Bonapartism and Bourbon legitimacy. It stresses the achievements of Bonaparte and, in this way, implicitly takes sides against the Bourbons. The same attitude was expressed by François Mignet's *History of the French Revolution from 1789 to 1814* (1856), which for some time was regarded as the most partisan product of the Bonapartist wing.

More important than the work of any of these men for the future of French historical scholarship, save possibly Jules Michelet, was François Guizot. Guizot was a mild liberal in his political views, or better perhaps, a moderate conservative. He was an important historian when he became minister under Louis-Philippe. Before he joined that government he had begun his *History of Civilization in Europe* (1885), a work which constitutes a triumph of condensation and on which his fame chiefly rests. As a minister he worked on behalf of historical scholarship, attempting to achieve the realization of his views of the tasks of history. He had said that the historian has a three-fold task. He must collect his facts and know how they are connected: that he called "historical anatomy." Secondly, he must discover the organization of societies and their life, the laws under which they live, and the rules of conduct by which they are governed: that is the "physiology of history." But his third task is to discover the "physiognomy" of history, the aspects of the daily tasks, the minute details of living which alone can tell us all we need to know about the civilization and culture of past ages. In order to provide French historians with materials on the basis of which these tasks could be performed, he organized the *Société de l'école des Chartes,* through whose labors the Ministry of Education began to publish in 1834 the series *Collection de Documents inédits sur l'histoire de France,* texts of important previously unpublished documents relating to French history. He also founded the *Société de l'histoire de France,* which counted among its members the most distinguished French historians and whose *Publications* (*Ouvrages publiés,* 1837-   ) contain in more than 350 volumes (to date) important source materials of various types. In general magnitude and importance for the making available of old documents in easily accessible form, the enterprises started by Guizot compare with the great collection of the *Monumenta Germaniae Historica,* started in Germany under the editorship of Georg Heinrich Pertz with the support of Baron vom Stein and continued later by Georg Waitz.

Both collections, the series initiated under the impetus of Guizot in France and the German *Monumenta,* are models of scientific historical research. They are the products not of one scholar but of the organized profession of workers in history in a country. Compiled with skill and scrupulousness, they are designed to become literary monuments not only of the past but also of historical scholarship of their countries. Although their initiation derived some of its impetus from the growing spirit of nationalism which fired the intellectuals of France, and above all, Germany, in the early nineteenth century, they are not so much the outflow of nationalistic or political bias upon history as they are the first large-scale realizations of scientific history on the European continent.

While the *Monumenta* were being planned and their execution begun, politically inspired history was being written in Germany as in France. Owing to the weakness of a divided Germany before the unification under Bismarck in 1871, tendencies of nationalism were stronger and more pronounced. We have already seen how Eichhorn and Leo, two leaders of German romanticism, were strong patriots. This was also true among their followers, for example Wilhelm von Giesebrecht, who wrote *Geschichte der Deutschen Kaiserzeit* (1855-58), which is no less distinguished by its scholarship than by its Teutonic fervor. Other nationalists were Johann Gustav Droysen, whose *Geschichte der Preussischen Politik*

(1868-86) was not merely a history but a eulogy of Prussianism; Heinrich von Sybel, whose *The Founding of the German Empire by William I* (1890-98) is a highly partisan defense of Bismarck and his overall policies, and, above all, Heinrich von Treitschke, whose nationalism was so blatant that he is often cited as the model of a historian with a strong nationalistic bias. His chauvinism was, however, not only expounded in the classroom and the historical treatise, but also from the rostrum of the Reichstag. Many expressions of a blind nationalism which were and are attributed to Treitschke do not appear in his books. Some were made by him in speeches, and some are merely legends which were fastened on him by his political adversaries. In spite of a strong Prussian bias, Treitschke's *Deutsche Geschichte im Neunzehnten Jahrhundert* (1896-99) is a work conceived on a large scale and executed with great skill and, apart from its strong bias, with great scientific fervor. Treitschke was not the last German nationalist historian. He had many imitators, especially during World War I and the Nazi period. In that latter time, German historical scholarship deteriorated to such an extent that we need not concern ourselves with it. But one of Treitschke's followers must be mentioned. This is Dietrich Schaefer, a strong monarchist and nationalist, but a gifted historian. His *Deutsche Geschichte* (10th ed., 1932) was an extremely popular work in the interwar period, and remains today a work cherished by many patriotically minded Germans.

But lest one should think that the only political influence on German historical writing in the nineteenth century was nationalistic, we must turn to some writers who approached history with ideas of social and political reform and among the most radical of whom were the founders of German socialism. First there was the school of historical jurisprudence. To be sure, this group of writers, the most outstanding among whom was Friedrich Karl von Savigny, did not approach history from an explicitly political standpoint. But their very concern with law, the reconstruction of the influence of the Roman law of equity and contract upon later development, and the role played by the popular Germanic laws in the strand of legal and constitutional development in Central Europe, had the result of making their over-all impact felt on the side of political moderation, constitutionalism, and cosmopolitanism. Savigny's main work was the *Geschichte des Romischen Rechts im Mittelalter* (2d. ed., 1834-51), but he was followed by many writers on the history of law and the historical development of constitutionalism. The most outstanding of his followers was Otto von Gierke, who wrote a monumental work on the development of German corporations, part of which has been translated. One portion was published in English under the title *Political Theories of the Middle Ages* (1900), with an introduction by Frederic W. Maitland. (Maitland's Introduction is an essay on medieval political theory of such high stature that this part of the book in itself justifies the translation.) Another portion of Gierke's *Das Deutsche Genossenschaftsrecht* (1868-73) was published under the editorship of Sir Ernest Barker and bears the title *Natural Law and the Theory of Society, 1500 to 1800*

(1934). Other outstanding members of the legal historical school of Germany were Rudolf Sohm and Ludwig Mitteis. The latter was also a papyrologist of repute and devoted much of his time to the study of Egyptian legal papyri from the second to the sixth centuries, by means of which he could trace the development of Roman law from its Republican antecedents to the codification of Justinian.

The impact of the legal-historical school had, on the whole, only a partial political slant, but there were also genuine liberals among the German historians of the Metternich period. Among them the most outstanding were Karl von Rotteck, whose *The History of the World* (new ed., 1883) constituted an attack on all suppression of liberty. The book was immensely popular and went through many editions. It was translated into most European languages. Another writer of similar persuasion was Friedrich C. Schlosser, whose main work was a *History of the Eighteenth Century and of the Nineteenth till the Overthrow of the French Empire* (1843-50). In addition to his fervent liberalism, Schlosser expressed abundant moral judgments. His books read in part like an application of the rules of Kantian moral philosophy to human history. A third German writer whose work was deeply imbued by liberal ideas was Schlosser's pupil, Georg Gottfried Gervinus. His main work was a *Geschichte des Neunzehnten Jahrhunderts* (1855-56), in which he attempted to trace the rise of liberalism, constitutionalism, and republicanism. These tendencies he traced back to the Protestant Reformation, and he represented the work of Luther as a struggle against the monarcho-aristocratic trends in the Catholic Church. Finally, Friedrich Christophe Dahlmann must be reckoned among the German historians whose over-all political partisanship was on the side of liberty. Dahlmann wrote on early German history, but his influence was more directly political than merely through historical books. He was the victim of a "purge" for his convictions when he was dismissed from his University (Göttingen) in 1837 for his political views in favor of constitutionalism. The next nine years he spent at Bonn warning the princes of the consequences they would face if they refused constitutional government to their peoples. His last public emergence was in 1848 when he battled manfully for a liberal Empire under Prussian hegemony.

Dahlmann represents a curious mixture of a liberal with a high degree of nationalist fervor in favor of Prussia. But though this may appear surprising today, such a position was by no means contradictory in the early nineteenth century. Prussia had introduced more far-reaching reforms under Stein and Hardenberg than any other Central European state; she was fostering the German customs union which had, on the whole, free-trade tendencies; the Hohenzollerns favored industrialization, and the over-all treatment of the middle classes, especially in the western part of the Prussian dominions (Westphalia and the Rhine Province), was on the whole more liberal than many of the small states which filled Central and Southern Germany. Moreover, in internal German politics Prussia was the great and only equal antagonist of

Austria, which before 1848 was regarded as the very center of reactionary absolutism. Hence a sentiment favoring Prussia and freedom at the same time was not considered inconsistent, and many members of the German left shared Dahlmann's attitude. Among them was Ferdinand von Lassalle who was not a historian but a politician. Among them was also Friedrich Engels whose work, *The Condition of the Working Class in England in 1844* (1887), is perhaps the most characteristic work of historical analysis from the extreme left. Among these writers should also be counted Engels' friend and collaborator Karl Marx, who was as much a historian as an economist. Marx's *The Eighteenth Brumaire of Louis Bonaparte* (1898) or his writings on the Crimean War, which appeared as news releases and were collected under the title *The Eastern Question* (1897), are historical accounts with a strong socialist political flavor.

Socialist historiography made considerable headway in Germany after the establishment and growth of the socialist party. Although in the fields of economics and philosophy the socialists of the late 1890's and early 1900's turned out some very respectable works, they did not achieve as high a level of output quantitatively and qualitatively in the field of history. The best socialist historical work was probably Eduard Bernstein's *Die Geschichte der Berliner Arbeiter-Bewegung* (1907-10). Other writings of merit were the works by Franz Mehring, *The Lessing Legend* (1938), *Geschichte der Deutschen Socialdemokratie* (1897-98), and, above all, his biography of *Karl Marx* (1935). This last work is still probably the best biography of the great socialist leader. A slight socialist influence was also exercised in the early works of Werner Sombart, especially his *Socialism and the Social Movement* (tr. from 6th German ed., 1909).

Whereas in France conservative and liberal historical writers were fairly evenly balanced, and whereas in Germany conservative and nationalistic writers predominated, on the whole, in Britain and the United States it was the liberals who held the center of the stage. In the first half of the nineteenth century, the great Whig "triumvirate" was made up of Henry Hallam, Thomas Babington Macaulay, and George Grote. Of these three, the first two wrote on English history and the third on classical antiquity. Hallam's chief work was his *The Constitutional History of England from the Accession of Henry VII to the Death of George II* (5th ed., 1846). This book was a political manifesto, particularly so since it appeared at a time when the Tory hegemony was as yet unbroken in England. It was a severe blow to "personal government," and it extols the moderate parliamentarism of the Whig revolution of 1688. It was an immensely popular book among the educated. It was read at the universities, quoted in Parliament, studied as a guide by the youthful Queen Victoria, and translated under the auspices of Guizot into French, a document of liberalism and textbook for friends of constitutional liberty everywhere.

For those who found Hallam's three stout volumes tough going, there was an immensely more readable popularization of his views in Thomas Babington Macaulay's *Essays, Critical and Miscellaneous* (1843). In terms of sheer readability, these essays belong to the most fluent English prose ever written. Macaulay also wrote *The History of England from the Accession of James the Second* (5th ed., 1849), which remained unfinished at the time of his death. When he wrote this book, he expressed the ambition of writing a work which would "for a few days supersede the last fashionable novel on the tables of young ladies." This ambition was satisfied; when the first two volumes of the *History* appeared they were best sellers and sold in quantities not much below those of *Waverly*. Macaulay had worked hard on this book, and this explains the slowness of its completion. His nephew tells us that "he could not rest until every paragraph concluded with a telling sentence, and every sentence flowed like running water."

Next to Hallam and Macaulay there were a number of minor figures. Harriet Martineau wrote a popular *History of the Thirty Years' Peace, A.D. 1816-1846* (1877-78), which was a liberal interpretation of her own times. A successor to these Whig historians was John R. Green, who wrote after the middle of the century. Green's *History of the English People* (1878-80) was the classic account of British history written from the liberal camp. There were also some opponents of the Whig view of history. Among them was, above all, Sir Archibald Alison, who wrote a *History of Europe from the Commencement of the French Revolution* . . . (1837-42), which he himself declared to be a great effort on behalf of the Conservative cause. Another conservative writer was William Napier, whose *History of the War in the Peninsula* . . . (new ed., 1851) was a document extolling the Duke of Wellington and the conservative cause in general.

Finally, there were historians in Britain who may be compared to the vigorous nationalists in Germany and France. These men tended to study the Germanic or Celtic origins of Britain and to concentrate in their work on the fashioning of the British race. Outstanding among them were John M. Kemble, whose *The Saxons in England* (1849) stressed the superiority of the Anglo-Saxon stock. It also became famous in Germany where it was used to support the contention of the civilizing mission of the Teutonic tribes. A follower of Kemble was Edward A. Freeman, who presented the Anglo-Saxon theory in his *History of the Norman Conquest of England* (1867-79). The peak of the pro-Teutonic interpretation of English history is to be found, however, in the work of the poet-historian Charles Kingsley, *The Roman and the Teuton* (1864). This book, though conceived as a piece of historical writing is, in reality, a piece of special pleading, in which the "young and virile children of the Teutonic forest" are extolled and contrasted with decadent Romans of a "dying empire."

The liberal-conservative struggle was extended in England also to the field of history of antiquity. The Teutonic theory could not be applied to that field, if we overlook the wholly unscientific attempt of Kingsley to contrast an Arminius and an Alaric with a Diocletian and other "degenerate" rulers of Rome. Just as in the field of modern history a Hallam and a Macaulay confronted an Alison, so in the field of Greek history the radical George Grote confronted the Tory William Mitford. Both wrote works entitled *History of Greece,* but whereas Mitford's (1829) was quoted by the Tories with approval, Grote's avowed purpose in writing his book (new ed., 1869-70) was to provide a "juster view" of Greek history. The result is an exalted praise of Athenian democracy and an unconcealed hostility not only against the Persian kings, but also against Philip and Alexander of Macedon, the "destroyers of Greek freedom." The Macedonians are represented as quasi-Asiatic barbarians, and it is their conquest of Greece which forever extinguishes the lamp of true Greek civilization. It was neither Mitford nor Grote who wrote the most scholarly and most objective history of Greece among Englishmen of his day, but Grote's friend, Connop Thirlwall, who had studied the scientific approach of the Germans and was using with greatest advantage the lessons he had learned from men like Barthold Georg Niebuhr, the disciples of Niebuhr, and the forerunners of Theodor Mommsen. With Thirlwall's work the rigorous scientific spirit enters, for the first time, the writing of the history of antiquity in England. After this work it spread to other fields and conquered English historical writing soon after the middle of the century.

An important aid to the scientific approach of English history was given by the publication of source materials. We have seen how the German series of the *Monumenta Germaniae Historica* and in France the *Documents inédits* prepared by the members of the *Ecole des Chartes* formed important collections of valuable sources that were indispensable prerequisites for the scientific approach to history. Britain also had its series of such publications. But whereas in Germany and France these enterprises were centralized and inspired by official and semi-official sources, in Britain only a small part of these publications were brought out by the efforts of the government. To be sure, in 1800 a Record Commission was established and charged with the editing of Britain's historical sources, but the Commission remained in a deplorable state of inactivity. In 1837 the Commission was discontinued, and the historical records were placed under the supervision of the Master of the Rolls. Again nothing much was done, until in 1857 Lord Romilly, the then Master of the Rolls, could attract some funds from the government for the editing of important documents. Romilly was fortunate in finding two men who were indefatigable in the work of making these documents accessible to the public, Thomas D. Hardy and Bishop William Stubbs. The collection, which constituted a publishing venture lasting 54 years, is known under the title of *Chronicles and Memorials of Great Britain and Ireland during the Middle Ages*. It also has a Latin title, *Rerum Britannicarum Medii Aevi Scriptores,* but it is usually referred to under its short title of *Rolls Series*. In addition to the official *Rolls Series,* a number of private collections have been made under the auspices of several societies. For example, the Camden Society published a long series of historical sources, the Early English Text Society of literary sources, the Selden Society of legal sources, and the Hakluyt Society of sources on voyages and explorations. Also, an exhaustive historical record of the various counties of Britain was begun in 1900 in the series of the *Victoria History of the Counties of England,* which is as yet incomplete.

As in Britain, the dominant political bias in the early American historical works comes from the liberal rather than the conservative side. In fact, due to its beginnings in a revolution against monarchy and as a consequence of its democratic traditions, the history of America was seen by many of its early protagonists as an experiment in setting up a government based on freedom and equality. These sentiments play a strong role in American historiography. Although the early period of American history witnessed the struggle between the Jeffersonians and the more conservative Federalists, and later the struggle of the democratic Jacksonians and their more conservative Whig opponents, American historians were, on the whole, too much under the impact of the revolutionary beginnings of this nation to write history in a strictly conservative vein. The most characteristic of the early American historians was George Bancroft, a Jeffersonian Democrat. Though he studied in Germany, where he came under the influence of Hegel, Savigny, and Boeckh in Berlin and Heeren in Göttingen, he returned to the United States fully inspired to "venerate the masses" and to listen to "the popular voice, which is all powerful with us; this is our oracle." Bancroft's main work was *A History of the United States from the Discovery of The American Continent* (1834-75). This is a work filled with a nationalist fervor and a deep love of liberty and democracy. The settlement of the United States was pictured as consisting of a constant stream of refugees from secular and religious oppression. The standard of freedom waved forever on the American shore and the banner of slavery on the other side of the Atlantic. Bancroft, who also extolled the Puritans, was followed by John G. Palfrey, who wrote *A History of New England* (1858-90), in which the Bancroftian formula was applied to a local region and a particular religious group. Bancroft and Palfrey were followed by a long string of others, chief among them John Fiske, whose hero was not the Anglo-Saxon or the Puritan, but rather the member of the middle class. The over-all impact of Bancroft's interpretation lasted to the very end of the nineteenth century; one of its last exponents was Frederick J. Turner, whose thesis is set out in a collection of his papers entitled *The Frontier in American History* (1920). In this collection of papers Turner attempts to explain American free and egalitarian institutions by the impact of the frontier and life on the frontier. Though Turner was a historical writer fully in the scientific tradition, his work is still strongly influenced by the over-all assumption of the peculiar liberalistic bias which may be felt in most of American historiography of the nineteenth century.

The anti-monarchical bias of American historians led them to investigate the history of liberal movements and the struggle against abolutism and tyranny everywhere. William Prescott turned to the history of Spain. His first work, *History of the Reign of Ferdinand and Isabella, the Catholic* (10th ed., 1848-49), was an account of the conquest of the Iberian peninsula by the Catholic kings. Here is a description of the struggle of a powerful force of progress against a decaying outpost of a once vigorous and forward-looking race. Though less outspokenly liberal than the work of Bancroft and Palfrey, Prescott's sympathies are with the Catholic kings as they destroy an ancient moribund civilization, and he is duly critical of the inquisition which they allowed. Prescott later turned to the history of the Spanish conquest of America, and we shall return to this aspect of his work—which is the best known and makes up his most popular writings—below. Prescott was followed by John L. Motley, whose *Rise of the Dutch Republic* was a work fully in the spirit of Bancroft. An even later American historian, Henry Charles Lea, whose work is free from much of the romanticism of Bancroft and Motley and who properly belongs in the scientific tradition of historians, wrote *A History of the Inquisition of the Middle Ages* (1888), and *A History of the Inquisition of Spain* (1906-07), as well as other related topics of religious history. The overbearing impact of these works is also a description of the excess to which tyranny and absolute power may lead, and it is not surprising that Lea's contributions won high praise from a liberal historian like Lord Acton.

SCIENTIFIC HISTORY

By the middle of the nineteenth century the trend of history everywhere had reached a new stage, the stage of "scientific history." Since history had become a subject taught and studied at the universities, and since the scientific spirit had invaded the universities in the course of secularization and the great increase of biological, physical, and chemical research, historians tended to approach history from a scientific standpoint. This transition to scientific history was made the easier since philology and the study of law were carried on according to increasingly more stringent scientific canons, and since one aspect of the study of philology and law, especially in Germany, was the history of languages and literatures and of legal institutions. It is therefore not surprising that history, which originally had been an occupation largely of amateurs, became more and more a reserve for specialists. To be sure, men like Macaulay or Prescott could not be called professionals in the strict sense. But the age of the amateur historian was passing fast, and by the end of the nineteenth century he was the rare exception.

Textbooks and Popular Works—The growth and development of scientific history had a number of consequences. Above all, history was written primarily for the specialist rather than for the general reader. This means that works of history tended to treat more specialized subjects and to concentrate on periods and persons who had attracted little attention earlier. Whereas the main efforts of earlier historians had been devoted to painting a large canvas, writers on historical subjects now concerned themselves with minute and accurate miniatures. This is not to say that great and general historical works were not written any more, but they formed a rather small proportion of the total literary output of historians. Another aspect of this development was the need for popularizations. These took on two forms: the historical work for the general reader and the college or university textbook. The textbook became mandatory, because courses in schools were regularized, and a standard account of an historical priod or a national history had to be made available to students. As in other fields of social science, textbooks in history varied much in general quality and scope. Some of the best texts, as for example, Samuel Eliot Morison and Henry S. Commager's *The Growth of the American Republic* (4th ed., 1950), approach the general level of a treatise; others are pedestrian and too much confined to barren reporting of events to be much more than elaborate compilations of chronologies with some interspersed text.

The writing of historical works destined for the general reader was a more complex and difficult problem. History is the only social science still regarded as a field for general reading and in which felicity of style and beauty of expression are appreciated. The peculiar position of history as a field of literature in present-day American civilization is attested, among other things, in that historical works, more often than works in other social sciences, are reviewed in such general media as *The Saturday Review* or the *New York Times Book Review*. In addition, history is one of the fields in which literary prizes, for example, the Pulitzer Prize, are given, and historical works in general outsell those in other social sciences. Now it is not the specialized historical study which enjoys this position, nor the textbook, which is usually shunned by the general reader. The general reader is most interested in general histories or in biographies. The last fifty or seventy years have therefore witnessed, jointly with the growth of history as a science, the publication of many historical works addressed not to the specialist but to the general reader. These works, like literary works in general, are again of greatly varying quality. Some "popular" histories have become important works in their own right. For example, Charles A. and Mary R. Beard's *The Rise of American Civilization* (1927) is a work primarily addressed to the general reader which, because of its special interpretation of American history, has found a place on the shelf of the scholar also. Another example is George M. Trevelyan's *Illustrated English Social History* (1949-52), whose popularity has been eminent in Britain and which has been thought worthy of inclusion in a paperback reprint series of qualitatively eminent works. Often works whose chief audience was intended to be the scholarly world have been accepted by general readers as a "popular" work. Examples for this are also numerous. Perhaps the best-known instance is the popular appeal of Arnold Toynbee's *A Study of History,* a work which deals not with a historical period or the history of a country or institution, but which contains a philosophy of history. Other works falling in this group are Johan Huizinga's *The Waning of the Middle Ages* (1924), which has also been reprinted in a paperback edition, George Gordon Coulton's *Medieval Panorama* (1938), or Richard H. Tawney's *Religion and the Rise of Capitalism* (1926).

In addition to works like those mentioned just now, several series of historical works have attained considerable popularity. Among them are *The Rivers of America* series, which contains monographic studies of the history and geography, folklore, and human life on and around a river, or several series of national histories, such as, for example, the *Oxford History of England* (1934-) or the *Cambridge Modern History* (1902-12). Moreover, there have been published an abundance of special histories in the field of the arts, literature, and music and a number of popular histories of various institutions. Examples are Lewis Mumford's *Technics and Civilization* (1934), which is a history of practical arts, George H. Sabine's *A History of Political Theory* (rev. ed. 1950), and with special reference to popular culture, histories of fashion, histories of sports and pastimes, and histories of cleanliness and household practices.

Local History—A second result of the introduction of scientific thinking and methods in historical study and writing was the vast development of local history. Of course, here also forerunners may be found. For example, we find histories of cities or parts of countries as far back as the seventeenth century. Examples are John Stow's *The Survay of London,* which is a mixture of history, topography, folklore, law, and custom, and which was first published in 1618, or Robert Plot's *The Natural History of Oxford-shire,* which was first published in 1677 and is also a mixture of history, topography, folklore, and other things. But a short perusal of any bibliography of the history of the sixteenth or seventeenth century of Britain, France, or any other country (e.g., Godfrey Davies, *Bibliography of British History: Stuart Period, 1603-1714,* [1928]) will reveal the great scarcity of local histories in this period. Compare this with such extensive enterprises as the *Victoria History of the Counties of England* (1900-) or the massive many-volumed series of publications issued by many State Historical Societies in the United States, e.g., *Collections of the Illinois State Historical Library* or the *John Watts de Peyster Publication Fund Series* of the New York Historical Society. A list of these state and local historical societies and their publications is available in a handbook entitled *Historical Societies in the United States and Canada* (1944). The attention given to state and local history in the United States can be appraised also by consulting the annual bibliographies appearing under the title *Writings on American History,* compiled from 1902 to 1940 by Grace Gardner Griffin and continued after her death by the National Historical Publications Commission.

One does not go far wrong in regarding as the "father" of local history Gilbert White, whose *The Natural History and Antiquities of Selborne* has become a classic. It was first published in 1789 and has seen numerous editions since. In the "advertisement" to his book, White outlines a program for the writing of local history. He says that "the idea of *parochial history* . . . ought to consist of natural productions and occurrences, as well as antiquities. . . . If stationary men would pay some attention to the districts on which they reside, and would publish their thoughts respecting the objects that surround them, from such materials might be drawn the most complete county-histories, which are still wanting in several parts of this kingdom, and in particular in the county of Southampton." White's admonition has been followed, and in Britain, as well as in other parts of Europe, but also to a very great extent in the United States, "stationary men" have concerned themselves with the history of the "districts on which they reside," and we have gained from this concern an abundant flow of local history. Though few local histories produced since White wrote have attained the fame of his book, several works that are concerned with the history of towns, states, or regions have attained considerable attention and have served as models. An example of an excellent history of a city is Asa Briggs' recent *History of Birmingham, Borough and City, 1865-1938* (1952); an excellent state history is Oscar and Mary F. Handlin's *Commonwealth* (1947), which deals with a crucial period in the history of Massachusetts; and among regional histories we have such works as Walter Prescott Webb's *The Great Plains* (1931), Bernard DeVoto's *Across the Wide Missouri* (1947), or Van Wyck Brooks's several volumes of New England history. Even Mark Twain's *Life on the Mississippi* (1883) should be regarded as a local history, especially if Gilbert White's prescription is applied to it. Twain reports in this book on "natural production and occurrences" and even on some "antiquities" of the Mississippi River region.

But the bulk of local history is contained in the publications of local or regional historical associations, much of it in the form of articles or monographs. In Britain and the United States interest in local history is also manifest by the formation not merely of State Historical Societies and similar public, semi-public, and quasi-public associations, but also by the formation of private associations concerned with the exploration of the history of a region, province, or locality. Examples are the Mississippi Valley Historical Association, which now, however, has extended its field of interest to all phases of American history, or the Thoresby Society, which is concerned with the history of the city of Leeds and the surrounding parts of Yorkshire.

Scientific Method in History–A third result of the growth of the scientific spirit in history has been the standardization and development of rigorous rules of historical method. First generally accepted rules of evidence were gradually developed. What "facts" should be accepted by historians, and how could historical "facts" be established? What rules are to be followed if two witnesses to an event give different accounts of it? Many of these problems and other related ones had troubled earlier historians very little. In part they were not concerned with establishing the "incontrovertible facts" of a historical episode with the same degree of confidence as modern historians, and in part questions of the verification of historical facts were often beyond their competence, since they had few unquestioned texts on which to base their conclusions. Again, this does not mean that forgeries in documents or intentionally or unintentionally false statements had not been discovered earlier. Perhaps one of the most memorable events in the history of historical method is the discovery by Lorenzo Valla that the *Donation de Constantine* was a forgery. But though we find several exceptions of this kind before the development of scientific methods of evidence in historical scholarship, the criticism applied to texts, the attempt to interpret the correct meaning of texts, and the inferences required to reconcile inconsistencies and to judge between divergent statements are activities with which only modern historians are familiar. The methods which are properly applied to historical documents, the rules of historical method, have often been described. The most fundamental book in this field is a famous study by a German author, Ernst Bernheim: *Lehrbuch der historischen Methode* (1889). All the later and more accessible works in English are based upon the principles laid down by Bernheim and must be considered as adaptations of the problems which he discussed. Among recent American works which outline historical method in a lucid and clear fashion may be mentioned Louis Gottschalk's *Understanding History* (1950) and Edward Maslin Hulme's *History and Its Neighbors* (1942).

The application of scientific method to history has not confined itself to rules of textual criticism but has drawn in other sciences as well. In some instances the modern historian may be likened almost to a detective. In order to test the genuineness of a document, he may use chemistry in testing the paper and inks, X-ray photography to determine erasures or other defects, the application of various solutions to bring out partly or totally faded passages, and similar techniques. Some discoveries which have been made by these and other methods are quite startling and have brought considerable new insights, forcing historians in some instances to revise accepted views. For example, one of the most disputed problems in the history of book-making is the question of the priority of the invention of movable type. What did Gutenberg actually invent, and when did he apply first whatever invention he actually made? It is known that Gutenberg printed editions of the Latin primer of Donatus before he turned to printing the Bible. But copies of Gutenberg's various editions of Donatus were rare and hard to come by. A language primer used by generations of learners was more easily destroyed than a big voluminous Bible. Also, the over-all value of a copy of a Donatus was much less, and the book was constantly reprinted, so that little importance was attached to any one copy. Partly damaged copies of this work were thus used by early bookbinders as a filler for the leather covers of other books, and scholars have extracted various early versions of Gutenberg's books from the bindings of later works which often were of little value. In this way the steps by which Gutenberg arrived at his invention could be traced more accurately, and although the question of the invention of movable type is not yet finally solved, more information and surer knowledge has been attained about it by the "detective" work of historical scholars than we would have otherwise. Another startling example of how a valuable manuscript was discovered inside the coverage of another book is reported by Professor P. Wolff of the University of Toulouse. Professor Wolff found a valuable fourteenth-century tax list of Toulouse in the binding of another work. On the basis of this list many questions of the history of that city which up to then were little understood could be explained more fully and accurately.

In the search for more accurate knowledge, historians have also drawn upon the researches of some related disciplines. It is not necessary to go into a full description of such disciplines as diplomatics, numismatics, paleography, and other sciences and crafts which are used as aids by historians. Their main purposes and methods are discussed in any good book on historical method (such as the ones mentioned earlier) or in general reference works such as, for example, the *Encyclopaedia Britannica.*

A fourth result of the trend toward scientific history has been the growing concern of historians with the history of institutions, culture, and civilization and various other forms of the expression of the human intellect. Whereas up to the middle of the nineteenth century most history was political, military, or dynastic history, this branch of history has now declined to relatively small proportions. Much more attention is paid to economic and social, to cultural and intellectual history, and though it would be difficult to make an accurate estimate, more than half the current output of historical works is concerned with problems of the history of institutions other than war or government. This development will be discussed further below in connection with the description of the various branches of modern historical literature.

Reference Works–A fifth result of the transition to scientific history has been the vast increase of reference works in history. It is impossible to give here a complete or even approximately complete list of historical reference works. All that can be done is to draw attention to some general types of such works. Apart from general encyclopedias, dictionaries, and general bibliographies of various kinds, there have been developed by historians a number of specialized works of reference to be used by historians or others interested in history. First, there are specialized bibliographies of historical works relating to a given period or a given country. Examples were already cited when mention was made of Godfrey Davies' *Bibliography of British History: Stuart Period, 1603-1714* (1928) and Grace Gardner Griffin's series, *Writings on American History* (1902-). The former is one volume in a series of books that are to provide bibliographical guides to the various periods of British history. The second is an annual bibliography of books and periodical articles on all periods and localities in American history.

In addition to specialized bibliographies referring to historical works, there have been published encyclopedias or dictionaries relating particularly to history and especially to biography. The most noteworthy example is again a British work, the *Dictionary of National Biography* (1908-09), which was compiled under the editorship of Leslie Stephen and has been brought up to date from time to time by the publication of supplementary volumes. Using this work as a model, a *Dictionary of American Biography* (1928-37) has been published.

A third type of reference work is the history of historical writings. A number of books have been composed on the works of historians and their opinions, biases, and viewpoints. These are not merely biographical sketches of historians and their works but reflect the various trends and changes in approach of historians in different ages and periods. A pathbreaking work in this field was published in 1911 in Germany by Eduard Fueter, *Geschichte der neueren Historiographie,* which presents a history of historical writing from the Renaissance on. A large American work on the same topic is James W. Thompson, *A History of Historical Writing* (1942).

Three shorter works belonging in this group should be mentioned. First there is a very informative work by Harry E. Barnes, *A History of Historical Writing* (1937), which gives within the compass of one volume an excellent survey of historical schools and a list of historians and their chief works. An example that is less "factual" and more "interpretative" in over-all character is George P. Gooch's *History and Historians in the Nineteenth Century* (1913), and a third example, which is primarily philosophical and concerned mostly with an interpretation of the underlying values held by historians at various periods, is Robin G. Collingwood's *The Idea of History* (1946). Each of these books is in its way a highly representative example of the various ways in which historians have approached the growth and development of their own discipline.

Other reference sources are lists and encyclopedias of dates and lists of genealogies of rulers. The first impetus to these kinds of publications was given by a German author, Karl Ploetz, but in the meantime more modern dictionaries and encyclopedias of dates and genealogies have been published in the United States. Outstanding among them is *An Encyclopedia of World History* (rev. ed., 1952), edited by William Langer, as well as some more specialized dictionaries, such as, for example, *The American Dictionary of Dates, 1458-1920* (1921), compiled by Charles Ripley Damon, and *Encyclopedia of American History* (1953), edited by Richard Brandon Morris. This last work is a list of historical events in chronological order with some description of some of the later developments arising from the event listed.

Codification in History—Finally, the growth of scientific history has led to the need of and the desire for codification of historical knowledge accumulated at various periods. This means that at various periods historians felt that the time had come for them to take stock of all the accumulated knowledge which historians have stored up in journal articles and monographs, in books, government reports, and research memoranda. Much of this knowledge is scattered in various, sometimes ephemeral, media; much of it is published in various parts of the world in many languages. It was felt that at some time all this accumulated knowledge should be sifted and an appraisal be made of what knowledge could be considered as well established and what was still uncertain or under discussion. One means of aiding this process of codification was the calling of international historical conferences. To date ten such conferences have been called, and in each of them the progress of historical research in the various participating countries was reported. Another means of aiding this process is the publication, under the auspices of UNESCO, of a *Journal of World History* (1953-). But the actual task of codification is not fully accomplished by these means. It is accomplished rather by the publication of large encyclopedic works which contain a fairly definitive statement of the status of historical research on different problems. One of the first attempts of such a codification as this was the *Cambridge Modern History* (1902-12), which was planned by Lord Acton and which was published in the first decade of the twentieth century. This was followed up by the *Cambridge Medieval History* (1911-36) and the *Cambridge Ancient History* (1923-39). A further work of codification, the *Cambridge Economic History of Europe* (1941-), is now in the course of publication, and so far two volumes have appeared.

Another form of codification is the publication of a series of volumes relating to the history of a country or a civilization. One such set for Britain is the *Oxford History of England* (1934-), which appeared in the interwar period. Another work, on a much larger scale, is a French work edited by Henri Berr under the over-all title *L'Evolution de l'humanité*. This project, which was also begun after World War I, is not yet finished, since most of the volumes relating to modern history are still lacking. The provisional character of a work of codification on such a large scale becomes apparent, if one considers that some of the volumes published some twenty years ago have been brought out in a second revised edition at a time when some of the projected later volumes have not yet been written. Some of the earlier volumes of this series were also brought out in English translations under the general title of the series, *The History of Civilization*.

The series which have been described so far are devoted chiefly to universal history or European history. In the field of universal history the most recent codification is being carried on in a series of volumes published under the auspices of UNESCO. In Europe the codification of national histories of various countries is also being undertaken presently. For example, in Spain an impressive series of historical works on the history of Spain is being published currently under the general editorship of Gonzalo Menéndez Pidal, and in France a codification of the history of commerce, *Histoire du Commerce* (1950-55), under the general editorship of Jacques Lacour-Gayet, has just been brought to completion in six volumes. In the United States codification of this kind is rarer, but there exist two or three such attempts which are of considerable value. In the period before World War I, a series of 28 volumes under the editorship of Albert B. Hart, *The American Nation* (1904-18), was brought out. In 1918 there appeared, under the editorship of Allen Johnson, the first 50 volumes of *The Chronicles of America Series,* which may be considered as a codification and popularization at the same time; and in the interwar period there appeared the most scholarly and scientific codification of American history: the series *A History of American Life* (1927-), under the editorship of Arthur M. Schlesinger and Dixon R. Fox.

Codification may also occur in somewhat less ambitious forms than these large collections in many volumes. Some of the best texts in history, for example Morison and Commager's *The Growth of the American Republic* (4th ed., 1950) or Ephraim Lipson's *The Economic History of England* (5th ed., 1929-31), may properly be regarded as instances of such codification on a less grandiose scale. In addition, some works which are not destined to be texts but written as conscious summaries of the state of knowledge in a given field of history at a given period, and which must also be considered as codifications, are not uncommon. Among the best works of this kind may be counted Elie Halévy's *A History of the English People* (1924-34), William Langer's *The Diplomacy of Imperialism 1890-1902* (2d ed., 1951), or Chester W. Wright's *Economic History of the United States* (1941).

Scientific History in the Late Nineteenth and Twentieth Century —We have interrupted the account of the development of historiography with the discussion of the over-all impact of the new trend toward scientific history. Before we finish this chapter it is still necessary to give a short account of the main figures of this movement and of the varieties of historical works to which this development led. There is common agreement that the man who is responsible for the introduction of the scientific spirit into history is the German historian Leopold von Ranke. Ranke stands in more than one way at the watershed of two periods of historiography. He was the "first" scientific historian, and he was the last (or at least one of the last) universal historians. Ranke's collected works comprise scores of volumes (the exact number depends upon the edition one selects), and he wrote on modern and medieval history, on the history of Germany, France, Britain, Italy, and other countries, on secular and ecclesiastical history. Ranke's fame began with his first work, written in 1824, translated under the title *A History of the Latin and Teutonic Nations from 1494 to 1514* (1887). But his most popular works were his *The History of the Popes* (1912) and his *History of the Reformation in Germany* (1905), whose fame is due partly to the fact that they dealt with important questions weaving together the political and the religious, but partly also because Ranke's peculiar genius could convey more clearly than his predecessors the thought and conflicts of conscience of the men he wrote about.

Ranke had many disciples in Germany, and through the critical method of documentary research insisted upon by him and his further insistence on interpreting historical events by taking account of the "spirit of an age," he influenced historical scholarship all over the world. Among his chief disciples in Germany was Georg Waitz, who, after the death of Georg Heinrich Pertz, became the editor of the *Monumenta* and under whose editorship this vast collection saw its most fertile period. He indirectly influenced Theodor Mommsen, whose researches on Roman history and the history of Roman law introduced a new era for the study of the history of antiquity. His *The History of Rome* (new ed., 1870) is still a work which has scarcely been superseded by more recent research. Another historian who was influenced by Ranke, though he was not a direct disciple of his, was the Swiss Jakob Burckhardt. His chief work was *The Civilisation of the Renaissance in Italy* (1892), a work which exhibits more clearly than almost any other the deep penetration of the spirit of a past age by an historian. The list of German historians who were immediate and intermediate disciples of Ranke is too long to enumerate. It may suffice if we mention the two outstanding German historians of this century who have continued to work in Ranke's footsteps. They are Friedrich Meinecke, whose *Weltbürgertum und Nationalstaat* (5th ed., 1919) has become a modern classic, and Franz Schnabel, whose *Deutsche Geschichte im Neunzehnten Jahrhundert* (1929) is the only German work which, in terms of penetration and comprehensiveness, can be placed alongside Halévy's *History of the English People.*

In France the same spirit as that fostered by Ranke in Germany was exerted primarily through the impact of the historians associated with the *Ecole des Chartes.* There are few overtowering figures in France in the last half of the nineteenth century comparable with a Mommsen or a Waitz. A very much read historian was Hippolyte Taine, whose *Les Origines de la France Contemporaine* (16th ed., 1888) was not so much a work which excelled by its scientific perfection as by the fluency of its expression and the novelty of some of the views expressed. Perhaps the most remarkable achievement of French historiography of that time, apart from specialized monographs, was the historical investigation of the great French Revolution, to which Alphonse Aulard devoted his life. Aulard's work was in part superseded by the more recent work on the revolution by the socialist Jean Jaurès and the liberal Albert Mathiez. Another eminent historian of that period was Numa Denis Fustel de Coulanges, who studied the political institutions of ancient Gaul and whose work, *The Ancient City* (7th ed., 1889), has become a classic model of interpretation of the political and social development of the urban community in ancient Greece.

Again, it would be impossible to list all the modern French historians who have made great contributions to scientific history, and any selection among them betrays the particular preferences and perhaps biases of the writer of these lines. However, there is general agreement that among the most notable achievements of French historiography in our generation are the works by Marc Bloch, *La Société Féodale* (1939), a brilliantly insightful study of European society in the early medieval period, and Fernand Braudel's *La Méditerranée et le monde méditerranéen à l'Epoque de Philippe II* (1949), an account of the history of southern Europe during the period when Spain still commanded a supreme political position in Europe and in the world. One cannot omit from a list of modern French historians the name of Lucien Febvre. Though he has not produced a work quite commensurate in stature with those of Bloch or Braudel, he has exerted a powerful influence on French historical study and writing through his teaching and lecturing and through the many articles and notes in learned journals which he has published. One of his main works, *A Geographical Introduction to History* (1925), betrays the breadth of his learning, and he may be regarded as one of the very last French historians with universal interests.

In Britain the impact of the German development toward scientific history was more pronounced than in France. In part this may have been due to a long and thoughtful essay Macaulay had published on "Ranke's *History of the Popes*." In part it was, no doubt, due to the influence of Lord Acton, who never produced a major book himself, but whose main influence was exercised through conversation, correspondence, and a few essays in literary and historical journals. Acton himself was a pupil of another great German historian, Johann Döllinger, whose *History of the Church* (1840-42) made the latter one of the outstanding church historians of his day. Döllinger worked entirely in the scientific tradition of Ranke and his school, and Acton brought his master's ideas to Britain. Among the most notable achievements of British scientific history in the later nineteenth century were the works of Samuel R. Gardiner, who concentrated his research on the seventeenth century and whose *The Thirty Years War, 1618-1648* (1874), as well as other works on Cromwell and his time, have become standard treatises for that period. Simultaneous with Gardiner's work appeared the writings of William E. H. Lecky. Lecky had been much influenced in his general outlook by Henry Thomas Buckle, who had set out to write a *History of Civilization in England* (new ed., 1872) along rationalist lines, of which, however, only the first two volumes were published before his death. They form not a history but merely the prolegomena to one and may be compared in more than one sense with the famous *Prolegomena* to the history of the Muslim world which 500 years earlier Ibn Khaldun had written. Lecky accepted Buckle's rationalist outlook and published a *History of the Rise and Influence of the Spirit of Rationalism in Europe* (1866) and a *History of European Morals, from Augustus to Charlemagne* (1869), which are important contributions to the history of ideas and at the same time betray the growing trend toward the history of civilization and culture. A third great British historian of the late nineteenth century was Mandell Creighton who devoted his life work to a study of the history of Italy and the Papacy. His *History of the Papacy During the Period of the Reformation* (1887-94), though not based on the careful exploration and sifting of archival materials, drew on the many printed sources and renders an excellent balanced picture of that controversial subject.

As in the case of Germany and France, the output of historical works in contemporary Britain is both large and often on a high level. Again it is difficult to select any one or two works as the best and most representative. Among works which in recent years have been received with general approval and which exhibit British historical scholarship at its best are Charles W. Previté-Orton's posthumously published *The Shorter Cambridge Medieval History* (1952), Steven Runciman's *A History of the Crusades* (1951-54), George N. Clark's *The Seventeenth Century* (1929), and John B. Bury's *A History of Greece to the Death of Alexander the Great* (1900).

In the United States, as in Britain, the influence of German historiography was noticeable. Many American historians of the later nineteenth century followed George Bancroft's example and studied at German universities. But in converting the lessons they learned into actual historiography, they also drew on American traditions of historical writing. Among these traditions was the view that the history of the United States was primarily a history of the American people rather than their rulers or a special elite. Among American historians who were particularly important in creating a scientific attitude towards history in the United States were Henry B. Adams, who founded the history department at Johns Hopkins University, and John W. Burgess, who founded the Faculty of Political Science at Columbia University. Though Burgess himself was interested chiefly in problems of political science, one of his students, Herbert Levi Osgood, became the author of one of the most scholarly works in American historiography, a seven-volume history of the English colonies in America (*The American Colonies in the Seventeenth Century,* [1904-07]; *The American Colonies in the Eighteenth Century,* [1924]). Another American historian of note who was, in turn, Osgood's pupil, was George Louis Beer, whose work, *The Commercial Policy of England toward the American Colonies,* has scarcely been superseded though it was published in 1893. The more recent period in American history was treated at that time in a study of wide scope by John B. McMaster, whose work has already the flavor of a social history. Among the writers of the twentieth century, primary attention must be paid to Henry Adams, whose work, *Mont Saint Michel and Chartres* (1904), is an attempt to evaluate the culture of the Middle Ages; James H. Breasted, whose works on the history of ancient Egypt may be regarded as the foundation of the study of the ancient river civilizations in this country and whose influence made itself felt in the brilliant work of some of his students at the Oriental Institute at the University of Chicago. An excellent example of this branch of historiography is John Albert Wilson's *The Burden of Egypt* (1951). American works as Charles Homer Haskins' *Studies in Medieval Culture* (1929) or Lynn Thorndike's *The History of Medieval Europe* (1917) are works of great scholarship and penetration on the intellectual history of the Middle Ages. Ferdinand Schevill's work on the *History of Florence* (1936) is an excellent study of that famous city, and John U. Nef's *War and Human Progress* (1950) is a work not only of great scholarship but also of deep philosophical penetration. But the largest output of American historians was in the field of the history of their own country. Charles A. Beard's *An Economic Interpretation of the Constitution of the United States* (1913) was a novel approach to American history that caused much debate, and the work of Allan Nevins on the middle period of American history and of Carl L. Becker on *The Declaration of Independence* (1922) are historical works which less have revolutionized historical scholarship in any external fashion perhaps, but which have brought model scholarship and penetrating analysis to bear on the problems selected for discussion. American historians have also devoted a good deal of attention to the writing of biography. Though the output of biographies is immense, several fairly definitive works of central characters in American history have been produced in the last fifty years. Most notable among them are Douglas Southall Freeman's *George Washington, A Biography* (1948-57), Carl Sandburg's *Abraham Lincoln* (1954), and Carl C. van Doren's *Benjamin Franklin* (1938).

This rapid survey of historical scholarship and writing of the last hundred years in several of the major countries could be supplemented by similar lists of works and writers in other countries of Europe and the western hemisphere. But the British, American, French, and German works which were briefly mentioned may be regarded as typical examples of the type of writings which are to be found in larger or smaller scope in all languages, and the approach exhibited in these works is characteristic of the kind of historical scholarship everywhere. It is, of course, true that in totalitarian countries a good deal of biased and even totally falsified history is produced, but this output need hardly be regarded as having any serious scholarly pretensions, though it is presented by the official spokesmen of totalitarian countries as "true science." The essential quality of such writing is excellently discussed in Klaus Mehnert's *Stalin versus Marx* (1952), in which the tortuous byways traveled by recent Soviet historians in their effort to falsify the picture of Russian and European history are described.

One of the most hopeful achievements of modern historiography has been not only the development of precise methods and the general improvement of historical scholarship, but also the tendency to broaden the scope of historical investigation to all aspects of human life. Whereas political, military, and naval history have not been completely forgotten, and works like Alfred T. Mahan's *The Influence of Sea Power Upon*

History, 1660-1783 (1890) or Winston Churchill's *The Second World War* (1948-54) belong to the most highly appreciated historical writings of the recent period, other fields of history have grown by leaps and bounds. The first inroad in the predominance of political and dynastic history was made by the historical treatment of law. We have already seen how men like Savigny and Mommsen and Waitz emphasized this aspect of historical study. But the historical study of law also became common in English-speaking countries, and Frederic W. Maitland and Frederick Pollock's *The History of English Law Before the Time of Edward I* (1895) is an outstanding achievement in this field. Other notable works in this field on a smaller scope are Albert V. Dicey's *Lectures on the Relation Between Law and Public Opinion in England during the Nineteenth Century* (1905) and Charles H. McIlwain's *The Growth of Political Thought in the West* (1932).

After legal history came economic history. There are close relations in the historical treatment of legal and economic questions, and once historians were firmly embarked upon the historical study of law they were naturally driven to explore the evolution of economic institutions. In this field again Germany led the way. The work of Wilhelm Roscher, Bruno Hildebrand, and Gustav Schmoller provided models in this field and will be discussed in more detail in the chapter on Economics. Among English-speaking historians, William James Ashley was one of the most gifted practitioners of this branch of history. His *An Introduction to English Economic History and Theory* (2d ed. 1892-93) was one of the first works of its kind. In the last 50 years this branch of history has expanded to such an extent that economic history and even a sub-branch of it, business history, have become to be regarded as disciplines of their own.

The next step taken led to the history of society in general and from there to the history of culture and civilization and the history of ideas. In this last realm secular and religious historians found a point of common interest. With the beginning of the second half of the twentieth century historical writing moved along on a broad front. No episode, no social institution, no set of ideas or beliefs seemed too unimportant to historians to deserve careful and erudite investigation and analysis. It is the conviction of the historical profession in all civilized countries that along this path greater insight not only into man's past but also into human and social problems of the present will be achieved.

CHAPTER III

Geography

THE CHARACTER OF GEOGRAPHY

Geography shares with the other social sciences the task of understanding man in society. As a social science, it is anthropocentric and concerned primarily with answering the question: why do men act in certain ways at certain times and in certain places? Although an ancient field of knowledge, its character as a modern discipline has only just begun to emerge, and it has tended to be afflicted with a wealth of definitions. Furthermore, because the word "geography" refers not only to the discipline, but also to certain characteristics of a place, usually the "natural" or "physical" qualities of that place, its nature has been unclear to laymen and even to other scholars.

Some insights into the role geographers play as social scientists may be gained through consideration of some of the numerous definitions of the field of geography. These definitions and the work of geographers in general are dealt with at length in Preston E. James's and Clarence F. Jones's *American Geography: Inventory and Prospect* (1954), and in Richard Hartshorne's *The Nature of Geography* (1939). The volumes of James and Jones and Hartshorne are both methodological in nature. For a recent volume illustrating the broad interests of geographers and their relations with other fields of knowledge, see William L. Thomas, Jr.'s *Man's Role in Changing the Face of the Earth* (1956).

Geography as a Compendium of Facts—It generally is acknowledged that modern geographical study developed out of the interests of men about the characteristics of foreign places. A common conception—or misconception—among laymen has followed that geographers compile facts about places, particularly countries. This compilation is assumed to include such items as the areal dimensions, boundaries, cities, rivers, mountains, population, railways, and imports and exports of countries and continents. Geography, as taught in many of the elementary schools of this country at least, has been represented by listings of these unco-ordinated "geographical" facts which are memorized by children without explanation or synthesis.

Unfortunately, the idea of geography as unco-ordinated areal description has not been restricted to popular or semi-popular literature, or even to the elementary schools. Some college textbooks still consist largely of country-by-country descriptions and listings of these "geographical" facts.

The objections to the concept of geography as an encyclopedic compendium are several. The mere listing of facts without a frame of reference cannot lead to generalizations about them. An area is not simply a receptacle full of unrelated phenomena. The lack of organizational principles and a problem focus militates against contributions to scientific knowledge. Furthermore, the selection of facts may vary with each observer, and an emphasis on much that is unique rather than characteristic has been the almost inevitable result. In sum, the geographer is no more concerned with fact accumulation than any of his colleagues in the other sciences.

Geography as the Study of Environmental Influences–The influence that nature exerts on mankind also has been a focus of attention for centuries. The idea that the "natural environment" directly influences and even dominates man's activities may be found scattered through the writings of the ancients. The most important modern presentation of this viewpoint is in Friedrich Ratzel's *Anthropogeographie* (1882-91), the influence of which has permeated geographic thinking to this day. Ratzel's fundamental thesis was that the elements of the "natural" or "geographic" environment–climate, soils, topography, geologic structure, and water bodies, and their arrangement over the earth–determine or have determined, within rigid bounds, the activities of men. This environmental determinism is found in the writings of Ellen Churchill Semple, Ellsworth Huntington, and the German geopoliticians. It is discussed by Oscar H. K. Spate, in an article, "Toynbee and Huntington: A Study of Determinism," *Geographical Journal* (1952), and questioned by Robert S. Platt in his "Determinism in Geography," *Annals, Associations of American Geographers* (1948), and in "Environmentalism Versus Geography," *American Journal of Sociology* (1948). In these works of the environmentalists the history of people and states is interpreted in terms of the dominant influences that natural conditions have exerted through time. Although there are only a few remaining proponents of this point of view active in geographic work today, the stigma of environmental determinism upon geography has been difficult to remove, and there still are references in the social literature which identify this deterministic outlook as the core concept of the field.

The major limitations and objections to this definition of geography lie in its basic assumption that natural conditions continuously dominate human events. This assumption cannot be proven, but it permits a simple explanation for an enormous variety of complex social phenomena. Ratzel himself, in later writings, recognized the dangers of such facile explanations and shifted his emphasis from the "natural" to the "cultural" environment. It cannot be denied, of course, that a sudden and catastrophic change in nature, the water supply for example, may be the immediate cause for a migration of peoples or a radical change in social organization, but causal relations of this kind cannot be assumed and even when proven must be considered episodic, not continuous.

Geography as the Study of Man-Nature Relationships–The uncompromisingly deterministic view of geographic study gradually was modified, especially by the French geographers, to the point where geography became defined as a kind of human ecology, the study of man and the "natural" environment, in which there was assumed an interplay of forces both natural and cultural. This concept has had numerous supporters in the United States and abroad and is still held as a useful definition by many geographers. This view is well presented by John M. Mogey in *The Study of Geography* (1950). The question arises, however, as to whether a science may deal primarily with assumed relationships not precisely defined, rather than with the reality basic to those relationships. Furthermore, since the relationships are *assumed* to exist, the geographer may in effect be *directed* by his conception of them, even though his conceptions may in fact remain unverified hypotheses. The result has been a kind of determinism which is less apparent but no less strong than environmental determinism itself.

A further difficulty lies in defining the "natural" environment. The "natural" environment is generally divided into elements such as climate, soils, bedrock, landforms, water bodies, vegetation, and animal life. Each of these elements, however, with the exception of climate, may be modified strongly by men, and even climate, particularly microclimate, is not immune to change. A soil under cultivation, for example, becomes both a "natural" and "cultural" element. As for climate, many studies which have claimed to link human events with the "natural" environment have in effect subscribed to the more limited concept of climatic determinism. Therefore, the "natural" environment may be regarded as only a hypothetical construct of limited utility; its use had led to a kind of dualism between a "cultural" environment on the one hand and a "natural" environment on the other. In reality, however, there is only one physical environment, composed of various elements both natural and cultural. This argument does not propose to minimize the significance of climate, landforms, soils, minerals, and vegetation in the study of societies; rather it opposes grouping them into a "natural" class alone. The artificial separation of the unitary physical environment into two major segments often has led to a substantial distortion of reality, not only in some works of geographers, but commonly also in studies by social scientists.

Geography as the Study of Landscape—The definition of geography as the study of landscape is associated also with the French school of geography. According to this conception, geographers describe and trace the historical development of the "physical" landscape and thereby explain it. This "physical" landscape is composed of two aspects, the "natural" landscape which was in existence before man entered the scene, and the "cultural" landscape which man imposed over the natural base. The existing landscape complex is predominantly cultural and is explained by tracing its evolution from the natural to the present state. A notable American statement of this view is contained in Carl O. Sauer's *The Morphology of Landscape* (1925). To a considerable degree, also, it is associated with studies in historical geography of a sort most characteristic of European geographers, such as, for example, H. C. Darby, "The Changing English Landscape," *Geographical Journal* (1951).

Among the difficulties accruing to this definition of geography is the confusion associated with the meanings of the word "landscape," of which there are at least two: one nearly synonymous with the term "area"; the other pertaining to all the phenomena of the earth surface as viewed from a single point.

A second drawback is the maintenance of a "natural"–"cultural" landscape dichotomy, as in the case of the "natural" and "cultural" environments. Furthermore, if the "natural" landscapes refer to associations of physical phenomena on the surface of the earth before the coming of man, it can only be reconstructed historically, a difficult task at best. Geography, therefore, would become in effect only one aspect of history.

A final objection is the limit placed upon the subject matter of the geographer. If his study is restricted to the material phenomena of the earth's surface, he must ignore those characteristics of area that are not directly visible, although they may be of great significance to regional characterization. Emphasis is placed on form, not function, even though functional relations may be of far greater importance to the understanding of an areal complex than the physical forms that superficially compose it.

Geography as the Science of Distribution—A last definition tends to overlap all others: geography as the science of distributions, or the description and explanation of all distributions on the surface of the earth. It is sometimes shortened to "the study of the where of things," or enlarged to "the study of earth patterns."

Geographers, it is true, *are* concerned with distributions and the "where" of things. However, interest in distributions *per se* is not restricted to geographers alone. Each of the systematic sciences is concerned with the distributions of the phenomena it studies—geologists with the distributions of rock formations; the pedolist with soil distributions; botanists with plant distributions; demographers wth population distributions. It may be that these specialists use geographic techniques in examining their distributions, but this does not make them geographers. In like manner, geographers who try to concern themselves with *all* distributions inevitably cross into fields of special interest where their knowledge is less than that of experts in those fields.

It follows that the study of areal distributions is *not* the exclusive function of geography, although geographers have a special concern with them. In practice, the geographer often borrows the distributional findings of specialists in other fields and uses them for his own ends. In other words, the study of distributions is a necessary but not sufficient aspect of geographic methodology.

A Realistic Definition of Geography—Wellington Jones has defined geography as *the study of the human occupance of regions.* According to this definition, geography is concerned with the ways in which men occupy the surface of the earth, organize themselves spatially, and utilize the world's resources, themselves irregularly distributed, in short, with the areal organization of society. Most important, this definition is consistent with both historical developments and current trends in geographic thought and practice.

The geographer asks the following kinds of questions: How do people occupy the land in particular areas? What are the distinctive characteristics of this occupance? How do the occupance patterns of one area differ from those of other areas? In what ways may the localized associations of phenomena which characterize regional occupance be explained?

From these questions it is clear that the geographer is concerned with characterizing the human occupance of the earth's surface and with the actualities and potentialities of that occupance. His basic assumptions are two: (1) that societies are based upon a terrestrial fundament, the elements of which enter into some causal relationship with each other and with the cultural elements within the social complex, and (2) that the study of these localized associations of phenomena upon that fundament provides one key to the understanding of society. These assumptions act as a distinguishing feature of geographical research.

However, no groups of observable phenomena are restricted to the geographer alone. On the contrary, both factual and conceptual materials are shared or borrowed by him whenever necessary. For this reason, geography may be considered in part a synthetic science, seeking its understanding of the areal differentiation of human occupance by whatever means become available. Thus, geographers may deal with problems that overlap the other social sciences as well as certain of the natural sciences.

The Methodology of Geography—The assumptions of the geographer give both direction and purpose to his research. Since he assumes that the areal organization of society, an amalgam of elements both natural and cultural in origin, possesses comprehensibility as well as a basic logic, it follows that the areal analysis of this organization into its elements is a necessary prerequisite to understanding it. The major procedure of the geographer then, as he works from field and other data that can be areally described or summarized in the form of maps or diagrams, is a process of *areal analysis*. This process centers about the map as a tool for analysis, augmented by statistical data amenable to cartographic presentation and organization, and about the "field" as a natural laboratory.

Once the various elements and distributional patterns of the areal complex are separated out, they can be compared with each other empirically in terms of their areal similarities, differences, and relationships. The specific direction in which this analysis and comparison proceeds depends upon the problem at hand. For example, in a study of settlement forms in a rural area, the coincidence in areal distribution between particular types of barns and ethnic origins of farmers may be of great significance. On the other hand the correlations between distributions of telephones and types of barns probably will be of inconsequential importance.

The second major aspect of geographic methodology may be subsumed under the heading of *areal synthesis*. This procedure involves the integration of diverse elements resulting from the areal analysis process into associations and systems meaningful in terms of particular research problems. Again, the map is a major tool for synthesis, and by means of it areal correlations and relationships can be portrayed effectively and compared with other associations in area.

Let us take, for example, the dairy industry as a model in describing the geographical approach and method.

It is common knowledge that there are dairy farms scattered throughout the world. Even in China on the peripheries of the larger coastal cities there are small dairy farms supplying the local urban market. It is known also that there are concentrations of dairying activity in various places which sometimes are known as "dairying regions" or as "milk sheds." One of these is found in southern Wisconsin and northern Illinois. The concern of the geographer centers about such questions as: How can such concentrations be defined? What are the areal associations which make for or hinder the practice of dairying activities? In what ways is the area once defined related to its surroundings? What general principles regarding the location, internal patterns, and external patterns of such an area can be established?

From field observations the geographer discovers that the basic economic unit, the dairy farm, is characterized by particular associations of areal phenomena, just as the broader, and at the same time more abstract, area of predominant dairying activity is thus characterized. From such field observations and borrowed information an index can be established for the identification of dominant dairying activity, a ratio, say, between the acreage in non-forage crops and the number of head of livestock per farm unit. Since the field study of every farm in the area may be impossible, even by rapid reconnaissance, the geographer may turn to the *U. S. Census of Agriculture,* and, using data for minor civil divisions, he can distinguish those areas in which the ratio is high from those in whch it is low. By intensive field reconnaissance in doubtful areas and the use of aerial photographs for checking crop combinations usually found in association with the basic dairying units, he can create a so-called isopleth map showing, by lines of equal intensity, the quantitative distribution of dairying activities.

Once the outline of a region of concentration are established, the areal analysis continues with the breakdown of the areal complex into its elements: the units of land division, the pattern of transportation, the localization of processing plants and service functions, the distributions and dimensions of markets within and without the area, the natural qualities of the land (soils, drainage, relief, and climate). From such an analysis there evolve certain dynamic areal patterns and relationships which are associated with the dairying industry in this part of the world.

Once the interrelationships within the region, as compounded in the areal associations characterizing dairying, are analyzed, the relations between the region and surrounding areas can be examined in terms of accessibility and commodity flows. In this way the area of dairying becomes more and more specific as it takes on special characteristics derived from its unique position on the earth's surface. It becomes an increasingly comprehensible functional unit within which the dominant form of human occupance is identified and explained.

Even as the specificity of the region is being explored, moreover, it can be compared with other regions where the dominant agricultural activity is dairying. Thus, the area under first analysis is compared with the dairy regions of the eastern United States and northern Europe, for example, in an attempt to discover the features they share in common. If it can be determined that in each of these well-demarcated regions dairying is characterized by and associated with certain natural and cultural conditions, then a class of areas entitled "regions of dairying" can be established. The determination of broad regional standards for the industry permits the consideration of other major questions: What changes in the localized associations will lead to increased efficiency in the uses of land? What rearrangements of occupance patterns will alter the balance of the current system in what ways? Are the characteristics of the complex transferable to other areas which differ radically, for example, in their climate? In this way an infinite variety of new problems are posed which can be pursued as knowledge increases and data become available.

Let us take briefly another example, this time a topic less apparently related to regional occupance: shipping. What is the geographical approach to shipping?

A distinctive feature of every portion of the earth's surface is its location, or its accessibility. Each area of relative homogeneity, whether defined in terms of dairying or manufacturing or political organization, possesses qualities of location and accessibility. The geographer looks at shipping as one measure of accessibility, and the study of patterns of shipping services and functions helps him to characterize given regions as to their functions and associated problems of occupance.

Furthermore, shipping is based on the carriage of commodities, and trade is a major element in the economic-geographic complex of regions. For this reason the comparative study of shipping and trade as an aspect of circulation and spatial interaction serves to distinguish among economic regions and lends insights into their functioning economies.

In summary, the geographer possesses a distinctive approach to problems in area, an approach which demands the analysis of areal complexes, the comparison and relating of elements within area, the explanation and synthesis into areal associations of these elements within a problem framework, the comparison of given areal associations with others elsewhere, and finally the examination of the relations between a given area and its surroundings, as set in the world order. The procedures of areal analysis, comparison, areal synthesis, and comparison, which the geographer employs on differing levels and scales, is his trade mark, one which he is constantly refining and expanding.

The geographic approach and method is not restricted to a narrow subject matter but may in fact be applied to a vast array of problems which may be examined in turn from differing viewpoints by systematic specialists in other disciplines. Conversely, other scholars may use the geographic approach and geographic tools, in much the same manner that non-historians may utilize the tools and concepts of historical methodology and may, indeed, even write history. Just as the study of history provides one major key to the understanding of men in society, so does geography as a discipline concerned with areal organization contribute to the increased comprehension of the ways men live, think, and act.

SYSTEMATIC AND REGIONAL GEOGRAPHY

Geographic knowledge customarily is organized in two ways: one systematic and one regional. This traditional division has developed from two basic considerations: (1) the need to recognize and study particular phenomena as they are distributed areally around the world, and (2) the attempt to recognize and study associations of phenomena within a particular area. The distinction between the two methods of organization, however, is more a matter of purpose or emphasis than of differing subject matters. Relatively few geographical studies can be classified simply under one or the other methods, although differences in scale or degree of generalization in any geographic study will tend to place it primarily in one of the two categories.

Systematic Geography–Systematic geography is concerned with the geographic aspects of particular phenomena, that is, with the distribution of a phenomenon as it relates to other areally-distributed phenomena and as it contributes to an understanding of areal differences in human occupance. This is not the same concern that basically motivates the specialist in a systematic science. For example, the soil scientist, like the geographer, is concerned with the distribution of the various kinds of soils over the earth. He is interested, however, primarily in the distributional study not as a means for understanding areal differentiation and organization in general, but as a way to further understand the nature of soils. The soils geographer on the other hand examines distributions of soils in terms of the part they play in differentiating one area of human activity from another, in their relation to patterns of agriculture, forestry, settlement, and transportation. The soils geographer may borrow information from the soil scientist regarding the nature of soils. At the same time his aim is to generalize, if possible, concerning the relations that particular groupings or arrangements of soils have to other areally distributed phenomena.

Regional Geography—The regional concept is the logical result of attempts to organize knowledge concerning differences from place to place in the ways men have occupied the surface of the earth. It differs from systematic geography in that it emphasizes the localized association of phenomena, rather than the specific elements in such associations. Regional geography, however, deals with the same patterns of distribution as does systematic geography and utilizes the facts and generalizations developed by systematic geography; but its prime function is the welding of these facts and generalizations into systems of regional differentiation. The regional geographer, therefore, is a systematizer and integrator of given data into systems of regions.

The region based upon specific criteria which recur in more than one place is known as a *generic region.* It is a type of relatively homogeneous area which can be defined in terms of certain characteristics. To take an example from physical geography, the "tropical rainforest region" can be identified in terms of its associations of vegetation, soils, and climate. It occurs in several parts of the world. Such a regional concept is, of course, a generalization. As such, it is also in a certain sense a distortion of reality. No two "tropical rainforest regions" are identical. The class, "tropical rainforest region," is based upon only a few of the phenomena which exist, in reality, within the areas thus defined. To take another example, in the "region of dairying" in northern Illinois and southern Wisconsin, there are numerous non-dairying activities, as evidenced by cash-grain and specialized farms, recreational facilities, and small industries in towns. The dairying region, however, is defined in terms of the dominant activity, as indicated by percentage of land area devoted to dairying uses or percentage of labor force engaged in dairying. As a generalization, however, the generic region provides a tool for the solution of problems in area and provides one means for comparing localized associations wherever they may occur.

However, each generic region has an additional quality, that of situation. Every portion of the earth's surface is distinct from every other part on the basis of relative location—only one association of elements can occupy a point at any one time. It is perfectly plain, for example, that Chicago is the only metropolis at the southern end of Lake Michigan, that this city is bound to its hinterland by a web of highways and railways following certain known routes, that it acts as a focus of activities for a commensurable tributary area. In another case, the importance of the Great Lakes to American heavy industry is a characteristic in large part of the locational happenstance of these water bodies. Since certain attributes of the city and the lakes are unique to them, it follows that they must also be studied in terms of their uniqueness.

Whenever the unique aspect of a region becomes more significant than its generic aspect, it can be thought of as a *specific region.* The corn belt of the United States is a *specific region*. Insofar as there may be other areas in which the corn-hog associations of the Corn Belt may be found, it partakes of certain qualities of the generic region as well.

In another case, the so-called "Chicago region" refers to that point of the United States, the nerve-center and focal point of which is the city of Chicago. In certain respects this region is generic, since it belongs to the broad class of "metropolitan regions." In a perhaps more significant sense, it is a specific region, since there is only one Chicago and one hinterland in reciprocal and unique relation with each other. The Chicago region also is an example of a sub-type of specific region, the so-called *nodal region* or *functional region,* a concept much used in the field of urban and settlement geography. The nodal region particularly is a dynamic concept, concerned with the ever-changing relations among a complex of settlements differentiated from each other by specialized forms and functions and associated in a hierarchical system based on size and multiplicity of functions.

The concept of the geographic region, therefore, extends from the region based upon its uniformity with regard to a single, areally distributed criterion to the highly complex areal unit defined in terms of its functional organization. As the areal unit becomes increasingly complex, it also becomes increasingly difficult to describe, analyze, and generalize about. Therefore, much regional geographic study retains, perforce, a highly subjective and artistic quality, in much the same fashion that many studies of human behavior are highly intuitive in their interpretations.

Finally, it should be emphasized that various kinds of regions overlap and that regional systems suitable for one kind of study may not be suitable for another. Furthermore, the drawing of regional boundaries may be extremely difficult, except perhaps where political units act as the basis for a regional system. In some instances a numerical standard provides a relatively simple regional limit, as in the case, say, of population densities. Where nodal regions are being examined, however, the areal extent of relations between focal point and hinterland varies both with the kind of relationship involved and with time. In such cases, the boundary may be little more than a very broad and fluctuating zone which merges with areas partly associated with other nodal regions; and the identification of the regional focus or core becomes the pressing and significant geographical task.

Few regional studies, moreover, can be called "complete"; indeed, it is impossible to deal with *all* elements of the occupance pattern and relations within a given area. In fact, all generic regional studies may be described as "systematic" studies as well, since they deal with the areal similarities and differences of certain phenomena only. It is for this reason that the greater number of geographical studies can be described as being *both* systematic and regional, since they tend to concentrate on the regional qualities of certain types of localized associations or elements within those associations. The typical geographical study, then, can seldom be fitted with one or the other of the systematic-regional dichotomy, since it partakes of the qualities of both. A discussion of this question may be found in Robert S. Platt, "Regionalism in World Order," *Social Education* (1944). Most general geography texts use a world regional system based upon climate. However, Richard Joel Russell's and Fred B. Kniffen's *Culture Worlds* (1951) is organized on the basis of "culture regions," a concept akin to the anthropologists' "culture area."

SYSTEMATIC SUBDIVISIONS OF GEOGRAPHY

Physical Geography—Traditionally the geographer has worked from the land—in its broadest sense—and passed on to the problems of human occupance which are his major concern. Physical geography, therefore, has provided a traditional basis for geography in general. Commonly, it includes the study of the geography of soils, landforms, water, vegetations, minerals, and climate. In studying these phenomena the geographer is concerned not with their genetic aspects, but with their distributions and interrelations both among themselves and with the occupance features in area. It is this interest that has led to the description of geography as a bridge between the natural and social sciences.

Although the orientation of physical geography is toward the "use" aspect of the elements within it, its concentration on natural elements grants it a certain autonomy from the other subdivisions of systematic geography. This autonomy is evidenced by the considerable literature in so-called "pure" physical geography. This literature may be classified into three groups: (1) that which is basically descriptive, (2) that which is concerned with natural processes and the genesis of natural elements, and (3) that which attempts to generalize regarding the areal relations among two or more such elements. The first and second of these classes are not necessarily geographical; the second may more properly be considered geology, geomorphology, or climatology. The third type of study is geographical in that it is concerned with the nature of localized associations, although when these lack a "use" orientation, they may be considered peripheral to the core of geographical understanding.

Economic Geography—Except for physical geography, economic geography has been historically the most important of the various subdivisions. The larger number of texts in elementary geography are basically physical and economic geography, and the literature in the latter field is more extensive than that in any other. Its breadth of interest is huge, and the literature ranges from world-wide studies of individual commodities to the regional associations of economic phenomena in particular areas. Some of the principal texts in world economic geography are organized regionally as, for example, Earl Case and Daniel Bergsmark, *College Geography* (3rd ed., 1949). In contrast, Lester E. Klimm, Otis P. Starkey, and Norman F. Hall, in *Introductory Economic Geography* (3rd ed., 1956) use a topical or systematic outline. Studies of the geography of commodities usually emphasize the significance of those commodities to other aspects of the economic geography of an area, as, for example, David S. Campbell's *The Geography of the Coffee Industry of Puerto Rico* (1947).

Economic geography may be subdivided in turn into various parts: agricultural geography, industrial geography, transportation geography, commercial geography, and the like. All of these are closely related and overlap. For example, Chauncy D. Harris, in "Growing Food by Decree in Soviet Russia," *Foreign Affairs* (1955), analyzes the agricultural geography of the Soviet Union as it relates to the total Soviet economy; and Edward Louis Ullman analyzes the "Railroad Pattern of the United States," *Geographical Review* (1949), as it relates to the internal trade of the nation and the location of industry.

Since economics deals with the general problem of maximizing resource utilization, it is not strange that economic geography should encompass problems dealing with natural resource utilization and conservation. Although the evaluation of natural resources is not a topic restricted to economic geographers alone, it has come to be a major zone of interest to them. Joe Russell Whitaker and Edward A. Ackerman, in *American Resources, Their Management and Conservation* (1951), give an excellent general coverage of the field, and Ackerman's *Japan's Natural Resources and Their Relation to Japan's Economic Future* (1953) is an exemplary detailed assessment of problems of resource use for that country.

Political Geography–The nation-state also provides a framework within which the geographer studies human occupance in area. In political geography, the state itself may be considered a region based on the criterion of its homogeneous political structure. The political geographer deals with the geographical aspects of political organization, that is, with those aspects of power relations which are significant for differentiating one area of human occupance from another.

Contributions to the field range from the sweeping general hypotheses of Halford J. Mackinder in his *Democratic Ideals and Reality* (1919) to systematic monographs on boundaries and studies of specific political problems. Examples are Stephen Barr Jones, *Boundary-Making, A Handbook for Statesmen, Treaty Editors, and Boundary Commissioners* (1945); Derwent S. Whittlesey, *The Earth and State* (1939); William East and A. E. Moodie, editors, *The Changing World* (1956); Jean Gottmann, "Geography and International Relations," *World Politics* (1951); and the excellent high-school-level text by Stephen Barr Jones and Marion Fisher Murphy, *Geography and World Affairs* (1950).

Political geography is not the same as geopolitics, although some of the works of the German geopoliticians and their followers have been sound political geography. Insofar as much geopolitical thinking is based upon an organic concept of the state and the ideological dominance of chauvinism and militarism, geopolitics has fallen into disrepute among most geographers, although the term has become common enough to provide it with the inertia of popular use.

Historical Geography—"*Historical geography* . . . is not a branch of geography comparable to economic or political geography. Neither is it the geography of history, nor the history of geography. It is rather another geography complete in all its branches." (Richard Hartshorne, *The Nature of Geography* [1939], pp. 184-5.) Historical geography, in a phrase, is the study of the geography of past times, in effect a non-modern geography. The reconstruction and evaluation of conditions of geographical significance in particular time periods provides the major problem for the historical geographer. For example, the *Domesday Book*, with its data on property holdings and land use in the England of the post-Norman invasion period, is the basis for current British studies under H. C. Darby in the historical geography of that time. An example of this literature on the United States is Ralph Hall Brown's *Historical Geography of the United States* (1948). In studies of historical geography the distinction between history and geography may become virtually non-existent, a problem discussed by H. C. Darby in "On the Relations of Geography and History," in *Transactions and Papers, Institute of British Geographers* (1953).

One special aspect of historical geography traces the patterns of human occupance in a particular locality over a long period of time. Studies of this sort are known as studies in "sequent occupance." Derwent Whittlesey, in "Sequent Occupance," *Annals, Association of American Geographers* (1929), discusses this approach in general terms, and a study by Robert B. Hall, "Tokaido: Road and Region," *Geographical Review* (1937), exemplifies its application to a particular case.

Many studies in "historical geography" have been in reality geographical interpretations of history, and there still is work in this field on-going by both geographers and historians. A well known example is the work by Ellen Churchill Semple, *The Geography of the Mediterranean Region: Its Relation to Ancient History* (1931).

Urban Geography—One of the more rapidly growing subdivisions of geography concerns itself with the geography of urbanism. Urban geography deals with the city as a distinctive kind of area or region the significance of which is all out of proportion to the size of the site it occupies. There are three major aspects of urban geography. The first deals with the city in terms of its world and regional distribution and as one major feature of the world order, as exemplified in the studies by Mark Jefferson, "The Law of the Primate City," *Geographical Review* (1939); and Chauncy D. Harris and Edward Louis Ullman, "The Nature of Cities," *Annals, American Academy of Political and Social Science* (1945). The second concerns the functions of the city as it relates to a regional hinterland. Problems of this aspect of urban geography are also problems in the determination of the scope and functions of nodal regions. An example of this problem is dealt with by Howard J. Nelson in *The Livelihood Structure of Des Moines, Iowa* (University of Chicago, Department of Geography, Research Paper #4, 1949). The third aspect deals with the internal patterns and functions of cities or the various micro-regions of which a city is composed and the interrelations among them. Examples are the studies by Harold M. Mayer, "Patterns and Recent Trends of Chicago's Outlying Business Centers," *Journal of Land and Public Utility Economics* (1942), and Wesley A. Hotchkiss, *Areal Pattern of Religious Institutions in Cincinnati* (University of Chicago, Department of Geography, Research Paper #13, 1950).

The methods of study in urban geography present in microcosm the methods and viewpoints that characterize geography as a whole. Some urban geographers are concerned with the urban landscape and study its historical development. Others engage in areal analysis of the urban complex with a particular emphasis on areal differentiation based upon functions. Others specialize on particular aspects of the urban complex, such as transportation both within and without the city. Others will focus upon problems of planning. Examples of each of these approaches may be found in the lengthy series of doctoral dissertations in urban geography at the University of Chicago, where both urban geography and urban sociology received their initial impetus.

The distinction between urban geography and urban sociology never has been clear, especially with regard to studies of the internal organization of cities. Their zone of overlap is sometimes defined as urban ecology, although each field has its distinctive emphasis. The urban sociologist tends to concentrate on problems centering about the areal relations between social group and social group. The urban geographer emphasizes problems concerning the interrelations between micro-region and micro-region, on whatever basis they may be defined. Both geographers and sociologists publish articles on cities in their respective professional journals. An example is Edward Louis Ullman's "A Theory of Location for Cities," *American Journal of Sociology* (1941).

Cultural Geography–Cultural geography is one of the broadest and least well defined fields in systematic geography. The geographer is interested in all cultural manifestations which serve to differentiate one area of human occupance from another. The selection of cultural element-complexes is, however, frequently associated with livelihood activities, as demonstrated in Richard Joel Russell and Fred B. Kniffen, *Culture Worlds* (1951). In addition, there are numerous studies of settlement geography wherein the patterns and functions of settlements in regions are examined, such as G. T. Trewartha, "The Unincorporated Hamlet: One Element of the American Settlement Fabric," *Annals, Association of American Geographers* (1943). There also are studies of house types related to settlement geography which propose to use them as an index to cultural differentiation, as in the article by Fred B. Kniffen, "Louisiana House Types," *Annals. Association of American Geographers* (1936) and Joseph E. Spencer, "House Types of Southern Utah," *Geographical Review* (1945). Other works deal with such themes as the geography of religion, for example, as in Pierre Deffontaines, *Geographie et Religions* (1948), and demographic geography, as in Richard Hartshorne, "Racial Maps of the United States," *Geographical Review* (1938).

THE MAP

The most distinctive tool of the geographer is the map. Maps serve at least three functions: first, as a record for raw data as they are initially gathered and organized in field and library; second, as a means for separating out the elements of an area in the process of areal analysis and putting them together in new areal combinations; finally, as a means for expressing meaningfully the relations among patterns of phenomena over the earth.

All maps are generalizations, the extent of which varies directly with their scale. As scale increases, the closer the map approaches a reproduction of reality; as it becomes smaller, the distortion of reality increases. Despite this distortion, the map provides the geographer with a shorthand means for expanding his horizons beyond the limits imposed on direct observation.

The nature of the map varies with the data it portrays and the purpose for which it has been made. No map can show everything in an area no matter how large the scale. Thus, the information shown on maps is selected according to some criteria. Even the topographic map, with its wealth of natural and cultural information, is restricted to certain kinds of phenomena, and the general maps which appear in many atlases are even more restricted. In some cases landscape forms are the primary phenomena shown, as on topographic maps; in others intensity and frequency patterns are shown in a diagrammatic fashion, as on traffic or commodity-flow maps.

The geographer must be an expert in map utilization and designing techniques. Each geographical problem demands a different kind of map use, and the geographer must be able to create maps suitable to the problem under study. In this sphere, the geographer is distinct from the cartographer, although the final map demands the collaboration of both.

Maps are an ancient means of representing three-dimensional reality on a two-dimensional surface. Therefore, all maps are subject to distortion of some kind. The distortion of the earth's surface on a map may be in its shape, direction, or equivalence. Each kind of projection has its uses: one may portray the shapes of areas in middle latitudes with greater faithfulness; another may be characterized by true direction from its center; another will be most accurate about the poles. Any map user must be aware of the properties of maps in order to select the one best suited to the purpose for which it will be used.

For example, the Mercator projection, which until recent years was the most commonly used of all map projections, distorts the proportions of the extreme latitudes as compared with the equatorial latitudes and does not show the polar areas at all. Its shapes, however, are accurate, and its directions are true. Therefore, its chief value is as a navigation chart; distributions plotted on it are misleading. In recent years, distributions have been shown on the so-called "interrupted projections," such as the Goode's Homolosine Equal Area Projection. This projection retains good shape and equivalence of area, but may be difficult to use at first because the earth surface is cut into lobes and a sense of continuity may be lost. More detailed explanations of these and other projections may be found in a number of works, such as Erwin J. Raisz's *General Cartography* (1938) and Arthur H. Robinson's *The Look of Maps* (1952).

Most small-scale maps of the world or large portions of the earth surface are political maps or political and hypsometric maps. The first show the political divisions of the world and such features as large cities, rivers, and sometimes roads and railways. The second show the general topography of large areas by means of standardized colors denoting elevations in addition to the other information found on political maps. There are also some political and hypsometric set maps at medium scales, say, 1:4,000,000, covering a hemisphere or some large portion of the globe.

On much large scales there are sets of maps which emphasize topography and show differences in landforms by means of contour lines, shading, hachures, or combinations of all three. These maps generally are issued by special mapping agencies of various governments, such as the United States Geological Survey and the British Ordnance Survey. There is, however, a set covering much of the world and published by various agencies under international agreement at the relatively small scale of 1:1,000,000, the *International Map of the World.* Most topographic maps, however, are at scales of 1:250,000 or larger, the greater number being between the scales of 1:50,000 and 1:100,000. Those of the United States Geological Survey, which cover little more than half of this country, are chiefly at a scale of 1:62,500, although the Army Map Service is re-issuing them on a scale of 1:50,000.

The topographic map is not merely a landform and drainage map; a great wealth of other information is shown on each sheet. The symbols used for noting physical and cultural features are explained on the map itself or in readily available handbooks of instructional materials issued by the publishing agency. Skill in reading and interpreting these maps depends not only upon recognizing the symbolic representation, but also upon general and/or specific knowledge of the area covered by the map.

Much of the accuracy of the topographic map depends on the reliability of the "control" system upon which it is based. Every country possesses some kind of control grid composed of a network of triangles established by a carefully surveyed base line. The corners of triangles form points of locational control into which field data can be placed. In the United States a highly accurate triangulation grid has been completed by the U. S. Coast and Geodetic Survey, although increased precision of instruments and observations make occasional revision necessary. The control in other areas of the world may or may not be equally reliable. Most of Europe is well covered, but the greater part of Latin America, Asia, and Africa is sketchily mapped at the larger scales, if at all.

There are as many kinds of distribution maps as there are distributions. Most are in the form of single sheets, although geological and soil maps, for example, may come in sets. Of great interest to geographers are land utilization maps which classify land in particular areas according to its actual or potential use. In Great Britain a complete set of land utilization maps has been completed, based on the one-inch-to-one-mile topographic set published by the Ordnance Survey. City plans, maps of cultural phenomena, natural features, earth magnetism, traffic flow, and wholesale and retail service areas are to be found, each possessing its own characteristics.

The entire world ocean is covered by a series of charts published by the U. S. Hydrographic Office, a branch of the Department of the Navy. Territorial waters of the United States and its possessions, however, are charted by the U. S. Coast and Geodetic Survey. Many of the U. S. Hydrographic Office charts are compiled from surveys made by American navy vessels; others, the greater number, are derived from surveys and charts published by hydrographic offices of other countries, particularly by the British Admiralty.

The hydrographic charts show ocean depths and shorelines, which are given with a high degree of accuracy, along with prominent landmarks such as signal lights, buoys, channel markers, and the like. The Hydrographic Office also publishes *Sailing Directions* for various ocean areas which are to be used in conjunction with the charts.

The sources of maps are innumerable, ranging from governmental agencies, through large and reputable private publishers, to maps of explorers and field workers.

In the United States the major governmental map-producing agencies are the Army Map Service, the Coast and Geodetic Survey, Hydrographic Office of the Navy, and the U. S. Geological Survey. Each of these agencies issues indices to their published maps. Other government agencies which are important map producers are the Soil Conservation Service, the Forest Service, the Tennessee Valley Authority, the Army Corps of Engineers, and the Weather Bureau. The Army Map Service, founded in 1942, was responsible for the production of maps covering most of the world during the war years, and it is pursuing a program of distributing selected maps to educational repositories throughout the country. Most of its maps are reproduced from previously published map materials which have been checked and amended. The Coast and Geodetic Survey is in charge of triangulation control operations in the United States and possessions, the production of air navigation charts of the United States, and the charting of the territorial waters of the country. The Hydrographic Office produces hydrographic charts covering the world ocean, except for the shores of the United States. The U. S.

Geological Survey is responsible for the topographic mapping of the country and for the production of official geological maps. It works closely with state geographical and geological agencies in implementing these duties.

In other countries, similar agencies perform the same duties: in England, the British Ordnance Survey and the Geographical Section, General Staff, The War Office; in France, the Service Géographique de l'Armée; in Germany, the Reichsamt für Landesaufnahme; in India, the Survey of India; in Japan and its former possessions, the Imperial Land Survey; and so on. Each of these agencies has a characteristic technique for presentation, and the maps differ widely in appearance, scale, and reliability.

In addition, there are large private map publishers. In the United States, there are the scholarly American Geographical Society and such commercial agencies as the National Geographic Society, Rand McNally, Hammond, Weber-Costello, Jeppesen, Goushá, and Denoyer-Geppert, which are among the largest firms of this kind. In general, the caliber of private map production in the United States is well below that in western Europe and formerly even Japan.

OTHER GEOGRAPHICAL RESEARCH MATERIALS

Atlases and Gazetteers—An atlas is a group of maps bound together into one or more volumes. The atlas may be considered a special kind of book and can be filed as a book according to the area it covers. On the other hand, there are specialized atlases which cannot be fitted easily into an areal classification or which would be more useful if filed according to a subject matter classification. Agricultural, industrial, mineral, geological, or linguistic atlases are of this type.

General world atlases differ considerably in quality, just as maps do. The American atlases in common use for general reference fail to approach the quality of most European publications. The handiest of the American atlases which give some indication of areal realities and relationships is *Goodes World Atlas* (9th ed., 1953). Slightly larger is the excellent *American Oxford Atlas* (1951). For more detailed coverage it is necessary to consult such atlases as the British *Times Atlas of the World* (1955-), the German *Stieler's Handatlas* (1925), the *Allgemeiner Handatlas* (1881) of Richard Andree, the Soviet *Atlas Mira* (1954), and the *Atlante Internazionale* (1956) of the Touring Club Italiano, all of which are available in this country. The Soviet Union is covered in great detail in the two-volume *Great Soviet World Atlas, (Bolshoi Sovetskii Atlas Mira,* 1937-39). An English translation of the text and legends of volume I was published in 1940. Other nations have published atlases, official and unofficial, covering their territories and possessions—China, Japan, the French colonies, and Canada among others—and India is preparing a National Atlas.

Different forms of place names, as they occur in various languages, present a problem that must be dealt with in the use of maps. The study of place names, toponymics, has been developing in recent years in the United States about the work of the U. S. Board on Geographic Names of the Department of Interior. Although the Board has not prepared a world gazetteer, it has published its rulings covering place names in a number of countries.

Most atlases incorporate a useful gazetteer within their bindings, but these seldom are up-to-date or standardized among themselves. Separate gazetteers also are compiled, such as the great *Columbia Lippincott Gazetteer of the World* (1952). The Army Map Service has compiled a series of gazetteers for many areas covered by its maps, and these are as complete in the areas they cover as any other major source. For handier use *Webster's Geographical Dictionary* (1955) is recommended.

Research Aids and Publications–The infinite variety of materials of geographical interest presents a constant challenge to both the geographer and the librarian. A most useful aid to both is the book by John K. Wright and Elizabeth T. Platt, *Aids to Geographical Research* (2d ed., 1947), which compiles under subject and area headings many major sources of geographical information. A valuable 41-page introduction describes the nature and problems of the use of geographical materials.

There are also numerous geographic journals, exclusive of those peripheral to geography. In the United States, the chief ones are the *Annals, Association of American Geographers* (1911-), the *Geographical Review* (1916-), published by the American Geographical Society, *Economic Geography* (1925-), and the *Journal of Geography* (1902-), the last-named primarily a teacher's journal. Foreign countries are in turn represented by one or more similar journals. In Britain, the leading geographical periodical is the Royal Geographical Society's *Geographical Journal* (1883-). *A Comprehensive Checklist of Serials of Geographic Value* (1949), has been compiled by Chauncy D. Harris and Jerome Fellmann, which lists these journals by country and supplies pertinent information concerning their publication as well as holdings in the United States.

Bibliographies concerning geographical materials are, or have been, maintained by agencies in three countries. The American Geographical Society publishes its *Current Geographical Publication* (1938-), which lists accessions of the Society arranged under area and topical headings. In France, there is published the *Bibliographie Geographique Internationale* (1915-), an annual summary by areas and topics of the geographical literature of the world. In Germany before the war, there appeared the *Geographisches Jahrbuch* (1866-), covering separate areas or topics in individual volumes, which appeared irregularly and covered several years of the pertinent geographical literature.

C H A P T E R IV

Political Science

Introduction—Like all literature, writings on politics follow fashion. New styles, topics, aims come to dominate the creative imagination of successive generations. Fashions, of course, are not arbitrary. They are themselves symptoms of temporary predispositions and orientations stemming from and being responses to new conditions. The dilemma faced by the writer on politics is obvious. Politics—whether as vocation or hobby—is absorbing, and rarely does it permit that aloofness from fashion, if not passion, that is the ideal of scientific inquiry. Karl Mannheim, in *Ideology and Utopia* (1936), went further than any other contemporary writer in tackling the problem of interest and disinterest in political knowledge. He succeeded in opening our eyes to the complexity of the dilemma, making us perhaps more humble in our aspirations, but he hardly led us out of our predicament.

Yet, in politics at least, predicaments need not be counsels of despair. In fact, if politics means anything, it means making choices and taking sides, even though, as Mr. Justice Holmes once put it, we may have to wager our salvation on some unproved hypothesis. This, perhaps, is the fashion of our own day: that, at last, political inquiry has been freed from "the quest for certainty," and that we are willing to settle for what is hypothetical or, at most, probable. Within such a frame of reference, there is nothing doctrinaire or dogmatic about inclusions or exclusions from what one may declare to be the limits of a field of knowledge.

For the body of literature, past and present, dealing with government and politics, past and present, is huge, and selections must be made. This review of some of the literature—and it does not pretend to anything more than a review—is intended to be suggestive rather than exhaustive. It is not a bibliography of politics. It is not a report on all the problems, issues, and trends in political literature. It is almost wholly confined to American writings, with references to foreign literature only if influences on American thinking can be traced. It ignores the rich mass of periodical writing which, in some areas, may be more important than books. This essay, then, is just one political scientist's appraisal of some works which, it seems to him, are crucial in surveying the state of the literature on politics. While some of these books are mentioned because they appear to be outstanding contributions to the continuing re-orientation of political thinking and research, others are cited only because they may be typical or some major tendency in the literature, and still others are introduced because they may serve the purpose of further reference. Excluded are political novels, journalistic writings, biographies, and autobiographies, not because they necessarily fail to convey important insights into political behavior, to present keen analyses of political phenomena, or to enrich our political wisdom, but because they are not political science.

This limitation does not mean that the author pretends to know what the nature of political science is—for he is admittedly allergic to a statement of essences. But it is also not to be implied that he embraces an operational definition of the discipline—to the effect that political science is what those calling themselves political scientists do. As a reader is entitled to knowledge of a writer's observational standpoint, candor requires the author to suggest that his own commitments are to what is usually referred to as the "political behavior approach." The characteristics of this approach were summarized by the author and two colleagues, Samuel J. Eldersveld and Morris Janowitz, in *Political Behavior: A Reader in Theory and Research* (1956), as follows:

1. It specifies as the unit or object of both theoretical and empirical analysis the behavior of persons and social groups rather than events, structures, institutions, or ideologies. It is, of course, concerned with these latter phenomena, but only as categories of analysis in terms of which social interaction takes place in typically political situations.

2. It seeks to place political theory and research in a frame of reference common to that of social psychology, sociology, and cultural anthropology. This interdisciplinary focus follows inevitably from a concern with behavior—overt or symbolic. Even though the particular transactions studied are limited to those carried out in pursuit of political roles and political goals, political behavior is assumed to be a function of personality, social organization, and society.

3. It stresses the mutual interdependence of theory and research. Theoretical questions need to be stated in operational terms for purposes of empirical research. And, in turn, empirical findings should have a bearing on the development of political theory. Its empiricism is, therefore, quite unlike the "brute facts" approach of an earlier descriptive empiricism. It is self-consciously theory-oriented.

4. It tries to develop rigorous research design and to apply precise methods of analysis to political behavior problems. It is concerned with the formulation and derivation of testable hypotheses, operational definitions, problems of experimental or *post-facto* design, reliability of instruments and criteria of validation, and other features of scientific procedure. It is in this respect that the political behavior approach differs most conspicuously from the more conventional approaches of political science. Yet, it does not assume that the procedures of the scientific method can be simplistically and mechanically applied to the analysis of the political process.

Politics as Science: The State of Affairs—Although politics is probably as old as social man himself, political science as an academic discipline is a relatively recent and predominantly American phenomenon. Most pre-literate forms of social organization required some set of norms, rules, or customs which were of binding decisional character or could serve as bases for communal decisions. There were systems of social ordering, involving superior-subordinate or, perhaps, equalitarian relationships. Even customary social relations, not evidently depending on explicit rule-making, probably called for authoritative interpretations by men. Sanctions of one kind or another, in the form of rewards or punishment, were likely to be present in the simplest political relationships. Decisions had to be made, accepted, and enforced, if the social life of the community was to survive the hazards of an environment whose control was often beyond the technological know-how of the community. Indeed, politics, like primitive religion, was probably a part of man's efforts to come to grips with the environment.

Whether one prefers to trace political science back to Plato and Aristotle, or to the more empirically-minded Machiavelli, or to the establishment of independent academic departments of political science in the late nineteenth century, or to Charles Merriam's *New Aspects of Politics* (1925), is largely a matter of taste. Unfortunately, political scientists have expended an inordinate amount of time and effort disputing the origins and nature of their discipline. And the colloquy is likely to continue for some time to come. If, therefore, at mid-century, political scientists are agreed on anything, it is probably on the muddled state of their science. Political scientists are riding off in many directions, evidently on the assumption that if you don't know where you are going, any road will take you there. One need only consult the volume entitled *Contemporary Political Science, A Survey of Methods, Research and Teaching,* published in 1950 by UNESCO's Department of Social Sciences, with contributions by scholars from many countries; or the report entitled *Goals for Political Science* (1951), prepared by the American Political Science Association's Committee for the Advancement of Teaching (which, in due course, was properly raked over the coals by another set of political scientists in the Association's official journal); or a good many books and articles concerned with the scope and methods of political science, a body of literature that since World War I has reached formidable proportions, but which, in general, reverberates with the same old arguments, no matter what side a writer may be on.

This is not a plea for further efforts to define the "scope" of political science—efforts which, hindsight suggests, have occupied the attention of the profession more than the harvest warranted. For "scope" is a deceptive term which seems to imply that the topics to be handled under a given title can be clearly delimited by simply drawing boundaries. But a scientific enterprise cannot be located in space, for it is a series of ever-changing methods of inquiry and sets of data which are being tested in the solution of problems, theoretical and practical. As problems, observational standpoints, and sought-after solutions change, the discipline will also appear differently, and boundaries and methods tend to shift with such changes, more or less swiftly, subject only to cultural lags and, more often than not, the resistance of vested disciplinary interests.

One might argue, paradoxical as it may seem, that the health of a discipline can be judged by the concern it shows with its unsolved problems. To admit one's difficulties and weaknesses is not proof of infirmity, but a prerequisite of youth and growth. Unlike economics, equipped with a central instrument of analysis–the price system–which enables the economist to develop useful theorems explaining a few of the facts of economic life, political science has been unable to evolve a central model that could serve as a reasonably stable point of departure into political inquiry. In its 1951 report, the Association's Committee for the Advancement of Teaching recommended that "increased attention be given to conceptual and systematic political science as the factor around which all other elements should adhere," but to date relatively little work has been done toward what, it seems clear, is by no means an acceptable goal for all political scientists.

There are those who find the scientific enterprise obnoxious and take the position that the proper study of politics is concerned with ideal values, and that, on the practical side, politics is an art. Their point of departure may be a justification of the State, in capital letters, perhaps well exemplified by Bernard Bosanquet's *The Philosophical Theory of the State* (1899); or it may be a defense of the individual and his associations against the State, such as the earlier work of Harold J. Laski, best expressed in *A Grammar of Politics* (1925). Poles apart in their moral predispositions, monist and pluralist idealists agree that politics is a matter of values, immune to any laws of cause and effect.

At the other extreme in modern political science are those whom, for want of a better name, one may call "brute empiricists." Baconian in orientation, physical science of an earlier time serves them as a model. Their method is inductive inference of the causal effects of political phenomena. They insist on the observation of uniformities as a necessary condition of prediction and experimental verification. Representative of this tendency is Stuart A. Rice's *Quantitative Methods in Politics* (1928), which is distinguished by the great care taken in the application of investigatory techniques, something which cannot be said for many other studies of a similar orientation. Yet, the results of this kind of inquiry have been rather limited sets of discontinuous low-level generalizations, of little theoretical use, or, in its more enthusiastic phase, the premature statement of dubious "laws," such as William B. Munro's "law of the pendulum" in *The Invisible Government* (1928), at most a return to Aristotle's observation of the cyclical movement of governmental forms.

It may be that earlier failures to find receptivity in the profession for systematic models agitate against renewed efforts in this direction. A work such as George E. G. Catlin's *The Science and Method of Politics* (1927), perhaps the only systematic attempt to investigate the assumptions of political science as science, had no influence whatsoever on the course of the discipline, possibly because its strongly individualistic and Hobbesian premises did not square with immediate realities as experienced by most political scientists. Harold D. Lasswell and Abraham Kaplan's *Power and Society* (1950), while in sympathy with the aim of developing systematic models for political science, is largely concerned with formulating empirically usable sets of interdependent definitions and mutually reinforcing operational hypotheses.

More recently, in *The Political System* (1953), David Easton has critically analyzed political science from the point of view of the need for a comprehensive conceptual framework which would permit the simultaneous, systematic ordering of both institutional data and facts of political behavior, but his proposal for an equilibrium theory of politics—by no means a new idea—has been received with some skepticism. In fact, even those who fancy themselves as belonging to the avant-garde of political scientists, often called "political behaviorists," are prone to advise against what they evidently consider premature system-building. As stated in *Political Behavior: A Reader in Theory and Research* (1956), edited by Heinz Eulau, Samuel J. Eldersveld, and Morris Janowitz, "the political behavior approach as been essentially catholic and eclectic. Although the ultimate objective of some of its practitioners may be the construction of 'systematic theory,' it has remained eminently pragmatic in application."

There are, of course, persuasive reasons for caution. A systematic theory must not only be internally consistent, but it must be in keeping with the accepted record of facts which it presumably brings into meaningful relationship. Yet, the record of political facts that is known resembles a jigsaw puzzle in which many pieces are missing. Moreover, existing empirical studies are fragmentary, often cast in contradictory frames of reference, and produced at intervals of time over many decades. The task of system-building with materials of such heterogeneous origin and substance is precarious. But if he ignores the hard facts, the systematizer is likely to be lost out of sight by his more drudging colleagues. As will be seen later on, the estrangement of theory and empirical research, even on lower levels of investigation, has been and still largely is the most fatal flaw of contemporary political science.

It has come to be realized, therefore, that the choice is not one between system-building, unencumbered by research, and empirical inquiry, unencumbered by theory. Rather, it is more and more recognized that systematic formulation and empirical research must go hand in hand. And while theory-building may be more difficult than empirical investigation, research is more time-consuming. In other words, systematization must adjust itself to the pace set by research, just as research must seek continuing theoretical enlightenment. Fortunately, one can point to a number of recent enterprises which seem to heed this injunction. It is also interesting to note that many of these undertakings have been co-operative ventures, evidently on the realization that no single scholar, working alone, can come to grips with the complexities of politics. But one must also name in this connection the work of individual scholars, such as David Apter's *The Gold Coast in Transition* (1955), a self-consciously interdisciplinary structural-functional analysis of "political institutional transfer." On the other hand, research not consciously fertilized by theory, no matter how grandiose in design or number of collaborators, is likely to be disjointed. As an example, one might mention the work carried out by a team of scholars at the Brookings Institution, in co-operation with political scientists throughout the country, and reported in five massive volumes edited by Paul T. David, Malcolm Moos, and Ralph Goldman, *Presidential Nominating Politics in 1952* (1954). While these volumes are full of much interesting information, they are devoid of theoretical significance from the point of view of a systematic politics.

All this does not mean, of course, that political science has not progressed in the last sixty years or so. Actually, the record is impressive, and recent developments suggest the vitality of the discipline. But this should not be cause for self-satisfaction. The history of political science as an independent field of inquiry can be written as a history of successive emancipations from earlier limitations and false starts. Yet, these successive emancipations have been additive rather than cumulative: the old survives with the new, and the old acquires new defenders as the new relies on old apostles. It is impossible to say, therefore, that anything has been disproven as long as conventional tests of proof—the requisites of scientific status in any field of knowledge—are not commonly accepted by political scientists, or, in fact, are rejected by some as altogether irrelevant in political inquiry.

There are those impatient with "method." Given the aridity and the scholasticism of much methodological discussion, their impatience is understandable, though not justified. What they are saying, in effect, is that the results matter, and not the processes of inquiry by which the results are obtained. But if political science as disciplined discourse is to differ from other forms of political communication, the processes by which findings are made and conclusions reached must be replicable, either logically or empirically. There are, admittedly, standards of excellence for political philosophy, for political polemics, for political fiction, or for political guidance. But they differ from those canons of scientific method by which a political science must be judged.

Political Theory: The Lost Frontier—Perhaps the most pervasive feature of political science as it emerged in the late nineteenth century from its age-old marriage with moral philosophy, history, and public law is the separation of theory and empirical research. With positivism already regnant in both history and law since the second quarter of the century, the mid- and late-Victorian complacency, characterized by an easy and naive belief in the inevitability of progress and liberty under law, was congenial to the eschewal of ethical sentiments. This development is understandable. Positivism is the response of men living in an era (and aura) in which problems of ultimate ends are believed to be rooted in man himself or his natural and social environment. Moreover, the social order may seem stable and be taken for granted, so that, when decisions must be made for the community, they appear to involve choices of means rather than ends. But with the elimination of questions of value from political disquisitions, positivism also exorcised empirically relevant theory. What now went as theory was largely a combination of imported, abstract German ideas about the nature of the State, a concept really alien to the American experience, Austinian notions of sovereignty that their exponents found troublesome to reconcile with federal institutions and other facts of American life, and evolutionary doctrines about races and nations. Yet, the study of political institutions was quite unencumbered by these "theoretical" excogitations, being concerned with descriptive, historical, and formalistic analyses of governmental structures and constitutional principles. Works such as Woodrow Wilson's *The State* (1889) or John W. Burgess' *Political Science and Comparative Constitutional Law* (1890-91) are of interest today mainly to antiquarians.

But the stage was set for making theory peripheral to the core enterprise. Theory in American political science, as elsewhere, came to mean the history of political philosophies. William A. Dunning's three volumes—*A History of Political Theories, Ancient and Mediaeval* (1902), *A History of Political Theories, from Luther to Montesquieu* (1905), and *A History of Political Theories, from Rousseau to Spencer* (1920)—set the tone for a long series of similar works, of more or less originality, describing the contents of the classical texts and avoiding critical assessment. In due time, similar histories were written for particular countries, notably the United States, England, France, and Germany. Or the precedents were traced for particular concepts, such as Charles E. Merriam's *A History of the Theory of Sovereignty since Rousseau* (1900) or Francis Coker's *Organismic Theories of the State* (1910). To this may be added a still growing body of studies on particular political philosophers, with a strong dose of biography and historical-environmental data added to make textual exegesis more palatable. But once the pragmatic reaction set in against the empty formalism and legalism of the earlier political science, theory was left hanging in mid-air, with neither its feet firmly rooted in contemporary political facts, nor its head in the frankly speculative heaven of metaphysics.

This is not intended to suggest anything said about politics before 1800 or 1900 is not relevant for present investigation. To commit the classics to oblivion—if that were possible—would only mean a reversal of the attitude of those who believe that nothing significant has been written about politics since Plato, Aristotle, and Thomas Aquinas. The issue is certainly not one of the moderns versus the ancients. The real issue is the uses to which classical as well as modern political writings are to be put. It is for this reason that study of the classics must necessarily take account of the state of the discipline within which these writings find their problematic focus, theoretical status, and methodological apparatus. Otherwise it is impossible to specify criteria needed to determine whether or not a literary production falls within a designated critical orbit.

For those able and willing to give the classics another try—for whatever reason—most of them are available in cheap editions. The "spell of Plato" may best be caught in the *Republic,* written about 380 B.C., a weird mixture of utopian writing, elitist predilections, and metaphysical speculation about human purposes from which, by an admittedly rigorous logical procedure, an ethical absolutism is derived. The *Republic* represents a genre of idealist political writing which has survived to the present day and which sees the definition of the ideal political community as the major task of political thinking. This type of political literature undoubtedly provides important data for political science, but it is not political science unless the notion of "science" is deprived of all meaning. It supplies data for political science not because of the eternal verities to which it aspires, but rather because it is symptomatic of the reactions of highly sensitive and intelligent men to times of stress and strain. It is of importance in understanding the history of the political intellect, and it is important because it symbolizes the aspirations of men for a better life and because it has driven men on to action, no matter how mistaken their assumptions and how dangerous their behavior.

More profitable from the point of view of modern political science is Aristotle's *Politics* which dates from about 350 B.C. Aristotle combined logic with empirical observations in creating the method of comparative analysis of political institutions. There is, of course, much that is nonsense in the *Politics* and even more that is irrelevant except for antiquarian interest, but the modern political scientist finds here a first classification of governmental structures, a theory of governmental change, an appreciation of custom and tradition as powerful forces in political behavior, the beginnings of social class analysis, and an ethics of political responsibility.

In Thomas Aquinas' *Summa Theologica,* written about 1250 A.D., the natural law doctrine of the Stoic philosophers was integrated into the Christian teaching of divine order, combined with the Aristotelian emphasis on customary norms or common law, and supplemented by a just regard for the sound legal positivism of the Roman jurists. The resulting synthesis represented a *tour de force* of considerable intellectual achievement and influence, notably on the emergence of constitutionalism.

The intellectual ferment of the Renaissance produced, in Niccolò Machiavelli, the first of the modern political theorists. His *Prince,* which first appeared in 1513, is one of the most controversial books in political theory and remains a monument to the liberation of man's mind from medieval preoccupations with metaphysics and religion. Often denounced as the work of an amoral charlatan, it is a dispassionate analysis—except for the last, possibly forged, chapter—of the political style of the Renaissance, a clear-headed appraisal of the role of political power in human affairs, and a keen dissection of the problem of means and ends in political conduct. The book oozed the spirit of a changing times. The *Prince* represents a kind of political writing that has come in for much criticism, by both idealists and empiricists, but its propositions are neither purely descriptive nor dogmatically absolute. Rather, as close reading will show, they usually are cast in terms of hypothetical statement—"if you want this, then do that," and the success of action is made dependent on a great many conditions which might interfere with desired consequences. In other words, the statements made by this genre are not only tentative, subject to verification in practice, but the probability that expected results will occur is made contingent on the presence or absence of specified circumstances. It is for this reason that Machiavelli's *Prince,* on the surface so little sanguine about the possibilities of an ethics of responsibility, may be considered a precursor of the theoretical-empirical method of our own day.

By comparison with the *Prince,* Jean Bodin's *Republic* of 1576 seems unduly cryptic, but Bodin freed political theory from its bondage to theology and presented a secular conception of natural law and its ethical premises. His concept of sovereignty would become a central notion in political science and plague political theory down to the recent past; yet, if one appraises his theory of sovereignty, it appears eminently rooted in human reality, whereas later formulations seem depersonalized and metaphysical.

If Machiavelli's *Prince* was modern in that it represented the first truly empirical approach to the problem of power, Thomas Hobbes's *Leviathan* (1651) was modern in that it treated politics from the methodological standpoint of the new physical sciences. Deductive, logical, schematic, and comprehensive in his method, Hobbes related his "political system" to human behavior in general, approximating the structural-functional conceptions of recent social science. The fact that Hobbes ignored empirical observations may account, in part at least, for the relatively small influence of his work on the later course of political science. Instead, the *Leviathan* fell in disrepute as an argument in favor of absolute monarchy, though it is often noted that the *Leviathan* stimulated John Locke to write in 1690 his *Second Treatise of Civil Government,* which became the bible of eighteenth-century liberalism.

Both Hobbes's and Locke's works, like the third of what constitutes the great trilogy of the age, Jean Jacques Rousseau's *Social Contract,* which first appeared in France in 1762, are cast within the framework of natural law philosophy, with its assumptions about the omnipotence of human reason, its speculations about the contractual origins of civil society, and its contemporarily congenial individualism. If they cannot serve any longer as viable theories, they continue to be important polemical tracts of the times—Hobbes as the father of absolutism, Locke as the father of liberalism, and Rousseau as the father of nationalism.

Much neglected by historians of political theory is the work of Giovanni Battista Vico, whose *Principii d'una Scienza Nuova* (1725; 2d ed., 1730) is an expression of revolt against the ahistorical, speculative methods and findings of the natural law philosophers. Vico's approach impressed the Baron Charles Louis de Montesquieu, whose great *De l'esprit des loix* (1748) marks the modern revival of Aristotle's empirical, historical, and comparative analysis. Montesquieu is, of course, best known for his formulation of the principle of the separation of powers. His influence on American political thought is evident in *The Federalist* (1787-88), a series of essays by Alexander Hamilton, James Madison, and John Jay in favor of the new American Constitution. In England, Edmund Burke's subtle mixture of guarded liberalism in economics and equally guarded conservatism in politics is well expressed in his *Reflections on the Revolution in France* (1790).

Political thought in the outgoing eighteenth and nineteenth centuries moves along many roads. Conservatism, romantic and reactionary; liberalism, constitutional and utilitarian; socialism, utopian and "scientific"; nationalism, idealist and historical; individualism, anarchic and democratic; and other ideological formulations compete in the struggle for men's minds. Jeremy Bentham's *An Introduction to the Principles of Morals and Legislation* (1789) and later works postulated reform in terms of the principle of utility based on "pain and pleasure" as its "two sovereign masters." Georg W. F. Hegel's *Grundlinien der Philosophie des Rechts* (1821) marked the apotheosis of the "state." Liberalism found its most distinguished spokesman in John Stuart Mill, whose *On Liberty* (1859) and *Considerations on Representative Government* (1861) remain to this day unequaled as expressions of constitutional sanity. Karl Marx and Friedrich Engels, in *The Communist Manifesto* of 1848, combined the dialectic method and historical analysis in their theory of the inevitable class struggle. Everywhere change was in the air, and men everywhere sought to control the change in line with their preferences and predilections. Political theory was, above all, man's response to a rapidly changing world of industrialization, urbanization, and colonization. The Enlightenment's idea of progress was given powerful impetus by the discoveries of Darwin, and progress and evolution became almost synonymous in usage. The tremendous strides made in the natural sciences spurred on those dedicated to the study of human affairs. The time had come for the emergence of the social sciences as independent disciplines. And with it also came the decline of political theory.

Dunning's descriptive historicism dominated the scene for a generation, and it was not until 1937, when George H. Sabine published *A History of Political Theory,* that some fresh air would ventilate the moldy caves of historical scholarship. Before Sabine, Charles H. McIlwain, in a sophisticated introduction to *The Political Works of James I* (1918), had shown the possibilities of creative theoretical activity in the writing of the history of ideas, but his later *The Growth of Political Thought in the West* (1932) was more conventional. McIlwain tended to view political philosophies as rationalizations rather than as determinants of political action, but unlike Sabine he was not clear as to just what the important problems of a political theory really are. Instead, it was Sabine who reversed the trend in the study of political theory by reintroducing methodological rigor into the analysis of political ideas. As he pointed out in the preface to the revised edition of his book in 1950, "... any clear-headed theory of politics requires discrimination between states of fact, causal connections, formal implications, and the values or ends that a policy is designed to achieve. In any political philosophy all these factors are combined, but no combination can alter the fact that they are logically different and that conclusions about them are differently warranted." Yet, even after Sabine, most of those who call themselves "political theorists" seem to ignore this methodological injunction. They continue to present the work of a classical writer without discriminating between the various dimensions of theory—value statements, causal hypotheses, empirical data, epistemology, and techniques of obtaining political goals. When, in the early fifties, David Easton came to write his *The Political System* (1953) subtitled "an inquiry into the state of political science," he did not find wide acceptance of the Sabinian view among his colleagues.

The trouble with the classics is not that they are studied, for they should be studied, but rather it is the way they are studied. Unless the student of historical writings approaches his subject with some notion of just what he is after, and with some methodological sophistication, his work must necessarily remain without significance. If it is his attitude that all the really important things which need to be said about politics have already been said by the classics, his scholarship, no matter how erudite, will be uncreative from the point of view of theoretical progress. Historical scholarship is an activity essentially different from theory construction, be it concerned with value theory or causal theory. The objective of history-writing is narrative, either to tell us "how things have actually been," or to tell us "how things have come to be what they are." The objective of theory is either to clarify values and goals of public policy, or to advance causal propositions which can be empirically verified. Little has been done along these lines by political theorists who have taken the historical road. As an example of the former, one might mention William Y. Elliott's *The Pragmatic Revolt in Politics* (1928), with which one may partly disagree, but which does not pull its punches in its critique of pluralism; or Leo Strauss's masterful *The Political Philosophy of Hobbes: Its Basis and Its Genesis* (1952). As an example of the latter, there is Robert A. Dahl's recent *A Preface to Democratic Theory* (1956), which is an acute analysis of the causal propositions and functional hypotheses implicit in various historical formulations of democracy. A masterpiece of historical-theoretical writing is Otto von Gierke's *Das Deutsche Genossenschaftsrecht* (1868-73), part of which is available in an English translation by Frederic W. Maitland, *Political Theories of the Middle Ages* (1900).

The prevailing mode of dealing with theory is still either rejection of the premises on which propositions are based, or criticism of the logical procedures used in making deductions from major theoretical propositions, or, perhaps worse, selective quotation with the implicit attempt at ridicule. Articles and book reviews in the journals are still full of these kinds of diatribes. The technique is literary, and as one reads these tracts or articles of the critics, one is struck by the use of metaphor, loose assertion, flowery language, and often invective.

Of course, logical analysis and conceptual clarification are important ingredients of a viable political theory. A notable example is Thomas D. Weldon's analysis of classical political theory, *The Vocabulary of Politics* (1953). The book is a critique of classical styles of thinking with their real essences, absolute standards, and geometrical methods, as well as a plea for attention to meanings which change with changes in institutions, problems, and human aspirations. But the final test of a theory's validity does not lie either in polemical exegesis or even in logical analysis. It lies in the ability of the theory to withstand the rigorous test of empirical proof. This kind of test requires ingenuity, patience, and much drudgery. In part, of course, theorists must blame themselves if their work arouses nothing but verbal excoriation. Theories devoid of operational definitions and testable hypotheses are difficult to defend in the absence of proof. And, admittedly, the burden of proof lies with the theorist rather than with the critic. It is for this reason that, if political theory is to be freed from the jungle war of polemical disputation, political theorists have an obligation to be explicit about the character of the statements they make—whether they are propositions of fact or of value—and to remain within a range of factual data or value problems to which their theories presumably refer, as well as to provide for those lines of empirical inquiry which alone can prove or disprove their assertions.

And if academic political theory in its historical garb contributed little to a science of politics, it contributed even less to the reformulation of political values or the creation of new ones. Academic political theorists, though insistent on the need for a normative political philosophy, have not produced a single major piece of writing that might be considered a contribution to a political value system. Until recently, what creative value theory was produced was more likely to be the work of philosophers and intellectuals generally than of academic political theorists. Perhaps the most persistently creative political theorist on the American scene, whose work spans almost two generations and an ever-changing orientation, has been Walter Lippmann, by profession a journalist but at heart a teacher. From *A Preface to Politics* (1913), a hopeful plea for reform, through *A Preface to Morals* (1929), in search of a new political ethics, *An Inquiry into the Principles of the Good Society* (1937), an assessment of the problem of freedom and control, to the recent *Essays in the Public Philosophy* (1955), Lippmann articulated some of the major value problems of the century. John Dewey, a philosopher, in *The Public and its Problems* (1927), *Individualism, Old and New* (1930), and *Liberalism and Social Action* (1935), reconceptualized democratic liberalism in terms of pragmatic assumptions. Thomas V. Smith, another philosopher, contributed *The Democratic Way of Life* (1926), *Beyond Conscience* (1934), and *The Promise of American Politics* (1936). Max Lerner, though trained as a political scientist, formulated a program for liberals in *It is Later than You Think* (1938), *Ideas are Weapons* (1939), and *Ideas for the Ice Age* (1941). Recently, two political scientists, Louis Hartz, in *The Liberal Tradition in America* (1955), and Clinton Rossiter, in *Conservatism in America* (1955), have written creative re-appraisals of the American political tradition.

There has been some change, notably since World War II, under the impact of the fascist and communist challenges. An increasing number of political scientists have come to devote themselves to problems of public policy. Yet, those interested in the formulation of policy alternatives have not been political theorists, but students of public administration, international relations, or judicial processes. And while some of them may consciously see themselves as the descendants of the great classical theorists, their work hardly supports Leslie Lipson's assertion, in *The Great Issues of Politics* (1954), that "indispensable for understanding politics are the classic works of eminent thinkers which have stood the test of time."

The Core of Political Science: The Study of Government—The early separation of political theory from the main body of political science had profound effects on the formulations which were given the new discipline. Not only was the "state" accepted as the basic unit of analysis, eliminating from the focus of political science many political phenomena which did not fit its arbitrary definition, but the works which made some claim on comprehensiveness were little more than compilations of abstract principles, descriptions, and classifications of governmental institutions, powers, and tasks. Raymond G. Gettell's *Introduction to Political Science* (1910) or James W. Garner's *Introduction to Political Science* (1910) codified the early lore and proverbs. They are of little use because they were not based on careful analysis of the facts of political life and were, at best, syntheses of a wide and often contradictory assortment of concepts, ideas, and "data." Westel W. Willoughby, in a series of works including *An Examination of the Nature of the State* (1896), *The Fundamental Concepts of Public Law* (1924), and *The Ethical Basis of Political Authority* (1930), struck a more sophisticated note, combining legal analysis with search for origins, structural description with normative assessment, and statement of principles with supporting data. Willoughby's trilogy probably represents the most consistent and comprehensive statement of political science as conceived by the founding fathers of the discipline. Francis G. Wilson's *The Elements of Modern Politics* (1936), a late-comer of this genre of general works, brought the tradition up to date but also heralded its departure.

A more realistic approach was Harold J. Laski's *Grammar of Politics* (1925) which, however, was looked on in America more as a work in pluralist political theory than as a statement of political science. The pluralist standpoint is also present in the works of Robert M. MacIver, *The Modern State* (1926) and *The Web of Government* (1947), but in contrast to Laski's philosophical-speculative perspective, MacIver's orientation is rooted in sociological and anthropological institutional data. Arthur N. Holcombe's *Foundations of the Modern Commonwealth* (1923) and Edward M. Sait's *Political Institutions* (1938), still describing political principles and institutions, were frankly critical, though unable to transcend the traditional limitations set by acceptance of "the state" as the basic concept of analysis. Sait's book, in particular, was sensitive to "methods of approach," but it did not offer alternatives to description.

Of somewhat different caliber are two works which appeared in the thirties, Herman Finer's monumental two-volume *The Theory and Practice of Modern Government* (1932) and Carl J. Friedrich's *Constitutional Government and Politics* (1937). Though both retained the concept of the "state" to circumscribe the central object of political analysis, they drew on a broad range of data derived from what by then had become the sub-field of "comparative government" and skillfully integrated them into the theoretical formulations of the classics as handed down by the historians of political thought. There was still historical narration and legal description in these two works, but both took cognizance of the existence of pressure groups and public opinion phenomena as important ingredients of the political process.

Within the framework set by this tradition, political science in the first forty years of the century produced an abundance of historical, constitutional, and institutional studies on almost every conceivable subject related to government, whether on the local, state, national, or international level. The problems of constitution-making, constitutional interpretation, and constitutional change constituted the center of political investigation. They were supplemented by descriptive analyses of governmental structures, notably accenting the difference between the presidential and parliamentary systems of government and the difference between the unitary and federal forms of territorial organization. In later years, the differences between democratic and authoritarian governmental systems were given attention. Studies on the origin, nature, and structure of representation, the history and activities of political parties, the organization and procedures of legislative bodies, and the functions of administrative departments circumscribed the outer limits of this literature. Avoiding theory, the studies were often informative, sometimes insightful, rarely systematic, and never dynamic in character. Pretending to freedom from value judgments, they were nevertheless shot through with normative assumptions, depending on the writer's orientation. In due course, each of these concerns would become a specialization.

When in the late forties UNESCO undertook its survey of the state of political science, it was a basic assumption of the project that the development of political science has been very uneven in different parts of the world, and that, therefore, an international accounting might "bring to light causes of international as well as internal tension which might otherwise have remained unknown." Indeed, perusal of the UNESCO volume reveals that whereas American political science traveled the pragmatic route with little theoretical enlightenment ever since World War I, continental scholarship in political science remained historical, legal, and, above all, philosophical in orientation. Yet, from the beginning it had been realized that a political science that would not permit comparison of either political institutions or political behavior patterns would necessarily remain culture-bound and parochial. But at its worst, comparison became comparison of uncomparables, tending to reinforce preference for one's own traditional institutions; while at its best, comparison amounted to little more than parallel description of institutions in terms of low-level empirical concepts which were foisted on more or less systematic observations. In spite of lip service to the contrary, the study of comparative government, so-called, was a seriatim presentation of national institutions or organizational problems. The texts, from Abbott Lawrence Lowell's *Governments and Parties in Continental Europe* (3d ed., 1897) through James Bryce's *Modern Democracies* (1921) to Taylor Cole's well-edited *European Political Systems* (1953), to name only a few in a long list of books, are comparative in name only. This is not to imply that they were of inferior scholarship, but that scholarship treated foreign institutions within a methodological frame of reference that was largely set by concepts derived from English or American constitutional experience. There were, of course, exceptions, such as the works of Finer and Friedrich already mentioned. But students of comparative government were, more often than not, specialists on a single country, and the proliferation of works on particular countries, too extensive for citation here, is apt testimony of the continued attractiveness of the country-by-country approach. Or they produced a rich body of specialized works on the functioning of presumably unique institutions in a foreign country, such as Walter Sharp's *The French Civil Service* (1931), William Ivor Jennings' *Cabinet Government* (1936), or Arnold Brecht's *Federalism and Regionalism in Germany* (1945), to mention only a few works that are typical. More recently, under the impact of an interdisciplinary "area approach," political scientists have come to deal with foreign institutions in a more multi-dimensional setting, relating political forms and processes to the social structure and culture of a given country, such as Robert Scalapino's *Democracy and the Party Movement in Prewar Japan* (1953) or Merle Fainsod's *How Russia is Ruled* (1953), but even these studies fall short of the requirements of comparative analysis.

There is today much ferment among students of comparative government. Under the auspices of the Social Science Research Council, a Committee on Comparative Politics has recently begun to specify major types of research needs, delimit areas of ignorance, and concern itself with theoretical and methodological problems. These tendencies have been summarized and evaluated by Roy C. Macridis in his critical *The Study of Comparative Government* (1955).

It was in the nature of the American experience that constitutional law should claim the attention of political scientists bent on specialization. The great political conflicts in American history had been conflicts over the Constitution. And even if not really legal but political in character, conflicts between the President and Congress, or between the federal government and the states, were seen in a constitutional perspective. Constitutional problems arising out of the due process, equal protection of the laws, and contract clauses of the Constitution, as well as such constitutional grants as the commerce power and taxing power, were of interest to political scientists. Yet, if one expected a treatment of these matters by political scientists different from that of the lawyers, such as Walter Bagehot had undertaken in *The English Constitution* (1867), the literature, at least until recently, does not reveal it. This is true even of the most political of American constitutional issues, the problem of judicial review. Justice Marshall's denial of the politically creative role of the courts in *Marbury v. Madison* (1803), still defended over a hundred years later by Justice Roberts in *United States v. Butler* (1936), had been codified in Kent's, Story's, and Cooley's nineteenth-century commentaries, and their authority seemed insurmountable. The pervasiveness of the classical legal approach is evident in an early work of Edward S. Corwin, *The Doctrine of Judicial Review* (1914) and Charles G. Haines' *The American Doctrine of Judicial Supremacy* (1914, 2d ed., 1932).

When the break-through came by way of "sociological jurisprudence" and a new "legal realism," it was led by lawyers rather than by political scientists. Justice Benjamin Cardozo took a close look at what the judges really do when they interpret the law in *The Nature of the Judicial Process* (1921), which was followed by such works, all by lawyers, but of interest to political scientists, as Thurman Arnold's *The Symbols of Government* (1935) and *The Folklore of Capitalism* (1937), or the more psychologically-oriented work of Jerome Frank, in *Law and the Modern Mind* (1930) and *Courts on Trial* (1949). The spirit of the Rooseveltian attack on the judiciary is probably best expressed in the work of a participant observer, Robert H. Jackson's *The Struggle for Judicial Supremacy* (1941). But political scientists contributed little to the new orientation. An exception is Robert K. Carr's *The Supreme Court and Judicial Review* (1942), and Fred V. Cahill summarized and evaluated the ferment of a generation in *Judicial Legislation; A Study in American Legal Theory* (1952). Charles Herman Pritchett, in *The Roosevelt Court* (1948) and *Civil Liberties and the Vinson Court* (1954), among political scientists, dissected the semantics, political issues, and judicial attitudes of the Supreme Court personnel. More recently, a young political scientist, Victor G. Rosenblum, in *Law as a Political Instrument* (1955), has broken new ground in delineating the political and the legal in what is admittedly a matter of interdisciplinary concern.

Within the framework set by the historical approach and constitutional categories, political scientists specializing in "national government," "state government," and "local government" produced a formidable body of either descriptive or, in some cases, frankly remedial literature. The problems associated with federalism loomed large. Earlier writers took the defensive view in favor of what they considered the "historic balance" between the federal government and the states. Beginning with the nineteen-thirties, description and diagnosis were supplemented by engineering efforts to improve state-federal relations, the writers evidently recognizing that little was to be gained from posing concrete problems in terms of an abstract "centralization versus decentralization" dichotomy. Typical of the new approach were Jane Perry Clark's *The Rise of a New Federalism* (1938) and George C. S. Benson's *The New Centralization* (1941). Two recent volumes, *Studies in Federalism* (1954), edited by Robert R. Bowie and Carl J. Friedrich, and *Federalism: Mature and Emergent* (1955), edited by Arthur W. Macmahon, present sophisticated analyses of the political aspects of federalism throughout the world.

Second only to the problems arising out of the territorial division of powers in interest to political scientists were the problems stemming from the functional separation of powers between the President and Congress, particularly the President's role in legislation. James Hart discussed executive orders in *The Ordinance Making Powers of the President of the United States* (1925), but the leading book dealing generally with the President's influence on legislation was a broadly-gauged study by Edward S. Corwin, *The President, Office and Powers* (1940). Lawrence H. Chamberlain's *The President, Congress and Legislation* (1946) is suggestive, and Wilfred E. Binkley's *President and Congress* (1947) traced the relations of the two agencies through history. One may also mention two recent books which attest to the continuing interest in the office of the President, Edward S. Corwin and Louis W. Koenig's *The Presidency Today* (1956) and Clinton Rossiter's *The American Presidency* (1956).

In addition to the works on federalism and presidential politics, political scientists have produced an enormous body of monographic studies on almost every conceivable institutional and problematic area of American government and politics. In particular, studies of Congress have been abundant. If the earlier of these studies, such as Robert Luce's *Legislative Procedure* (1922) and *Legislative Assemblies* (1924), were concerned with description of legal powers and the procedural maze of the legislative process, interest has gradually shifted towards the need for organizational reforms, as in George B. Galloway's *Congress at the Crossroads* (1946), and, even more recently, to the political dimensions of the legislative process, as in James M. Burns's *Congress on Trial* (1949) or Bertram Gross's *The Legislative Struggle: A Study in Social*

Combat (1953). Gross interpreted the legislative process as a struggle among groups in conflict, as did Stephen K. Bailey in *Congress Makes a Law* (1950), a detailed study of how the Full Employment Act of 1946 progressed through the legislative maze from theoretical conception to final passage. Yet these studies are more concerned with the group nature of political conflict generally than with how legislators actually behave. A stab toward such explanation was made by Julius Turner, in *Party and Constituency: Pressures on Congress* (1952), who correlated roll call votes on crucial issues with the character of Congressmen's constituencies. Few, if any, of these studies advance a systematic theory of legislative behavior. Bailey, for instance, referred to his method as a "vector analysis," but this turns out to be at most a convenient metaphor to circumscribe "the interaction of ideas, institutions, interests, and individuals" as components of the policy-making process.

The literature on American state and local government is similar in approach to that on national government. Constitutional questions and the role of the governor as administrator and policy-maker are treated as if they were microscopic cases of the national pattern. State administrative reorganization, legislative reform, as well as the relations between the state and its municipalities appear as proper concerns of academic study. The literature is too extensive to be mentioned here.

The more specialized political scientists became, the greater also became the alienation of theory from research, and the less able were students of such sub-fields as constitutional law, comparative government, public administration, or international relations to take cognizance of significant theoretical and methodological formulations at what had become the fringe rather than the core of their discipline. The fate of Arthur F. Bentley's *The Process of Government* (1908), one of the most creative works in American political science, is symptomatic. Bentley, equally dissatisfied with the structural formalism, metaphysical theory of the state, and cant about civic virtue of what he called "a dead political science," had suggested as the "raw materials" of politics the activities and relationships of those social groups whose unending interactions constitute the political order. But Bentley's realism made no impact on the thinking of his contemporaries and had to be almost independently rediscovered by hard work twenty years later in the work of specialists on administrative and legislative politics. Such works as Peter Odegard's *Pressure Politics* (1928), Edward Pendleton Herring's *Group Representation Before Congress* (1929), or Elmer E. Schattschneider's *Politics, Pressures and the Tariff* (1935) were applications of Bentley's thought, but there is little indication that these authors drew directly on his subtle discussion of action and interaction, of functional relations and group processes as objects of inquiry. Moreover, the internal politics of the great associations whose activities impinge on the political system remained unexplored. Oliver Garceau's *The Political Life of the American Medical Association* (1941) broke new empirical ground in this respect, but it was not until David B. Truman's *The*

Governmental Process appeared in 1951 that Bentley's theoretical contributions were rewoven into the central fabric of political science.

Similarly, a work of the English political scientist Graham Wallas, *Human Nature in Politics,* which, like Bentley's book, appeared in 1908, remained unheeded, in spite of the fact that such classical theoretical works as Machiavelli's *Prince,* Hobbes's *Leviathan,* or Mill's *On Liberty* had been explicitly based on psychological premises concerning the nature of man. Here, too, the separation of theory and research proved costly. When, in 1922, Walter Lippmann published his *Public Opinion,* there was nothing in the literature of political science he could utilize other than Wallas' work, with the exception, perhaps, of Abbott Lawrence Lowell's *Public Opinion and Popular Government* (1913). But it is in the nature of the scientific enterprise that its different departments cannot coexist forever in splendid isolation. The separation of politics from the study of personality, just as its separation from the study of group processes, was bound to be ended. It was primarily due to the restless spirit of Charles E. Merriam that political science would, in due time, again become a "behavioral science" rather than remain a taxonomic undertaking. In *New Aspects of Politics* (1925), Merriam outlined what amounted to a major research program for a generation of political scientists. Merriam reasserted the propriety and desirability of applying psychological and sociological concepts and techniques to political investigation. He insisted on the need for minute inquiry and microscopic studies of political behavior carried on by advanced scientific methods. And, above all, he called for a rejuvenation of political theory as a guide in research and the verification of hypotheses through empirical proof.

Merriam's influence on the subsequent course of American political science was less a function of his many writings than of his teaching. Along with colleagues and a group of brilliant students Merriam founded in the twenties and thirties what may well be called a "school," but which was both something more and something less than a "school" in the narrow sense of the term. For Merriam was much too freewheeling a scholar to hamstring independent efforts. What the members of the "Chicago school" had in common was a revolt against the prevailing formal, legal, historical, and descriptive tradition. But each of its members charted his own course without being tied to a master's "line." Yet, they carried the "message" of revolt into a variety of sub-fields in which they became specialists. In the field of public administration, Leonard D. White was always sensitive to new trends, and Herbert A. Simon would add new dimensions to the discipline. In the field of international relations, Quincy Wright and Frederick L. Schumann contributed new approaches. Harold F. Gosnell, using voting statistics, showed the possibilities of rigorous treatment of such data as well as of experimentation, to be followed in due time by Valdimer O. Key, Jr. Charles Herman Pritchett would come to study the attitudes of Supreme Court justices by scrutinizing their decisions more systematically than had ever been done before. David B. Truman, Avery Leiserson, Alfred

De Grazia, and others would make important contributions toward a more behavioral orientation in political science.

Last, but by no means least, the most imaginative among the Chicago renovators is Harold D. Lasswell. His influence has steadily grown since his *Psychopathology and Politics* (1930), with its unashamed Freudian premises, dazzled an almost disbelieving profession. Once again, after many years of denial, the problems of human nature were reintroduced into the study of politics. Speaking in a language strange to most political scientists, Lasswell's analytical schema, even if not totally accepted, has come to be widely used in behavioral studies of the political process. One might mention here as an example a book by Alexander L. and Juliette L. George, *Woodrow Wilson and Colonel House* (1956), whose authors skillfully apply categories of personality analysis in a study of two important decision-makers.

While Lasswell is best known for his contribution to a psychology of politics, his active mind continued to extend the frontiers of political science in other respects as well. In *World Politics and Personal Insecurity* (1935), he elaborated his conception of "configurative analysis," pleading for a multi-dimensional approach. In *Politics: Who Gets What, When, How* (1936), influenced by Vilfredo Pareto and Gaetano Mosca, he elaborated what remains probably the sharpest non-legal and non-normative definition of politics:

> The study of politics is the study of influence and the influential. The science of politics states conditions; the philosophy of politics justifies preferences. This book, restricted to political analysis, declares no preferences. It states conditions.
>
> The influential are those who get the most of what there is to get. Available values may be classified as *deference, income, safety*. Those who get the most are *elite;* the rest are *mass*.

In spite of strong positivistic leanings, Lasswell recognized early the central significance of values in political inquiry. In *Psychopathology and Politics,* he advanced the notion of a "preventive politics" as a kind of medical approach to the attainment of democratic values. And in *Democracy Through Public Opinion* (1941), he began the effort to relate statements of fact to statements of value which led to the conception of political science as "policy science." His continuing interdisciplinary and methodological interests are best expressed in the volume of articles entitled *The Analysis of Political Behaviour: An Empirical Approach* (1948), notably an essay on "General Framework: Person, Personality, Group, Culture." Decision-making as both a procedural and substantive problem is given further attention in *Power and Personality* (1948), which also brings Lasswell's psycho-political approach up to date. Decisional processes and attempts at their systematization, as well as researches into the policy aspects of law, are to be found in a number of recent articles, as yet not brought together in book form. In the introduction to *Power and Society* (1950), Lasswell, in co-operation with

Abraham Kaplan, outlined his conception of a "framework for political inquiry." Finally, one must mention the work of Lasswell and many associates in the area of symbolic political behavior, chiefly by way of content analysis, some of which may be found in *Language of Politics* (1949).

Public Administration: Departure and Return—Among the subfields of political science, public administration was the first to break loose from its moorings in the mother discipline, but it seems also destined to be the first to return to the womb. In fact, it looks as if public administration is serving as a main channel through which a new body of knowledge, transcending disciplinary boundaries, is being funneled into the central current of political science. From psychology comes what is often referred to as the "human relations" approach, and from sociology comes a systematic orientation best characterized as "organizational theory." At the same time, the new tendencies were bound to encounter the ticklish problem of value. One may speculate on why this is so. One reason may well be that among those specializing in various branches of political science, students of public administration were most likely to participate in governmental activities. Hence, they were more likely to test their concepts and principles against the harsh realities of political life than were students of government in general or international relations, not to mention the historians of political theory. Both the New Deal and World War II attracted political scientists into government service to a degree not previously known, and here they were brought into closer contact with social scientists from other disciplines than in the faculty clubs of their universities.

Public administration is eminently concerned with the relationship between means and ends, between facts and values, between conduct and the goals of action. The basic model is one of rational action predicated on the correct calculation of those alternatives of conduct which are most conducive to the attainment of a given set of ends and with a minimum loss of other goals. The model clearly specifies the necessity of weighing both alternate goals as well as alternate means. In spite of the relative simplicity of this model, the history of public administration has been tortuous—a case of either too little or too much. In particular, the apparent discrepancy between the rational aspect of administrative structure and the "irrational action" of human beings is a source of bewilderment to many students of public administration.

Because, perhaps, the problem of values looms so large in public administration, the "founders" of the field developed a sharp division between policy and administration at the very beginning of the discipline. There were, of course, plausible reasons for this: in part, an independent study of public administration was the outcome of the demand for an impartial civil service and other governmental reforms unencumbered by politics; and, in part, it was a corollary in government of the scientific management movement in private business, with its emphasis on economy and efficiency; finally, it was possessed by the spirit of the progressive movement of the first decade which took progress for granted as the goal of human endeavor and inquired little into other possibilities. The most explicit statement of the desirability of separating politics from administration is one of the classics of American political science, Frank G. Goodnow's *Politics and Administration* (1900). Administration, Goodnow argued, should be separate not only from partisan politics, but also from policy-making in general. One might also mention an early essay by Woodrow Wilson, "The Study of Administration," which appeared in the *Political Science Quarterly* for 1887. The preoccupations of the scientific management movement are best caught in Frederick W. Taylor's *The Principles of Scientific Management,* first published in 1911 and reprinted many times since.

The general acceptance of the notion of progress, with its predilection for Jeffersonian ends which now, in the age of increasing urbanization, industrialization, and mechanization, could be best realized by Hamiltonian means, is best expressed in another classic, Herbert Croly's *The Promise of American Life* (1909), a book of some influence on the later course of American liberalism. Goodnow's distinction between politics and administration was further elaborated by William F. Willoughby who, in *The Government of Modern States* (rev. ed., 1936), conceived of administration as a "fourth branch," independent of the executive power but to be controlled by the legislature. This "theory" was never widely accepted. Yet, the early texts in the field, especially Leonard D. White's *Introduction to the Study of Public Administration* (1926)—a widely used book, continued to reflect the direction set by Goodnow.

The question, "administration for what?" was largely ignored. If not ignored, values were taken for granted. The lack of interest in the policy objectives of public administration was probably both cause and effect of the separation of politics and administration. Policy formation was considered a function of politics and its execution a matter of administration. It was apparently assumed that because means and ends could be separated logically, they could also be separated in practice. Politics was "dirty business," and "taking administration out of politics" meant progress. The model failed to meet either the realities of policy or those of administration. It provided a fragmentary view of the administrative process, as if administration could be removed from its political context. The research emphasis was on the formal structural aspects of administration, or on rather vague "principles" of desirable administrative conduct which, if only properly applied, would make for efficient performance.

Yet, it must be pointed out that those who first advanced the dichotomy of politics and administration were not political conservatives. Many of them were in the forefront of political reformers who advocated the city manager form of government, regulatory agencies, and such devices of direct democracy as the initiative and the referendum. It was only after their post-World War I descendants had left reform behind that administration was considered an end in itself, with its corresponding neglect of the political problems of representation and party responsibility.

A gradual shift in thinking about public administration, perhaps first heralded by Felix Frankfurter in *The Public and its Government* (1930), did come with the advent of the New Deal, to be consummated only after World War II. The problems created by the depression shattered the easy assumption that the ends of government could be taken for granted and that policy considerations could be strictly excluded from administration. Pragmatism, notably as expounded in John Dewey's *The Public and its Problems* (1927), penetrated the consciousness of students of public administration. Moreover, the old maladies of corruption had been largely remedied, and it was no longer to be feared that contact with politics and policy-making would besmirch the good name of public administration. The new tendencies were noted by Leonard D. White in *Trends in Public Administration* (1933).

In general, writers on public administration continued to discuss structural matters throughout the thirties, and an influential volume edited in 1937 by Luther Gulick and Lyndall Urwick, *Papers on the Science of Administration,* once more restated the traditional approach and its magic summary term of administrative functions, POSDCORB, i.e., planning, organizing, staffing, directing, co-ordinating, reporting, and budgeting. The verbal scholasticism of public administration is also evident in Schuyler Wallace's *Federal Departmentalization: A Critique of Theories of Organization* (1941), which reviews in great detail the arguments for and against administrative centralization. But other writers began to place public administration in its political context by emphasizing the nature of policy-making. Administrative matters were now consciously dealt with in the framework of specific governmental programs. Administration came to be viewed as a means to an end which could not be properly evaluated apart from the uses to which it was being put. John M. Gaus and Leonard O. Wolcott's *Public Administration and the United States Department of Agriculture* (1940) is conceived in terms of the newer approach. In a later theoretical work, *Reflections on Public Administration* (1947), Gaus referred to this orientation as "an ecological approach," for it builds "quite literally from the ground up; from the elements of a place–soil, climate, location, for example–to the people who live there–their numbers and ages and knowledge, and the ways of physical and social technology by which from the place and in relationship with one another, they get their living." The new orientation was given a near-manifesto form in a series of essays by John M. Gaus, Leonard D. White, and Marshall E. Dimock, *The Frontiers of Public Administration* (1936). Policy-making as a central facet of public administration is most explicitly admitted in a post-World War II volume of essays edited by Fritz Morstein Marx, *Elements of Public Administration* (1946), written mostly by younger political scientists who had some kind of governmental experience during the war. It is given its most complete formulation in Paul H. Appleby's *Policy and Administration* (1949). The various developments in the field from Goodnow on are ably discussed by Dwight Waldo in *The Administrative State: A Study of the Political Theory of American Public Administration* (1948).

Two problems in particular have continued to occupy the attention of students of public administration. One is the problem of "bureaucracy," the other the problem of the "public interest." The problem of bureaucracy, as seen by political scientists, involved the issues of administrative discretion and administrative responsibility. Administrative supremacy was first bitterly attacked in England, in Gordon Hewart's *The New Despotism* (1929), and in this country by James M. Beck in *Our Wonderland of Bureaucracy* (1932), but both substituted polemics for analysis. Early works such as Cecil T. Carr's *Delegated Legislation* (1921) or Frederick F. Blachly and Miriam E. Oatman's *Administrative Legislation and Adjudication* (1934) were primarily concerned with legislative specification of discretionary limits. John Dickinson's *Administrative Justice and the Supremacy of Law in the United States* (1927) is still an excellent work on the control of bureaucracy by the judiciary, and it was supplemented by James M. Landis' *The Administrative Process* (1938). Robert E. Cushman wrote a broad, historical study in *The Independent Regulatory Commissions* (1941), but Marver H. Bernstein's *Regulating Business by Independent Commission* (1955) is a more critical analysis of the problem of administrative control. Charles S. Hyneman favored democratic political control of the bureaucracy in a somewhat nostalgic *Bureaucracy in a Democracy* (1950), in contrast to the position taken by Carl J. Friedrich, in *Constitutional Government and Democracy* (rev. ed., 1950), that bureaucrats are ultimately subject only to a degree of self-limitation. That bureaucrats reflect the dominant political elite is essentially the argument of John D. Kingsley in a study of the British civil service, *Representative Bureaucracy* (1944). And that bureaucracy is never better or worse than the men who fill administrative positions seems to be the underlying theme of two works using the biographical approach, Edward Pendleton Herring's *Federal Commissioners: A Study of Their Careers and Qualifications* (1936) and Arthur W. Macmahon and John D. Millett's *Federal Administrators: A Biographical Approach to the Problem of Departmental Management* (1939).

In recent years the problems of bureaucratic behavior, and notably its pathology, have also come to occupy sociologists, whose point of departure has usually been the keen observations on bureaucracy of the German Max Weber, now available in English in a collection edited by H. H. Gerth and C. Wright Mills, *From Max Weber: Essays in Sociology* (1946), as well as in a translation by A. M. Henderson and Talcott Parsons, *The Theory of Social and Economic Organization* (1947). In this connection, a *Reader in Bureaucracy* (1952), edited by Robert K. Merton and associates, brings together in handy format the best theoretical and empirical work done on the sociology of bureaucracy. Other excellent studies are Reinhard Bendix' *Higher Civil Servants in American Society* (1949), Peter M. Blau's *The Dynamics of Bureaucracy* (1955) and *Bureaucracy in Modern Society* (1956), as well as a research study by a political scientist, Dwaine Marvick's *Career Perspectives in a Bureaucratic Setting* (1954).

How the "public interest"–a vague and ambiguous concept–comes to be formulated by administrators and legislators has given rise to a lively body of literature. Arthur F. Bentley's rather pessimistic conception of special interest groups pressing on one another was modified in terms of a "reconciliation" conception in Edward Pendleton Herring's now classical *Public Administration and the Public Interest* (1936), while Avery Leiserson, in *Administrative Regulation, A Study in Representation of Interests* (1942), suggested acceptance of administrative action by interest groups as the standard of whether or not the "public interest" has been met. More recently, Earl Latham, in *The Group Basis of Politics* (1952), and David B. Truman, in *The Governmental Process* (1951), have dealt with the problem of how policy-makers accommodate themselves to conflicting group pressures. But no systematic theory has as yet been evolved, though a supplementary "Note on Conceptual Scheme" in Martin Meyerson and Edward C. Banfield's *Politics, Planning, and the Public Interest* (1955) is suggestive.

The tendencies which came to dominate public administration thinking in the middle thirties not only questioned the possibility (and desirability) of separating policy from administraton, but also indicated that the so-called "principles of administration"–especially "economy" and "efficiency"–were wanting as criteria of good administration in the face of the urgent problems that needed to be solved in depression America.

But it is easier to talk about the relationship between means and ends than to specify just how they are related. Any step in the direction of a solution to the problem of facts and values, even if incomplete, could be expected to have far-reaching consequences for administrative theory. The step was taken, in a frontal attack, by Herbert A. Simon in *Administrative Behavior: A Study of Decision-Making Processes in Administrative Organization* (1947). Although published after the war, Simon's book had been conceived in the early forties and represented by far the most radical critique of traditional public administration. Strongly influenced by logical empiricism, with its exclusion of statements of value as researchable topics, Simon once more seemed to introduce the separation of policy and administration. But this interpretation is incorrect. Rather, it was Simon's objective to bring logical clarity into what had been confused notions, in both the older approach as well as in the newer trends. Simon argued that while statements of value, at least at present, are beyond the pale of empirical proof, goals of policy can be translated into statements of fact which can be tested. And as the goals of public administration are mainly immediate rather than remote, the possibility of a science of administration was once more asserted. Indeed, statements of ultimate ends—freedom, justice, welfare, and other values of democratic ideology—are meaningless unless connected with relevant means propositions. Simon's work represented, therefore, a theoretical orientation which had been lost in the years since Goodnow made the distinction between policy and administration. While critical of what he called the "proverbs of administration," Simon offered a series of hypothetical propositions of empirical relevance. In particular, the concepts of "economy" and "efficiency" are shown to be serviceable as criteria of administrative effectiveness in the context of theoretically demonstrable means-ends "chain" constructs.

Simon's book represented a departure and new beginning in another respect. It brought administrative thinking into line with a psychology of human relations. Students of public administration had been aware of Mary Parker Follett's plea for attention to the motivations of individuals and groups in organizations, but her *The New State* (1918) was more likely to be cited than read, and her suggestive papers, collected by Henry Metcalf and Lyndall Urwick in *Dynamic Administration* (1942), had been heeded more by students of private than of public administration. The "human relations" approach proper had been developed at the Harvard Business School by Elton Mayo and his associates, had been stated first in Mayo's *The Human Problems of an Industrial Civilization* (1933), and was subjected to rigorous empirical research in the Hawthorne experiments, reported in Fritz J. Roethlisberger and William J. Dickson's *Management and the Worker* (1939). Meanwhile, in 1938, an enlightened business executive, Chester Barnard, in *The Functions of the Executive,* had drawn on his rich personal experiences in pointing to the importance of what since has come to be called "informal organization." These and other developments were exploited by Simon and his associates, Donald W. Smithburg and Victor A. Thompson, in a lively text, *Public Administration* (1950).

In recent years, too, students of other disciplines have begun to concern themselves with administrative and organizational problems, and they have brought to the study of administration a good deal of theoretical and methodological sophistication. One might mention Alexander H. Leighton's participant-observational *The Governing of Men* (1945), a study of a Japanese relocation camp by an anthropologically-trained psychiatrist; Philip Selznick's sociological *TVA and the Grass Roots* (1949), with its concept of "cooptation"; or Laura Thompson's *Culture in Crisis, A Study of the Hopi Indians* (1950), based on the findings of the "Indian Personality and Administration Research" sponsored by the Office of Indian Affairs and the Committee on Human Development at the University of Chicago. Edward C. Banfield, in *Government Project* (1951), a study of a federal government-sponsored co-operative farm in Arizona, demonstrated how documentary materials, combined with *post-facto* interviews, can be used in behavioral analysis. Seymour M. Lipset, Martin Trow, and James Coleman, in *Union Democracy* (1956), have shown the possibilities of organizational analysis for an understanding of political processes in private associations. The implications of the great increase in number, size, and complexity of organizations in modern times is treated by Kenneth E. Boulding, an economist, in *The Organizational Revolution, A Study in the Ethics of Economic Organization* (1953).

At present, two trends are noticeable in public administration. There is first an effort to reconstruct and report administrative experience in its historical dimension. This may take the form of comprehensive history-writing, such as Leonard D. White's *The Jeffersonians* (1951) and *The Jacksonians* (1954), or it may take the form of history-writing at a relatively low level of abstraction, represented by the volume of "cases" edited by Harold Stein, *Public Administration and Policy Development* (1952). Designed primarily for teaching purposes, these cases are detailed descriptions of complex administrative situations, but limited in time and scope.

The other trend, "organizational theory," is characteristic of the attempt to develop empirically-testable theoretical models of organizational behavior. In this connection, communication theory and the theory of games have become of interest to students of public administration and political science in general. Richard C. Snyder, H. W. Bruck, and Burton Sapin present a comprehensive model which takes account of motivation as an important variable in *Decision-making as an Approach to the Study of International Politics* (1954). A volume of lectures given at the Brookings Institution and collected in *Research Frontiers in Politics and Government* (1955) includes essays by Herbert A. Simon on "Recent Advances in Organization Theory" and by Richard C. Snyder on "Game Theory and the Analysis of Political Behavior." Robert A. Dahl and Charles E. Lindblom, a political scientist and an economist, respectively, in *Politics, Economics and Welfare* (1953), explore different types of decision-making–polyarchy, hierarchy, bargaining, and the price system–from the point of view of both organizational control and policy consequences.

Beyond the Horizon: International Politics–The study of international politics has been in almost constant ferment for a number of years. Part of the ferment is the gradual shift that has occurred in transferring the study of international politics from the domains of history and law to that of political science. And part of the ferment probably is the fact that with this transfer the study of international politics, while getting rid of some of the compulsions of the historians and the lawyers, has inherited many of the headaches of the political scientists.

Before World War I one can hardly speak of there having been an independent study of international politics. The relations among states were, of course, of interest to historians and international lawyers, but whereas the former were primarily concerned with diplomatic history, the latter were preoccupied with the legal agreements existing between "sovereign nations," their rights and duties under the body of international law, customary and positive, that had evolved since the dawn of the modern era. And if the lawyers built comprehensive and abstract legal systems which postulated a "family of nations," the historians dealt with concrete diplomatic events and sought after, in a hit-or-miss fashion, the "causes" of war, but seldom peace. Typical of the diplomatic approach was David J. Hill, *A History of Diplomacy in the International Development of Europe* (1905-14). The leading treatise of international law in the United States was John B. Moore's eight-volume *A Digest of International Law* (1906). The historical method employed by both historians and lawyers did not make for generalizations, not to mention theories of international intercourse. What theory there was, Frank M. Russell has shown in *Theories of International Relations* (1936), was largely of a normative, philosophical, or apologetic character.

The study of international relations proper began only after World War I. With the aims and functions of the League of Nations as its main focus, the between-wars approach was motivated by a hopeful moralism which, in the face of recurring disasters, was stubbornly intent on formulating and implementing the goals of the international society, largely through organizational and legal means. Great emphasis was placed on formal structures, techniques of peaceful adjustment of international conflicts, and legal commitments. Information from geography to economics, from history to ethics, was harnessed into service, but lack of methodological rigor tended to confuse untestable assertions with statements of fact. The huge literature of the period ranged from comprehensive texts such as Raymond Leslie Buell's *International Relations* (1925) or Clyde Eagleton's *International Government* (1932) to formal studies of the League, such as Sir Alfred Zimmern's *The League of Nations and the Rule of Law, 1918-1935* (1936), to specialized treatises on the judicial settlement of disputes, such as Hersh Lauterpacht's *The Function of Law in the International Community* (1933), to historical treatments of wars, such as Sidney B. Fay's two-volume *The Origins of the World War* (1928), and to particular problems, such as Parker T. Moon's *Imperialism and World Politics* (1926). Most of these books, in addition to special pleading in favor of some preferred remedy for the world's ills, showed great technical competence and were singularly free of nationalistic obsessions.

There was, of course, dissent from what to some scholars appeared to be an undue preoccupation with institutional gadgets by which presumably rational men would bring the international house into order. Frederick L. Schumann published his brilliant *International Politics* in 1933, treating the politics among nations in a "state system" lacking a common government as a struggle for power, emphasizing cultural and historical antecedents as well as the attitudes and behavior patterns of nationalism and imperialism, critically reviewing the foreign policies of the major powers in terms of alternatives open to policy-makers, but not neglecting the possibilities of international law, organization, and diplomacy. Charles A. Beard, long in the forefront of the iconoclasts, subjected the vague notion of "national interest" to ironic scrutiny in *The Idea of National Interest* (1934). Nicholas Spykman's *America's Strategy in World Politics,* opening up the problems of national security, was not published until 1942, though its author had cried out for more rigorous methodological procedures in the study of international politics throughout the thirties. Finally, in *Britain and France Between Two Wars* (1940), Arnold Wolfers not only interpreted the activities of the League of Nations in terms of the foreign policies of its two dominant members, but also related their foreign policies to the political interests and ideologies of the major political groups in the two nations.

The changing focus of research in international politics was characterized by an increasing tendency to emphasize the motivations of nations and their policy-makers, their capacity to carry through on commitments, and those internal psychological, industrial, geographic, and demographic variables which determine that capacity. Moreover, with the ascendancy of political scientists among students of international relations, very much the same questions came to be asked about international politics as are asked about domestic politics: what modes of behavior are common to all states, rather than what is unique in the foreign policy of a single state? What are the conditions requisite to what types of foreign policy? What makes for repetition in the behavior of nations? What are the processes of decision-making? How does domestic politics interact with foreign politics? In other words, the shift was one from description of formal governmental structures and philosophical speculation about the ends of policy to closer observation of political processes and decision-making situations. The tendency to break down the separation of international from domestic affairs, even in the treatment of international law, is evident in Philip C. Jessup's *A Modern Law of Nations* (1948), and the close relationship between domestic ideologies and foreign policy is at the heart of Charles Micaud's *The French Right and Nazi Germany, 1933-1939* (1943).

With this new orientation came a greater reliance on the interview, either of the intensive or the sample survey variety, and on quantitative content analysis of mass communications, as tools of inquiry, rather than on official documents, papers of state, or newspaper accounts. Thomas A. Bailey's *The Man in the Street* (1948) and a volume by Lester Markel and others, *Public Opinion and Foreign Policy* (1949), are more or less tendentious in that the former took an optimistic, the latter a pessimistic view of public opinion as a formative force in foreign policy-making. On the other hand, Gabriel A. Almond's *The American People and Foreign Policy* (1950) is free of such biases and a keen analysis of the sociological and psychological factors influencing public opinion on foreign policy. It describes the environment in which foreign policy decisions must be made, traces historic trends in the development of American culture and character-making for possible prediction of responses, and conceptualizes attitudes in terms of "moods" which contribute to the shifting quality of American foreign policy. As an example of the uses of content analysis in the study of foreign policy, perhaps most suggestive is *The "Prestige Papers"* (1952) by Ithiel de Sola Poole and others, a refined treatment of the editorial comment of some of the world's leading newspapers over a span of fifty years. Of course, the older approaches continue to be pursued with some tenacity.

Unfortunately, the reaction to the reformist orientation in international relations literature of the inter-war years resulted, first, in a rather futile and sterile debate over "realism versus idealism" in approaches to the study of international politics, and, second, in a tendency to ignore values altogether. As in other fields of human behavior, so in the study of international politics, the approach which ignores or denies the relevance of values and prides itself on its factual hard-headedness tends to smuggle in its values by the back door, with the difference that it is blind to its own value judgments. The "built-in" danger of what one may call "vulgar realism" may be exemplified by the work of an influential Englishman, Edward H. Carr. In *The Twenty Years' Crisis, 1919-1939* (1939) Carr succeeded in presenting a reasonably critical diagnosis of the international situation. But in the following *Conditions of Peace* (1942), the "naturalistic fallacy" of his realism appears as an unadulterated "wave-of-the-future" doctrine, with its justification of appeasement and appraisal of Hitler as a twentieth-century Napoleon. The implicit value scheme is that "what is, is good," and it is not only good, but will last. From a methodological point of view, this approach makes for great flexibility. In *The Soviet Impact on the Western World* (1947), a little book full of otherwise suggestive insights, Carr easily switched from Hitler to Stalin as the new savior: "The missionary role which had been filled in the first world war by American democracy and Woodrow Wilson had passed in the second world war to Soviet democracy and Marshal Stalin."

Carr's work indicates the danger of treating data without a scheme of clearly specified values. Fortunately, not all realist interpretation eschews the problem. As Thomas D. Weldon has shown in *States and Morals* (1947), a concern with values, as long as values are clearly distinguished from facts, does not necessarily mean lack of precision in systematic knowledge, but, on the contrary, contributes to the clarification of policy alternatives as they are circumscribed by the facts of the situation. In other words, given the existence of an international state system, national goals are a legitimate point of departure in the study of those forces and tendencies which shape the behavior of nation states. Outstanding proponents of this type of "realism" are William T. R. Fox, *The Super-Powers* (1944), and Hans Morgenthau, *Politics Among Nations* (1948). More recently, George F. Kennan's *American Diplomacy, 1900-1950* (1951) has been hailed as an example of this realism. Yet, in accepting "power" as the goal toward which foreign policies are oriented, this modified realistic approach tends to hypostatize a single value into a principle of interpretation which may not find general acceptance. Moreover, as John H. Herz has pointed out in a fine theoretical study, *Political Realism and Political Idealism* (1951), implicit in both the realist and idealist views of international politics are hypotheses about human nature which come to be treated as if they were analytical models. The difficulty with either a model which postulates an ideal world system without conflict, or a power model which is predicated on the assumption of continued conflict, is that neither comes to grips with those expectations concerning the foreseeable future in terms of which policy-makers must make their decisions.

But "realistic" need not refer to a model that makes certain assumptions about the nature of men and nations. It may refer merely to the observational position of the investigator, and in that sense the model does not either specify the preferences of the inquirer or postulate characteristics of the object of inquiry. Rather, the observer formulates alternate expectations about the shape of things to come and assesses these expectations in terms of a variety of values, among which maximization of power may be only one value. Such models were first suggested by Lasswell in *World Politics and Personal Insecurity* (1935) under the name of "developmental constructs," and some such models were presented in his *The World Revolution of Our Time, A Framework for Basic Policy Research* (1951). Hence, analysis of international politics comes to concern itself with the study of those forces and conditions which shape national expectations and values. This approach assumes that orientations toward power differ from culture to culture, and it avoids the assumption of "realism" that all men everywhere are equally power-motivated. On the level of research this approach traces changes in the distribution of crucial social and political characteristics of world elites and counter-elites which serve as indices of social and political change affecting the distribution of top political power in world society. One should consult in this connection Harold D. Lasswell, Daniel Lerner, and C. Easton Rothwell, *The Comparative Study of Elites* (1952).

International politics, as a field of scientific study, has come to mean, then, investigation of the influences that bear upon the shaping of foreign policies, the process of policy formulation and execution, as well as of the techniques required to adjust the differing foreign policies to each other. The focus of research, as in Quincy Wright's *A Study of War* (1942), has become both more systematic and interdisciplinary than it had previously been. A good index of the newer trends is the type of research articles which have been published in the journal *World Politics* since 1948. A theoretical application of the multi-dimensional method in the area of international organization is Werner Levi's excellent *Fundamentals of World Organization* (1950). The vast range and complexity of the problems facing foreign policy-makers is well documented in the series of volumes published between 1947 and 1954 by the Brookings Institution under the title *Major Problems of United States Foreign Policy*. Legislative and administrative aspects of American foreign policy-making are treated, respectively, in Robert A. Dahl's *Congress and Foreign Policy* (1950) and James L. McCamy's *The Administration of American Foreign Affairs* (1950). An increasing number of studies are concerned with the ideological dimensions of foreign policies. An excellent example is Nathan Leites' *A Study of Bolshevism* (1953).

Accompanying the trend toward more systematization has also been a wider recognition that international political behavior cannot be understood in terms of rational decision-making models alone, but that it is affected by largely unconscious, culture-bound preconceptions and the emotional flavor of the total political environment. Otto Klineberg, a social psychologist, in *Tensions Affecting International Understanding* (1950), surveyed and summarized the relevant literature, and increasing attention is paid by students of international politics to the "personality-in-culture" formulations of the cultural anthropologists. Gabriel A. Almond's *The Appeals of Communism* (1954) or Gardner Murphy's *In the Minds of Men* (1953) are particularly valuable from this point of view. Karl Deutsch, in *Nationalism and Social Communication* (1953), applied recent developments in communication theory to international analysis. The most ambitious effort to present a systematic, interdisciplinary model of interactional behavior in terms of a theory of action is *Decision-Making as an Approach to the Study of International Politics* (1954), by Richard C. Snyder, H. W. Bruck, and Burton Sapin.

The Party and the Vote: Behavioral Breakthrough—The problem of how governments are empowered was at the heart of much classical political theory. Whether the power of some men to rule over others was derived from divine authorization, customary legitimization, violent usurpation, or popular consent constituted central issues of different theories of representation. Harold F. Gosnell, in *Democracy, The Threshold of Freedom* (1948) and Alfred De Grazia, in *Public and Republic: Political Representation in America* (1951), have perceptively traced the course of theories of representation and their institutionalization in different electoral systems.

It is anomalous, therefore, that the study of the role of political parties in the representative process did not come into its own until fairly recently. Why this should be so is a matter of speculation. One reason might be that preoccupation with the extension of the franchise during the nineteenth and early twentieth centuries deflected students of democratic politics from attention to the role of political parties in popular government. Moreover, the reform movement's efforts to introduce the devices of direct democracy—initiative, referendum, and recall—were partly based on the biased assumption that parties were detrimental to a truly democratic politics. Finally, unlike in the case of governmental processes, neither constitutional nor other formal models were at hand to serve at least as initial points of departure in empirical study, and the construction of theoretical models was not thought of as a proper concern of political science.

In England, the emergence of Parliament during the eighteenth century as the locus of political power which was shared by Whigs and Tories enabled Henry Bolingbroke and Edmund Burke to sense the central significance of parties in the political process. Yet, the founders of the American Republic, though aware of the importance of parties, or factions, as they called them, did not cherish their development, even if they could not long avoid their manipulatory potentialities. To Alexis de Tocqueville, observing American politics in the early nineteenth century and reporting on his experiences in *Democracy in America* (1835-40), parties appeared as part and parcel of democratic life. The first extensive treatment of parties is to be found in the work of an Englishman, James Bryce's classical *American Commonwealth* (1888), followed in 1898 by Henry Jones Ford's *The Rise and Growth of American Politics.* The tradition set by foreigners, such as de Tocqueville and Bryce, in observing American politics has been continued by the Englishman Denis W. Brogan in *Politics in America* (1954). Systematic analysis of party solidarity by way of study of roll-call votes in selected sessions of Parliament, Congress, and some American state legislatures was first undertaken by Abbott Lawrence Lowell in *The Influence of Party upon Legislation in England and America* (1901). In 1902 appeared the Russian Moisei Ostrogorskii's critical treatise, *Democracy and The Organization of Political Parties,* which interpreted party as a means of expressing and manipulating mass public opinion in a democracy.

But with the turn of the century and the concurrent separation of political theory from the study of political institutions, with its attendant emphasis, first on formal-legalistic, and later on reformist approaches, party politics, if not misunderstood or even denounced, practically disappeared from scientific discourse. An acute, critical diagnosis of American politics, such as James Allen Smith's *The Spirit of American Government* (1907), just as the books of Arthur F. Bentley and Graham Wallas, did not cut the academic ice, and Charles A. Beard's *An Economic Interpretation of the Constitution of the United States* (1913), treating the interplay of factional politics and class interests in the creation of the basic American law, came to influence the study of contemporary party politics only in the twenties.

Without empirically relevant theoretical models available, the study of party politics proved elusive. Ostrogorskii had treated parties as organizational artifacts, and in 1915, in *Political Parties,* Robert Michels, taking as a premise the hierarchical ordering of all organizations, including even parties which, like the Social Democrats, prided themselves for their egalitarianism, had taken a dim view of their democratic potential. The subsequent course of the study of political parties has recently been traced and evaluated by Neil A. McDonald in an excellent little volume, *The Study of Political Parties* (1955). Whether conceptualized as groups, associations, organizations, or institutions, parties seem to defy pertinent analytical categories, or, if such categories are employed, they seem to do violence to some pertinent facts of party.

Arthur N. Holcombe's *Political Parties of Today* (1924) is the pioneering work in the recent study of American parties. By the time Holcombe came to write his book, studies of aggregate voting behavior had been undertaken, and they suggested the possibility of treating sectional groupings as units in the analysis of party politics. Though avoiding generalizations, Holcombe carefully specified sectional party shifts of power and examined their relationship to the functioning of the party system as a whole. In 1940, Edward Pendleton Herring, in an empirically attractive, but theoretically inconclusive, *The Politics of Democracy,* put the accent on the personal relations of party leaders. Valdimer O. Key, Jr. in *Politics, Parties and Pressure Groups* (1942), the best available text (which has gone through several editions), noted the psychological attachment of partisans to their party, while Elmer E. Schattschneider, in his imaginative *Party Government* (1942), considered party "the property of organization." None of these formulations are mutually inconsistent, but rather complementary, sustaining the hope for a systematic theory of party politics.

Fortunately, theoretical difficulties have not stood in the way of a fruitful body of empirical work which, hopefully, will fertilize future theoretical development. In fact, as the work on parties, unlike the work on government, was not bound to a rigidly legal model, it has shown greater flexibility in formulating middle-range hypothetical propositions. Moreover, in spite of sometimes strongly normative components in most interpretations, classification in terms of party functions and doctrinal differentiations has facilitated comparative analysis, as is attempted, though not completed, in a recent volume edited by Sigmund Neumann, *Modern Political Parties* (1956). Comparison has been most fruitfully executed by Valdimer O. Key, Jr. in *Southern Politics in State and Nation* (1949), a monumental effort to trace in great detail the variations of the Southern one-party system from state to state, utilizing interviews, voting statistics, and other social data. If *Southern Politics* was primarily descriptive, its recent—but partial—sequel for the North, *American State Politics: An Introduction* (1956), contains many hypotheses about the working of the American party system which are subjected to empirical test and contribute to a more systematic and less generalizing view of American party politics. Key's two books are, in many respects, testimony to David B. Truman's expression of frustration attendant on efforts to come to grips with party phenomena, in *The Governmental Process* (1951):

> The behavior patterns [of parties] are fluid and inconsistent. The term does not have the same meaning at the national, State, and local levels of government; it may not have the same meaning in two States or in two localities; finally, in the nation, in a single State, or in a single city the term may not have the same meaning at one point in time as at another, in one campaign year and in the next. It usually means in election campaigns something very different from what it means when applied to activities in a legislature.

In the absence of a systematic theoretical framework for the study of political parties, the historical approach continues to be attractive.

Wilfred E. Binkley's *American Political Parties: Their Natural History* (1943) is a lively account of American party history. Malcolm Moos, in *The Republicans* (1956), recently demonstrated the vitality of historical interpretation in a detailed study of one of the two major parties. Richard F. Hofstadter, a historian, in *The American Political Tradition and the Men Who Made It* (1948), utilized the life-histories of the great presidents in an interpretation of the unfolding drama of American political history. Descriptive case studies of the big-city political machines, such as Harold F. Gosnell's *Machine Politics: Chicago Model* (1937) or Roy V. Peel's *The Political Clubs of New York City* (1935), have been abundant. Life-histories have been used by Harold Zink in *City Bosses in the United States* (1930), and by Dayton D. McKean in a study of Frank Hague, *The Boss: The Hague Machine in Action* (1940). William Foote Whyte, a sociologist, presented a realistic study of the relationship between organized crime and politics in *Street Corner Society: The Social Structure of an Italian Slum* (1943). Other community studies, notably William Lloyd Warner's *Democracy in Jonesville* (1949) and Floyd Hunter's *Community Power Structure* (1953), contain valuable data on the relationship between local social structures and political behavior.

Abroad, notably in England and France, there has been renewed interest in the study of political parties since the last war. In France, Maurice Duverger, Georges E. Lavau, François Goguel, and Georges Dupeux have published insightful works on party politics and voting behavior. Unfortunately, only Duverger's work, *Political Parties* (1954), has been translated among the more general treatises. It is of interest because Duverger stresses the effect of different structural patterns of party systems as independent variables on both modes of leadership and public opinion phenomena. In England, which for decades had taken her party system for granted to such a degree that it was given relatively little scholarly attention, a series of detailed electoral studies were carried on since 1945 at Nuffield College in Oxford by Ronald B. MacCullum, Alison Readman, Herbert G. Nicholas, and David E. Butler, culminating in the latter's *The Electoral System in Britain, 1918-1951* (1953). Also noteworthy is a study by James F. S. Ross, *Elections and Electors; Studies in Democratic Representation* (1955).

Valuable aid in understanding party politics and the role of parties in the political process has come and is likely to continue to come from the increasing number of investigations into the voting behavior of the electorate. This is particularly true of the studies published after World War II. The tone of the earliest studies, using aggregate voting statistics, had been set by sociologists, and when, after about 1924, political scientists undertook similar studies, the main concern was with voter turn-out at the polls and voting preferences, which data were correlated with such other available demographic data as age, sex, race, education, income, religion, occupation, ethnic origin, or urban-rural residence, to test isolated, low-level hypotheses about the behavior of aggregate groupings. Other studies were satisfied with simple tabulations to permit broad generalizations and comparisons. While some of these studies were more pretentious than either methods employed or findings warranted, others exhibited great ingenuity in the use of classificatory and statistical techniques but were innocent of theoretical considerations.

Best known among these investigations is the pioneer work on political participation by Charles E. Merriam and Harold F. Gosnell, *Non-Voting* (1924). An experiment in the stimulation of voting was subsequently reported by Harold F. Gosnell in *Getting Out the Vote* (1927), and Gosnell continued these interests in *Why Europe Votes* (1930) and *Grass Roots Politics* (1942). Other works in the same or similar vein were Stuart A. Rice, *Farmers and Workers in American Politics* (1924) and *Quantitative Methods in Politics* (1928), James K. Pollock, *Voting Behavior: A Case Study* (1939) and, in co-operation with Samuel J. Eldersveld, *Michigan Politics in Transition* (1942). Trend analysis for the purpose of prediction is most frequently associated with the name of Louis H. Bean, *Ballot Behavior* (1940) and *How to Predict Elections* (1948). A broad canvass of national voting behavior through time is presented in two books by Cortez A. M. Ewing, *Presidential Elections, From Abraham Lincoln to Franklin D. Roosevelt* (1940), and *Congressional Elections, 1896-1944* (1947). This literature has been constructively criticized by Samuel J. Eldersveld in a sophisticated appraisal, "Theory and Method in Voting Behavior Research," reprinted in *Political Behavior: A Reader in Theory and Research* (1956), edited by Eulau, Eldersveld, and Janowitz.

Few of these earlier studies were of direct help in assessing the functioning of the American party system. Arthur N. Holcombe, as already mentioned, had examined sectional tensions in American party politics in his *Political Parties of Today* (1924). In his later *The Middle Classes in American Politics* (1940), Holcombe described the changing balance of power between urban and rural areas from the point of view of its effect on the party system. But it was not until Valdimer O. Key, Jr. revived the use of aggregate voting data that this type of analysis was purposefully used as a tool to gain insight into the structural and functional patterns of the American party system.

Aggregate voting studies were inherently incapable of either explaining the individual voter's motivations and perceptions or the effect of party activities on his behavior. If the dynamics of the party system were to be understood, the role of the voter in the functioning of the system and his behavior in the context of party activities had to be ascertained. This kind of study was made possible by the appearance of the representative sample survey, or "poll," from about 1936 on. By interviewing voters, students of electoral behavior were now able to reconstruct the motivational, attitudinal, and perceptual context in which voting as a decisional activity took shape. Moreover, the introduction of the so-called "panel method" of repeated interviews at various points in time permitted conceptualization of voting as a decisional process rather than as a simply momentary act.

Unfortunately, political scientists for some time not only failed to recognize the scientific potentialities of the interview survey and to acquire the skills necessary for its execution, but some of them were frankly hostile to the new technique, as evidenced by Lindsay Rogers' ill-advised attack, in *The Pollsters* (1949). Of course, the "failure" of the commercial polls in 1948—associated with the names of George Gallup, Elmo Roper, and Archibald Crossley—did not help matters, but quick action by a Committee on Analysis of Pre-election Polls and Forecasts of the Social Science Research Council in publishing its constructively critical report, *The Pre-election Polls of 1948* (1949) by Frederick Mosteller and others, tended to restore confidence in survey techniques. Perhaps more important is the fact that due to this initial hostility of political scientists, the study of voting behavior, temporarily at least, slipped out of their hands into those of sociologists and social psychologists. The result was, however, that while these studies derived their significance from the sociological or social psychological theories in terms of which they were conceived, they tended, as Valdimer O. Key, Jr., has remarked, "to take the politics out of the study of electoral behavior."

The pioneering study of Paul F. Lazarsfeld, Bernard Berelson, and Hazel Gaudet, *The People's Choice* (1944), reporting the results of panel-type interviews during the 1940 presidential campaign in Erie County, Ohio, seemed, it is true, unduly sociological in its crass assertion that "social characteristics determine political preference." But the Erie study, as well as its successor of 1948, the Elmira study, reported in Bernard Berelson, Paul F. Lazarsfeld, and William N. McPhee, *Voting* (1954), contain much of value for an understanding of the political party system and its operation—notably on the tendency of campaign activities to activate the voter and reinforce his preferences rather than convert him; on the operation of "cross-pressures" in the voting situation; on the role of the mass media of communication; on the nature of the decisional process as one of slow crystallization rather than of rational choice; or on the political consequences of primary-group relationships.

The most comprehensive study of the influence of party, party-related issues, and candidates on voting behavior was a national probability sample survey conducted both prior to and after the 1952 presidential election by the Survey Research Center of the University of Michigan, and reported by Angus Campbell, Warren E. Miller (a political scientist), and Gerald Gurin in *The Voter Decides* (1954). By examining how the voter relates himself to politics in terms of identifications, preferences, interests, and expectations, Campbell and his associates succeeded in presenting an image of the American party system, at least on the national level, as it is perceived by the electorate and seems to influence the electorate's behavior. Samuel A. Stouffer, using data collected by the Gallup and Roper organizations, has demonstrated the advantages of sample survey analysis for the study of mass phenomena in *Communism, Conformity, and Civil Liberties* (1955).

It is also interesting to note that the 1952 Michigan design was flexible enough to permit treatment of the data by a number of political scientists in terms of their own preoccupations, setting a precedent for the wider use of such data. Alfred De Grazia used the Michigan data in portraying in detail Western voting patterns in *The Western Public, 1952 and Beyond* (1954). Morris Janowitz, a sociologist, and Dwaine Marvick, a political scientist, re-analyzed the Michigan data on the basis of a competitive theory of democracy in *Competitive Pressure and Democratic Consent* (1956).

A recent summary and appraisal of voting studies, of the aggregate and survey type, both American and European, is an article, "The Psychology of Voting: An Analysis of Political Behavior," by Seymour M. Lipset and others, published in *Handbook of Social Psychology* (1954), edited by Gardner Lindzey.

Epilogue—In a moment of euphoric exultation, a distinguished political scientist and former president of the American Political Science Association, Peter H. Odegard, recently took "A New Look at Leviathan" (in a volume of essays, edited by Lynn T. White, *Frontiers of Knowledge in The Study of Man,* 1956):

> There is a new look in the study of politics; an increasing awareness of the baffling complexity of what since Aristotle has been called the queen of the sciences—the science of politics. No longer a hostage to history, and freed at last from its bondage to the lawyers as well as from the arid schematism of the political taxonomists, political science is in the process of becoming one of the central unifying forces for understanding why we behave like human beings. As the dominant mood of the interwar period was one of specialization and isolation among the major disciplines, so the mood of this postwar generation is one of specialization and integration.

Perhaps Professor Odegard is unduly hopeful. Certainly, those laboring in the vineyards of political behavior research can take heart from such acclaim. Certainly, too, it is true that much progress has been made in political science in recent years. But a sober, second look also suggests that Professor Odegard's picture is still more in the nature of a snapshot of a possible future than of a richly painted current canvas. In fact, there is no surer way to kill the newer trends than to "co-opt" the label "political behavior" without reservations. As one considers the requisites of behavioral research, one must recognize a continuing need for intellectual humility. For few are those who can say that they have fully mastered these requisites.

The qualifications for advancing a science of politics are exacting, and there is only small indication that political scientists even now receive the kind of research training necessary to meet them. On the contrary, these are those who, entranced by interview schedules, scales, indices, and statistical devices, undertake research without being aware of the many epistemological and methodological assumptions they make in using these techniques; there are those who, immersing themselves in just these assumptions, never come around to doing empirical research and substitute for it a new verbal scholasticism; and there are, finally, those who, though adequate technicians, are not sufficiently trained in political theory or acquainted with past institutional research, with the result that they do not ask any really significant questions. Yet, the future for a science of politics is bright, and Professor Odegard may have caught some of the rays.

C H A P T E R V

Economics

Introduction—In few other fields of social science are the varied modern uses of print so fully exemplified as in the field of economic analysis and practical economic activity. The importance of efficient economic activity to the individual and to the community is not new; from the beginning of time man has had to devote most of his waking hours to the task of getting his livelihood. Yet for many centuries these activities remained simple enough to be easily learned through simple instruction and early participation. Improvements came slowly and were easily absorbed into existing habits of work. The economic environment was limited almost entirely to the small self-contained community, and familiarity with its conditions was gained through the normal experiences of living in it. Under such circumstances the necessary communication among individuals working together or assuming responsibility for different tasks could be most effectively carried on orally. Even in primitive communities the methods of getting a living were influential in determining patterns of social organization, and changes in these methods brought about social changes; but again the adjustment was so "natural," and frequently so slight and so gradual, that the participants may scarcely have been aware of the relationship between the two.

While literature dealing with practical economic activities appeared in very early historic periods, it was not ubiquitous; and dependence upon it was very slight. Only in modern times have the increasing complexity of economic activities and the accompanying expansion of the economic environment necessitated the development of a variety of specialized forms of literature. At the same time, the difficulty of social and political adjustment to accelerating changes and the widespread awareness that the welfare of all is involved in decisions concerning economic policy have instigated a flood of publications discussing the desirability of various policy decisions. Such publications are intended usually for the general reader in the hope of influencing his attitudes and actions in relation to economic questions.

The relation of economics as a field of scientific investigation to these manifold economic activities is different from that of the natural sciences to the various technological fields in that the advancing knowledge of the economist is not "applied" in practical life in the same way. His attempts to develop and to validate generalizations concerning economic behavior create no new products or industries, but may be used to predict what will happen if certain economic policies are pursued. Thus the innumerable decisions which must be made by governmental agencies, by corporate bodies, by labor unions and other professional interest groups, and, ultimately, by individuals may be affected by knowledge of the economists' work.

In view of this situation a large body of economic literature is produced by governmental agencies on all levels, by business firms and international organizations. This material may be divided in two parts, one being concerned chiefly with the presentation of a certain viewpoint and, in extreme cases, with propaganda, the other centering on the authoritative presentation of current data. Those publications by governments and international organizations containing data have become one of the main sources of the facts upon which economic analysis is based. The forms in which these data are presented vary considerably. Some of it is compiled in annual serials, such as the *Statistical Abstract of the United States* (1878-) or the *Demographic Yearbook* (1948-) of the United Nations. Others appear in monthly serial publications, such as, for example, the *Survey of Current Business* (1921-) published by the U. S. Bureau of Foreign and Domestic Commerce or *International Financial Statistics* (1948-) published by the International Monetary Fund. Finally, factual data are published often in special books or monographs. For example, many of the printed reports on Congressional hearings include sections presenting basic economic data, and the United States government and other governments, as well as the United Nations and its specialized agencies, publish frequent studies of economic import. It goes without saying that the quality—both as concerns methods of compilation and forms of presentation—of these works varies considerably. In general, the governmental publications of the poorer, "underdeveloped" countries are less reliable and less skillfully presented than those of the richer, more economically advanced countries. However, even these somewhat less satisfactory data form an important reservoir of the raw data on which a good part of economic analysis and research is based.

The General Scope of Economics—There are almost as many definitions of the scope and subject matter of economics as there are writers on this topic. In earlier periods much stress was laid upon philosophical-deductive reasoning starting from a number of apparently obvious propositions of great generality (for instance, that every man is the best judge of his own welfare, or that in the process of everyone's striving toward his own profit the welfare of all will best be served). In recent times, more emphasis has been given to the finding of empirical relationships by means of either statistical or historical investigations. Definitions originating in the 1770's, the 1880's, and the 1940's exhibit in quasi-epigrammatic form the progress of economics as a social science since the middle of the eighteenth century. Adam Smith defined it as "the science of wealth"; for him its scope was limited to the study of the nature, causes, and external aspects of the wealth of nations. This view became less tenable as it became apparent that modification of wealth is a process in time and that therefore *income* rather than wealth might well be the more immediate object of study. Also, the borderline between economics and the other social sciences was not sharply drawn in the nineteenth century; and, in their desire to influence public policy, economists engaged in discussions remote from the study of wealth. As the practical value of some aspects of economics began to be recognized, there was some pressure for economic analysis of problems facing governments or businesses, and the literature of economics came to include such diverse topics as the management of business enterprises, collective bargaining, methods of evaluation of dutiable imports, and considerations of the allocation of consumers' expenditures among various items of consumption. The eminent English economist, Alfred Marshall, therefore defined economics as "the study of men in the ordinary business of life," and more recently an American economist is reputed to have said that "economics is what economists do."

In attempting to derive a somewhat narrower definition which will fit at the same time the total output of economic literature, a distinction should be made according to whether the primary emphasis of a work is ethical, political, or scientific. The first group comprises works which aim to exhibit the ways and means by which a particular moral imperative can be achieved in the realm of economic activity. The most obvious examples are works emanating from religious groups, such as the famous Encyclical of Pope Leo XIII, *Rerum Novarum* (1891), but much of the writing of various reform groups partakes of this character.

Political economic writings in the narrower sense are works written for the purpose of discussing the economic aspects of particular political measures. Political economic writings predominated in the seventeenth and eighteenth centuries and continue to form an important part of the literature of economics till today. As a consequence during most of the nineteenth century, economics was usually called political economy.

A good way to familiarize oneself with the scope of economics as it is conceived of in institutions of higher learning is to consult a textbook. The existing textbooks, which vary considerably in scope, may, in general, be divided into two groups: those like the works of Kenneth Boulding (*Economic Analysis,* 1941) or of Paul Samuelson (*Economics,* 1948), which are concerned chiefly with an exposition of the theoretical aspects of economics; and those like John Ise's *Economics* (1946), which are mainly descriptive and attempt to familiarize the student with economic institutions rather than with theoretical relationships.

Returning now to the problem of the definition of the distinguishing features of all economic problems, theoretical and applied, one might say that they all involve a process of maximization (or minimization) in the realm of social action. This may also be expressed by saying that an economic problem exists if some social end is given and has to be achieved with a minimum expenditure of means; or, if a set of means is given and a maximum result is to be achieved.

It is this core which constitutes the basic theoretical kernel of economic problems. Although this may sometimes be hidden in some of the works dealing with the application of economics, careful examination of such writings will usually reveal this core. However, only a relatively small proportion of the economic literature produced currently is devoted exclusively or even primarily to theoretical problems. This is not due to the fact that the major issues of economic theory have been established in a more or less permanent form, but rather to the intrinsic difficulty and the rigorously circumscribed appeal which purely theoretical works have. For this reason, theoretical works in economics are sometimes treated apart from others, and the field of economic theory is regarded as a specialty. In fact, it is a branch of economic analysis underlying all other works, and the writings in applied fields of economics all include explicitly or implicitly some theoretical portions.

Marshall's description of economics as the study of man in the ordinary business of life applies best perhaps to these manifold fields of applied economics. A classification of these fields has sometimes been undertaken, but no generally agreed upon categories have been established. Some sense of the over-all structure of the various fields can be obtained by consulting the list of special fields in economics drawn up by the American Economic Association. After citing some special subfields of economic theory and economic history, the following main areas of applied economics are mentioned: money, banking, and business finance; public finance; international economics; labor and industrial relations; land and agricultural economics; business organization; and public utilities and transportation. To these should be added perhaps the growing field of consumer economics.

The degree of theoretical content of many of these areas differs greatly. In international economics or monetary economics some very extensive theoretical works have been published, whereas in the field of business administration the bulk of the writing has been in applied economics. Some of the other fields occupy an intermediary position between these extremes. In a field like labor and industrial relations, for example, one can find such predominantly theoretical works as Paul H. Douglas' *The Theory of Wages* (1934) and such purely institutional and descriptive writings as Sidney and Beatrice Webb's *Industrial Democracy* (1897).

Economic reasoning, it is apparent, can and does take place in the simplest daily experiences of choice-making, requiring no elaborate analyses. The consumer shopping in the market is engaging in economic behavior as truly as is the large corporation deciding to cut production costs in order to meet lower prices. The former may use only the *Consumers' Research Bulletin* (1931-) for guidance, while the latter calls upon an entire battery of experts both in the flesh and in print.

The Development of Economic Analysis in Relation to the Evolution of Economic Institutions—It is evident from the foregoing discussion that economists have given their attention to a variety of different problems, and that different problems must be attacked with different methods. Most typically, however, in modern scientific analysis, the economist attempts to establish a relationship between variables which, as a rule, are measurable, so that the method is quantitative and the materials are statistical or other quantitative data. In each case, the nature of the problem and of the method used will determine the character of the resulting publication and therefore the size and composition of its potential reader-group. As we study the work of the economist, these points will become clear with respect to the development through time of the economist's interest in various problems as they emerge from a changing background of economic institutions, and with respect to the development of methods suitable for dealing with typical economic problems. While many of the titles cited as examples are worth knowing in themselves as landmarks in the development of economics, they should be examined here with two major questions in mind: (1) what materials were used in the writing of this book, and (2) who is likely to read this or similar works, and for what purpose?

The Ancient World—Although man has been concerned with economic problems, that is, with the allocation of scarce resources among alternative uses, since the inception of human culture, he solved these problems for a long time in a practical common-sense way without thinking much about them. To be sure, the economic relations of primitive peoples are by no means simple; but economic relations are influenced so powerfully by the given factors of the environment, and human economic activity is adapted so closely to these given factors, that the modes of production appear almost automatic.

When the first systematic studies into the economic organization of primitive peoples were made, a theory of unilinear evolution of economic and social relationships was assumed. This theory was first formulated in its most representative form by Lewis H. Morgan in 1877 in *Ancient Society*. More modern ethnographic studies have tended to cast doubt on Morgan's theory, and the conception of a uniform evolution of human social and economic organization has been abandoned. An analytical synthesis of primitive economic activity and that of highly developed peoples would be desirable; such works as Richard Thurnwald's *Economics in Primitive Communities* (1932), or Melville Herskovits' *Economic Anthropology* (2d. ed., 1952), are a significant beginning in this direction. Early attempts to provide an analytical-descriptive account of a "primitive" economy were made by Sol Tax, in *Penny Capitalism* (1953) and Cyril S. Belshaw in *In Search of Wealth* (1955). Works like these are of paramount importance also for practical policy makers, because of the growing contemporary interest in the economic advancement of so-called underdeveloped ideas.

When Morgan worked out his theory of cultural evolution, he treated the Greek and early Roman social organizations as representing a higher level of social evolution than the primitive socio-economic systems of the Australian aborigines, the American Indians, or the Polynesians. Morgan's researches, however, had already been preceded by a series of studies on ancient economic history. Arnold H. L. Heeren had been a pioneer in the field of studying ancient commercial and industrial development, but his *Historical Researches into the Politics, Intercourse, and Trade of the Principal Nations of Antiquity* (1833-34), first published in 1805 in Germany, suffered many shortcomings because he used as his chief sources only the written accounts of ancient writers. He drew heavily upon the writings of such men as Herodotus, Thucydides, Xenophon, Aristotle, Plutarch, and Pliny. His disciple and successor, August Boeckh, in *The Public Economy of Athens* (1828), enriched the study of ancient economic relations by his use of inscriptions in addition to the texts of classical authors. Inscriptions not only provided original, direct information which could be used to check some of the facts and many of the evaluations of the ancient authors, but also proved to be a new and fruitful source of information on economic matters. Further sources of information were uncovered by students of legal and constitutional history. The works of Theodor Mommsen, for example, his *History of Rome* (new ed., 1870), are as important for the economic activities and social relations of ancient Rome as they are for the political and legal history of the city and the empire.

The deciphering of new scripts, such as Egyptian hieroglyphs and Mesopotamian cuneiform, uncovered a mine of information on economic matters—on trade, prices, labor contracts, land tenure, etc. Egyptian papyri and Babylonian clay tablets were found to contain extensive data used for business or tax purposes; in Greece, temple documents yielded extensive tabulations of information relevant to the study of economic affairs. Some of the best recent accounts of ancient economic history, such as the works by Mikhail I. Rostovtsev, *The Social and Economic History of the Roman Empire* (1926) and *The Social and Economic History of the Hellenistic World* (1941); Fritz Heichelheim's *Wirtschaftsgeschichte des Altertums* (1938); and Arthur E. R. Boak's *Manpower Shortage and the Fall of the Roman Empire in the West* (1955) incorporate all these sources.

The Middle Ages—After the fall of the Western Roman Empire in the fifth century A.D., the main center of economic activity shifted first to Byzantium and later to Central and Western Europe. Up to the tenth century there were few documents produced which contain primary or even substantial economic significance, and the economic historian of these countries and periods is forced to piece together his evidence from often fragmentary and incomplete sources. The main documents which have been found useful are laws and imperial or royal decrees and ordinances and to a lesser extent in monastic and other chronicles and in personal letters and diaries. So, for example, some of the chief sources for Byzantine economic conditions are the so-called *praktika,* i.e., manorial inventories, of which some 25 dating from the eleventh to the fifteenth centuries have been found. Another important source of Byzantine economic relations is the *Book of the Prefect,* composed in the tenth century and containing an extensive regulation of urban industry and the guild system in Constantinople. It is on sources of this kind that modern accounts of the Byzantine economy are based. Some outstanding examples of this literature are Georgije Ostrogorskii's *History of the Byzantine State* (1956) and Gunnar Mickwitz' *Die Kartellfunktionen der Zünfte* (1936).

The sources for economic conditions in early medieval Europe are, on the whole, similar. Monastic inventories, laws, and, sometimes, letters or chronicles provide the main source for our knowledge of European economic conditions in Anglo-Saxon, Merovingian, and Carolingian times. The counterpart to the Byzantine *praktika* are monastic inventories of Western monasteries, among which the so-called *Polyptyque* of the Abbot Irmino of the Monastery of Saint-Germain-des-Prés is perhaps the best known. Another famous document from the same period is Charlemagne's regulation of the administration of royal domains, the *Capitulare de Villis.* The difficulties encountered in appraising the economic organization of early medieval Europe from sources such as these may be gauged by consulting Alfons Dopsch's *The Economic and Social Foundations of European Civilization* (1937) or the first two volumes of the *Cambridge Economic History of Europe* (1941-).

Canonist Economics—A sharp change in the medieval literature on economic subjects can be observed in the thirteenth century. This change may be attributed to two causes, one intellectual and the other socio-economic. The thirteenth century witnessed the full flowering of the philosophy of the Schoolmen, who found their master in Thomas Aquinas. The Thomistic philosophy, which was ecumenical in character, paid some attention to economic subjects. In contrast with the modern scientific point of view, which pushes moral factors into the background, the writings of Thomas and his followers treated economic problems from the moral viewpoint as a means of implementing the religious teachings of the Catholic Church.

At the same time, however, the development of towns devoted chiefly to trade and the beginnings of industry—notably in Italy and the Low Countries—made empirical study of several economic problems imperative. A society based overwhelmingly on agricultural production in the manor, with only a rudimentary division of labor and with very little trade, was not conducive to investigation of many basic economic questions. At the same time there were no large states; effective political control was exercised over regions no larger than a modern English county, or, at most, over what would be regarded on the Continent as a mere province. But by the thirteenth and still more by the fourteenth century, progress had been made in Western Europe toward the establishment of centralized power. In attempting to strengthen their own position and to weaken that of the nobility, monarchs extended privileges to the towns, thus stimulating trade and industry.

An important prop to royal power was the control of fiscal and monetary matters by the king. Trade required money and credit as indispensable instruments. And so it is not surprising that, from the fourteenth century on, the literature which deals with economic questions concentrates chiefly on the following topics: (1) the value and role of money and coinage; (2) the problem of "usury" or interest; (3) the question of revenue, taxes, and public debt; and (4) the regulation of internal and international trade. These four topics occupied the center of economic thinking until well into the eighteenth century. Only slowly did the notion arise that these problems were really subsidiary to questions of manpower (population), resources, capital formation, production, and the general mechanisms achieving the distribution of resources and income among the various economic units.

The problem of money and coinage was made acute by the frequent and arbitrary depreciation of coinage by princes for their personal enrichment. Here was a topic which offered an opportunity to voice moral judgments as well as views on the economic aspects of inflation. And this opportunity was grasped avidly by writers, among whom—as could be expected in the Christian Middle Ages—ecclesiastics were especially prominent. A considerable number of such tracts on monetary problems have been preserved. The most famous among them are probably Nicolas Oresme's tract on the change in the value of money which was composed in the fourteenth century, and Gabriel Biel's *Treatise on the Power and Utility of Moneys* (1930), which was first published in the middle of the sixteenth century. At that time the inflow of precious metals which followed upon the discovery of America had begun to play havoc with the value of standard coins and the stability of prices. Thus soon after Biel had written his work, which is still steeped in medieval thought and language, Jean Bodin composed his famous essay on the impact of the importation of American treasure on European prices under the title *The Response to the Paradoxes of Malestroit* (1947, from the 2d ed., 1578). The difference in spirit from Biel's treatise (and Malestroit's work to which Bodin's tract was an answer) is striking. Biel's and Malestroit's works are predominantly moral and hortative, whereas Bodin's book is distinctly analytical. It has, not undeservedly, been called the "first modern work on economics."

Works on public revenues, trade, and usury are almost as frequent as those on money, but there is no need to discuss this literature in detail. The best of it is described in such modern works as William James Ashley's *An Introduction to English Economic History and Theory* (2d ed., 1892-93) and in the Introduction, written in 1925, by Richard H. Tawney, to Thomas Wilson's *A Discourse upon Usury,* which was first published in 1572.

Mercantilism—Whereas in political and religious history the break between the medieval and the modern eras is fairly sharp, in economic history and above all in the history of ideas on economic subjects there is little change from the late Middle Ages until well into the eighteenth century. By that time Western Europe was on its way to industrialization, and the great powers had begun their expansion into colonial regions. Governments had developed the deliberately planned economic policies and practices which we call "mercantilism." Business and financial houses needed current and accurate information upon which to base their decisions. The Fuggers, bankers to the Holy Roman Emperors, met this need by collecting letters, dispatches, and news items from many sources and having a selection of them copied in order that their international banking decisions might be made upon the best information available—an interesting example of an early forerunner of the modern newspaper, or even the financial or business service. There is a modern compilation edited by Victor Klarwill, published under the title *The Fugger News-Letters* (1924-), which illustrates the kind of news about persons, events, and trade that was considered worth reporting.

The term "mercantilism" goes back to Adam Smith, who designated the period of economic thinking in which considerations of state power and a beneficent absolutism were closely allied with economic regulatory policies as the "mercantile system." This he confronted with a system in which economic forces were permitted to find expression without compulsion, on the basis of the self-interest of all individuals. Smith's *An Inquiry into the Nature and Causes of the Wealth of Nations* (1776) is, in part, a tract designed to display the vicious effects of mercantilism and the beneficial effects of a system of free competition and free trade. The *Wealth of Nations* became one of the most influential works in economics. The rising liberalist generation in early nineteenth-century England regarded this work with reverence and, with Karl Marx's *Das Kapital* (1867), it remains one of the most frequently cited books in economics.

Works such as those of Smith and Marx tend to echo and re-echo through the public at large, until large numbers of people accept and act upon the ideas without knowing where they originated. Thus, although Smith himself was not guilty of the error, his discussion of mercantilism gave rise to the belief that economic policies and results associated with mercantilism were identical throughout Europe. In truth, mercantilism varied considerably in theory, practice, and result, both as between various parts of Europe and as between different periods. But it would also be wrong to exaggerate such differences. Many elements are common to all, or almost all, works of the mercantilist age. Standing midway between the moralism of the Middle Ages and the scientism of the post-Smithian era, the chief common characteristic of all this literature is its moralistic pragmatism. Almost all works of the period can be grouped in two classes: (1) tracts of the day, concerning some immediate problem of economic policy; or (2) handbooks for princes and their ministers, compilations of rules and advice on how to govern and how to regulate economic affairs.

Another element which the writings of the mercantilists have in common is their political nature. This is understandable in view of the practical and topical nature of the tracts, the lingering traces of moralism, and the lack of any general theory. The authors of most economic tracts were spokesmen either for the government or for some group, class, church party, or faction which had an axe to grind. A third common characteristic of the mercantilist literature was its loose terminology. The cumbersome language employed by some writers often caused their works to remain unappreciated for a long time. Mercantilist literature was, and probably still is, a gold mine for the discovery of new, and often not insignificant, forerunners of later theories. A case in point is Isaac Gervaise's *The System or Theory of the Trade of the World* (1720), which was "rediscovered" in the 1920's by Professor Jacob Viner. The fact that Gervaise's very original tract remained unappreciated for more than two hundred years may be attributed in part to its rarity and slight outward appearance but in part also to its awkward and inelegant language.

From what has been said, it is not difficult to see that the economic works of the mercantilist writers present a serious bibliographic problem. Many were pamphlets which appeared anonymously. Many others were pirated, varying from edition to edition, and almost all of them quickly became scarce. The two most extensive collections of English mercantilist writings are those in the Library of the British Museum and in the Goldsmith Library of the London School of Economics. Three excellent bibliographies exist: *The Literature of Political Economy; A Classified Catalogue,* compiled by John R. McCulloch in 1845 and reprinted by the London School of Economics in 1938; Henry Higgs's *Bibliography of Economics, 1751-1775* (1935-); and Joseph Massie's *Bibliography of the Collection of Books and Tracts on Commerce, Currency and Poor Law, 1557-1763,* reprinted in 1937 by G. Harding's Bookshop, London.

In the United States, there are three extensive and valuable collections of mercantilist works. The most comprehensive is the Kress collection at Harvard University; the two others are the Wagner collection at Yale and the Seligman collection at Columbia. The catalog of the Kress collection is an important reference tool for economic writings antedating 1776.

In view of the undoubted value and the scarcity of some of the mercantilist tracts a number of them have been reprinted. The most notable enterprises along these lines are an Italian collection of reprints edited by Pietro Custodi, entitled *Scrittori Classici Italiani di Economia Politica* (50 vols., 1803-1816), and a series of reprints of classical and mercantilist English writers published by the Johns Hopkins University Press. To these collections should be added the reprints of the works of some of the most interesting and curious mercantilist writers, as, for example, William Petty's *Economic Writings,* which were published in two volumes in 1899, or Richard Cantillon's *Essai sur la nature du commerce en général* (1755) which was reprinted several times, the last time in an authoritative annotated edition in 1952.

Emergence of Scientific Economics—In Western Europe the age of mercantilism came to an end by the middle of the eighteenth century. In Germany and in parts of Italy it lingered on, but by the beginning of the nineteenth century mercantilism was largely extinct there also. The transition from mercantilist economics to what may be called modern economics was characterized by a profound change. Beginning with the Physiocrats in France and with Adam Smith in Britain, economics attains the status of an empirical science. This should not be interpreted to mean that all moralistic and ethical reasoning is foreign to Smith and his followers. In fact, part of the appeal of the *Wealth of Nations* lies in the occasional excursions into philosophy, in its frequent epigrammatic observations, and in the injection of casual observations on topics unrelated to his main argument. This is a quality the *Wealth of Nations* shares with other great works in economics, for example, Marx's *Das Kapital,* Alfred Marshall's *Principles of Economics* (1890), Karl Menger's *Principles of Economics* (1950), and John Maynard Keynes's *The General Theory of Employment, Interest and Money* (1936). But in spite of the frequent interest in philosophy, morals, and politics, the distinguishing quality of modern economics is that in method, structure, and general outlook it is scientific. Modern economists tended to develop a general systematic theory, whose propositions and theorems are derived from, or are reducible to, empirical observation. To the extent that this occurs in any field, the writers and the audience tend to become specialized, and the resulting publications are seldom read by any one but specialists. Popular thinking and scholarly thinking tend to draw apart unless there is a constant flow of communication, sometimes in the form of "popularizations," sometimes incidental to discussion of practical issues.

Even though a common characteristic of all modern economics is its scientific nature, it cannot be said that a uniform and generally accepted body of economic theory was developed from the first. In fact, the period from 1750 to 1920 saw the rise and decline of several schools in economics whose members often vehemently opposed one another's theories. These disagreements were based sometimes on differences concerning the data or initial assumptions considered appropriate as foundations for economic analysis, sometimes they turned on differences regarding the methods used or on the relationships established between variables. In the nineteenth century, sharp disagreements split the various schools of thought over rival theories or rival methods in economic analysis. The battle of socialism versus its critics, of free-traders versus protectionists, and the famous *Methodenstreit,* in which the relative merits of the historical against the analytical method in economics were argued, are examples of these disagreements.

The proposition that economic behavior obeys certain generally valid laws independent of time and space, that is, independent of a cultural framework, has not been and probably can not be proved. Economics is thus a "historical" science, in that the laws and generalizations of economic theory attain their validity only for given cultural and historical situations. Economic theories that are correct in one situation may be quite false in another. This is an important insight, because in economic discussions more than in any other social science the *relative* validity of generalizations is often ignored. Thus many popularizations of economic theories purport to state universally valid propositions, a weakness which is not always absent from more scholarly contributions.

Methods in Economics–Economists today tend to proceed in their research by a common method, which is in its chief aspects identical with the procedures of any empirical science, i.e., the testing of theories by relating them to empirically observable data.

Two major disagreements over method can be discerned in the history of economics. One is the disagreement over the proper kind of data to be used. This was the chief issue in the so-called *Methodenstreit* that raged in Germany and Austria in the last quarter of the nineteenth century. The second conflict was concerned with the place of psychological and sociological assumptions relevant to economics.

The *Methodenstreit* turned on the question whether economics was a theoretical or a historical science. A number of German economists, under the leadership of Gustav Schmoller, maintained that the concrete data on the sole basis of which economic analysis could proceed were unique in character, and that therefore general economic laws could not be derived, but that any economic situation had to be explained in terms of its historical antecedents. Karl Menger protested this view in his *Untersuchungen über die Methode der Socialwissenschaften* (1883). He acknowledged that economic phenomena could be studied historically but held that this research constituted the study of economic history, not of economic theory. As to the possibility and validity of the latter he said:

> We construct a body of theoretical economics by attempting to determine out of the stream of changing economic phenomena those which recur repetitively. For example, we examine the general nature of exchange, price, ground-rent, demand and supply, and the typical relations between these variables, for example the effect of an augmentation or diminution of supply and demand on prices, or the effect of an increase of population on ground-rent, etc. The science of economic history, on the contrary, shows us the nature and development of specific economic phenomena, for example, the present state and past development of the economy of a certain people or region, the present state and past development of a certain economic institution, such as prices, or ground-rent in a certain economy, etc.

It is perhaps astounding, from the vantage point of the present, to consider that such simple truths as were enunciated by Menger had to be stated explicitly. But in Germany theoretical economics had come to a complete standstill during the last quarter of the nineteenth century. After the clear separation between economic theory and economic history had been made, both branches developed fruitfully and began to contribute to each other. The victory of Menger's viewpoint was so complete that later economic and social historians even attempted generalizations in their own fields. General theories were applied not only to the relationship between specific concrete institutions, such as exchange, prices, rent, etc., but between entire economic systems and forms of social, political, and ideological organizations. Instead are provided by Max Weber's *The Protestant Ethic and the Spirit of Capitalism* (1930) and by Richard H. Tawney's *Religion and the Rise of Capitalism* (1926).

But the resolution of the *Methodenstreit* left the relationship between induction and deduction in economics (and social science in general) still to be settled. Psychological factors determining economic motives and behavior were implicit in the assumptions on which the structure of economic theory was built. In the nineteenth century the assumption of rational behavior, as interpreted by utilitarian philosophers, was not severely challenged. It is true that the historical school had stressed factors other than cold, calculating rationality in determining human behavior, for example, tradition, national character, religious persuasion, and political partisanship. But the historical school could not point to any integrated and defensible psychological theory which might replace utilitarian psychology.

In the twentieth century this situation has changed. Utilitarian psychology has been abandoned, the perfectly rational economic man is recognized as a fiction, and the applicability of economic theory to the real world of affairs has been questioned, because the postulates of that theory were deduced originally from assumptions concerning human motivation and behavior which have been rejected. This situation has brought to the fore two conflicting schools of thought. One school attempts to construct a new basis for economic theory by laying the psychological foundations on which a new economics can be constructed, which would presumably differ significantly from the old economics. Unfortunately the authors who attempt to do this do not agree as to what psychological theory is correct. Charles Reinold Noyes, in his *Economic Man in Relation to his Natural Environment* (1948), holds to a theory of physiological psychology, others, like Walter A. Weisskopf in his *The Psychology of Economics* (1955), subscribe to psychoanalytic theory, and still others to behaviorism, or Gestalt psychology. Since economists, as such, are hardly competent to decide between rival psychological theories, some denied the dependence of economic analysis on psychological assumptions altogether. This group declared that economics should confine itself to the analysis of the relationships between empirically observable data without attempting to penetrate into the psychological processes underlying these data. The chief representative of this point of view is Gustav Cassel, the author of *The Theory of Social Economy* (1924). But since Cassel's work the pendulum has swung back especially since modern economists have come to recognize more and more the importance of the role of people's expectations in economic analysis. In fact, a recent treatise on economic theory, embracing a new approach, by Oskar Morgenstern and John Von Neumann, *The Theory of Games and Economic Behavior* (1944), fully takes into account the element of choice and the role of expectations.

Hence the classical economists were correct in supposing that economics rests on a sub-stratum of psychological theory. Nevertheless, economic theory need not be wedded to any one psychological theory, nor are *all* propositions of psychology of concern to economics. It is sufficient if the assumption can be made that human behavior in certain practical areas is consistent. A second necessary assumption is that in given situations individuals pursue some end and in the same culture have similar ends if they are in similar situations. Recent studies in industrial and also entrepreneurial psychology have provided very fruitful hints as to the motivations of workers and entrepreneurs in typical situations. The conceptual apparatus developed by economic theory is perfectly capable of adjusting to these findings. Traditional devices of economic analysis can be used with alternative and mutually exclusive psychological assumptions.

This is so because economic theory as such deals only with the mutual relationships of variables. Its propositions are valid for a large series of different situations involving choices between alternatives and may therefore be stated in perfectly general (mathematical) terms. The meanings attributed to the mathematical symbols or concepts used in these abstract propositions are determined by observing and classifying real situations of choice. The real choices made by individuals vary, of course, with social structure, physical environment, institutions, and beliefs–in short, with the social and cultural frameworks in which choices are made. Hence it is of the utmost importance for economics that institutional frameworks be examined and their regularities ascertained. Of course, since institutional frameworks change with time and space, economics has a "historical" tinge; but this does not mean that historical economics or institutional economics is an adequate substitute for economic theory, for the fundamental formal principles of economic theory may be stated independently of any given set of historical or of institutional factors. The problem is to determine which parts of an economic theory depend exclusively on the original set of events from which it was inferred, and whether and to what extent the theoretical structure can be generalized so as to be applicable to new cases. One of the chief tasks of writers on economic theory, certainly since the 1890's, has been to reformulate basic propositions in such a form that they can be applied to the greatest number of conceivable cases. Economic theorems have become more and more independent of any particular psychological theory, and economists have tended more and more to state their theories in such concepts as find the widest applicability to different cultural and institutional frameworks.

This situation is commonly recognized by modern economists, and struggles over method in economics have died down. Among recent restatements of present-day methodological views are Lionel Robbins' *An Essay on the Nature and Significance of Economic Science* (1932) and Friedrich A. von Hayek's *The Counter-revolution of Science* (1952), which attacks scientism and historicism in terms applicable to social science in general.

The Present State of Economics—The fact that scientific economics is now fairly free from the confusion arising from differences of opinion as to the proper data or methods to be used, or as to the adequacy of underlying psychological assumptions, does not mean that there is today complete unanimity among economists or a high degree of homogeneity in the literature produced. There are still traces of the many different "schools of thought" which have flourished in economics, of the national differences arising from different institutional backgrounds and different intellectual traditions and habits, and of the many different purposes for which economic literature is produced.

Schools of Thought—This is not the place to discuss at length the doctrinal differences and peculiarities of the many historic schools of thought. They are treated in the article, "Economics," in the *Encyclopaedia of the Social Sciences* (1930-35) and at greater length in a number of treatises on the history of economic thought, of which a good example is Erich Roll's *A History of Economic Thought* (1938). All that will be attempted here is to relate the development of the major present-day schools of thought, or rather approaches to economics, to the principal currents of political, social, and philosophical ideas which influence contemporary economic literature.

The history of scientific economics displays two periods in which there appeared to be a high degree of unanimity concerning the fundamental principles of economic theory. The first period was in the early nineteenth century, the second began with the end of World War II. The first period is usually designated as the period of classical economics; it is the time when the doctrines of Adam Smith and his chief followers in England and France were seldom challenged. The general satisfaction with the theory of value, the cornerstone of classical economics, is perhaps best expressed by John Stuart Mill, who wrote that "happily there is nothing in the laws of value which remains for the present or any future writer to clear up; the theory of the subject is complete." This was written in 1848. In 1871 the entire classical theory of value, regarded as unassailable by Mill, was overthrown.

Classical economics, which placed the theories of value and production in the center of economic analysis, arose when the central figures in the economic process became more and more clearly the individual commercial and industrial entrepreneurs. It was in industry and trade that the bulk of the wealth of England was produced; and the decisions of the many thousands, and later millions, of independent entrepreneurs determined to an increasing extent the form and the amount of wealth produced. The philosophical basis of a hedonist utilitarianism and the political basis of a laisser-faire state show through classical economics in many places. But the reality of the early nineteenth century did not conform fully to the picture evolved by the philosophers and theorists. The problem of poverty arose in an acute form. Thomas R. Malthus' famous *An Essay on the Principle of Population* (1798) was concerned with the means of alleviating poverty and distress. He found that the interference with the natural processes of the free market would lead only to worse evils than those which such measures were designed to remove, and he advocated "moral restraint" or delayed marriage and chastity as the most effective, and indeed the only means, of improving the condition of the poor. The entire economic literature of the early nineteenth century, although profoundly concerned with the problem of poverty and the means to its alleviation, regarded relief by the political authorities and legislation designed to lessen poverty not only as futile, but sometimes as positively evil. For example, David Ricardo, who scarcely favored the landed interest, accepts fully Malthus' conclusions on population growth in his *On the Principles of Political Economy, and Taxation* (1817).

The alternative to the policy of laisser faire was the advocacy of measures to be taken by government with the purpose of regulating the "anarchic" conditions created by a free market system. It is probably not incorrect to say that the fundamental difference between various schools of thought in economics since the middle of the nineteenth century can be reduced to the conflict between advocates of traditional liberal policies and advocates of various degrees of "planning." Even the socialists, who have traditionally been regarded as advocates of the most complete system of regulation and planning, do not present a united front in this respect. Karl Marx, for instance, was never very specific about the bases for the economic organization of a socialist society; as to its political future, he predicted that the means of production would become the property of society (not the "state"), and that at this stage the functions of the state as a monopoly of power would come to an end, the function of government would consist purely in administering the socially owned resources—the picture of an anarchist utopia.

John Stuart Mill, exemplifying the classical economic theory, and Karl Marx, exemplifying the socialist economic theory, thus can be said to stand at a crucial point in the history of economic thought. From their time on, various assaults were made on the freely functioning, unregulated economy, some from the right and some from the left. Protectionist theories, theories of a modified paternalism by the state, theories supporting government-fostered economic development, theories embracing a large sector of legislation and regulation for purposes of social reform, theories stipulating the nationalization of sectors of the economy were the various alternatives to classical economic theory. Among the chief representatives of these theories were Henry George, *Progress and Poverty* (1879); Henry Charles Carey, *Principles of Social Science*

(1858-59); Friedrich List, *The National System of Political Economy* (1856); and Adolph H. G. Wagner, *Theoretische Sozialökonomik* (1907-09).

List and Wagner are representatives of the German historical school and Carey and George of the American social-reform movements. They laid the foundations for institutional economics, which drew strength in part from the work of Thorstein Veblen, chiefly his *Theory of the Leisure Class* (1899). Veblen himself cannot properly be called an economist. His works are stimulating and often satirical studies of sociological topics, with economic implications. The major contribution made by the dominant school of American institutionalism is doubtless the work of John Rogers Commons, whose chief works, *Legal Foundations of Capitalism* (1924) and *Institutional Economics: its Place in Political Economy* (1934), are probably the most profound writings issued from the institutional school. Yet the contribution they make to the main body of economic theory is minute, and their value consists in a discussion of the social relations and the legal forms and framework of governmental regulation affecting economic processes, rather than in a new or original analysis of these processes themselves. Appealing as they so frequently do to the hope for a better society, the works of such men as George, Carey, and Veblen have been the best sellers among economic works.

The strong influence of institutional thought in America has led to attempts at combining traditional economic theory with institutional theory. This approach was begun by Wesley C. Mitchell, the founder of the National Bureau of Economic Research. The Bureau is one of the chief private agencies in the United States collecting data of economic importance and publishing monographic studies reporting the results of this research. Mitchell's main role consisted in recognizing that in order to bring the more empirically minded institutional approach closer to the more theory-oriented neo-classical approach, it was of foremost importance to determine by careful, often detailed research what were the actual forms and patterns in which such economic institutions as firms, households, government departments, markets, and others functioned. Only on the basis of such empirical knowledge could a marriage between the institutional and the theoretical approach be achieved. The position of Mitchell has thus been one of intermediary, and he has been claimed by the traditional school as one of their followers and by the institutionalists as an institutionalist. In fact, Mitchell's writings covered a large area of economic topics, and he was not afraid to discuss some of the philosophical and ethical problems relevant for economics. His most characteristic work, containing essays of various hues, is *The Backward Art of Spending Money* (1937). His position as an empiricist and theorist is expressed in a book which he wrote jointly with Arthur F. Burns under the title *Measuring Business Cycles* (1946).

Finally, a new approach to what might best be called institutional economics has recently appeared in the United States. So far, this has not yet led to a widespread literature, but a few basic contributions have begun to come out. This new kind of "institutionalism" starts not from dissatisfaction with classical or neo-classical economic doctrines, but from the attempt to determine the place and function of economic activity within the framework of society as a whole and to ascertain the wider social determinants of economic actions. The general theoretical framework for this approach is set down in the work by Talcott Parsons and Neil J. Smelser, *Economy and Society* (1956), but it has found a number of applications to specific economic problems, e.g., in an article by Bert F. Hoselitz, "Social Structure and Economic Growth," *Economia Internazionale* (1953).

While writers of the social-reformist, the historical, and the institutional schools were at work, economic theory was developed further on the basis of its original classical formulation. The chief centers where most of the work was done were at first England and Austria, and Sweden and Italy a little later. The vigorous cultivation of economics in the first-named countries was due to the presence in each of a man of outstanding genius who attracted around himself a series of talented younger men and capable older co-workers. These two men were Alfred Marshall and Karl Menger. In England, the light of pioneer research in economic theory had never been quite extinguished and, after the death of Mill, John Ellott Cairnes and William Stanley Jevons had continued the tradition. Jevons shares with Menger and the French economist León Walras the honor of having first stated the principle of marginal analysis in a systematic and integrated form. The circle of scholars who were associated with Marshall includes some of the most eminent names in modern British economics. An interesting picture of the later days of this "Cambridge group" is given in Roy F. Harrod's *The Life of John Maynard Keynes* (1951). Both Harrod and Keynes were members of the group, along with Arthur Cecil Pigou, Dennis Holme Robertson, John R. Hicks, Joan and Edward A. G. Robinson, Ralph G. Hawtrey, and many others. It would be futile to attempt even a cursory analysis of the contributions of these writers. Together, they have done more than any other group to restate economic theory in all its branches in the form in which it has become generally accepted today.

The circle of men who assembled around Menger or were inspired by him was hardly less numerous or eminent than the Cambridge circle of Marshall. In fact, the Austrian doctrine had initially a wider international reputation and found more ready acceptance than the Cambridge school. Its chief early spokesmen were Eugene Böhm von Bawerk and Friedrich Wieser; its doctrines were introduced into Sweden by Knut Wicksell, into Italy by Maffeo Pantaleoni and Luigi Cossa, into Holland by Nikolaas G. Pierson. In France, Charles Gide and others spread the new doctrine, and in the United States, Simon N. Patten and Richard T. Ely received it with sympathy.

By the end of World War I, the synthesis of the Austrian and the English branch of economics based firmly on marginal analysis had been achieved, but it was not long before a new approach was developed which at first seemed to tear asunder the laboriously built edifice of economic theory. This new approach has often been designated as Keynesian economics, since John Maynard Keynes's *The General Theory of Employment, Interest, and Money* (1936) appeared to put forth a set of entirely new ideas and to lift discarded and heretical theories to a new level of respectability. In reality, the important contribution made by Keynes was essentially along the traditional lines of the Cambridge school, but its immediate impact on economic theory was profound because of the attention drawn by Keynes to macro-economic relationships.

Because the two alternative theoretical approaches, micro-economics and macro-economics, parallel the opposing points of view in the most important practical problem of the day, i.e., the extent of freedom or of planning desirable in the economic sphere, the difference should be clearly understood. An economic system, such as that of any modern capitalist country, can be viewed as being composed of a large number of decision-making units, which for convenience may be classified into two groups, firms and households. The firms buy productive resources and sell finished products to other firms and to households; the households sell productive resources and buy finished products. The firms make decisions with the purpose of maximizing money profit, the households with the aim of maximizing satisfaction. Now, the analysis of how these units will act if put under certain constraints, the grouping of firms into industries, etc., presents us with a simplified model of economic analysis following a micro-economic approach. The term "micro-economic" is applied because the smallest significant entity, the firm or household, is chosen as the starting point. In order to gain a full picture of the economic structure and processes of a society, various methods of aggregating the behavior of these entities have to be applied.

The approach which begins, so to speak, at the other end of the scale is the macro-economic approach. Instead of starting with the activity of the smallest decision-making unit, this approach starts with the examination of the major *aggregate* variables relevant to economic analysis, such as national income, national savings, total consumption, and total investment. It disregards in its first approximation the distributive aspects of these variables and the effect of various policy measures on them. The macro-economic approach can be more directly related to governmental regulatory practices than the micro-economic approach, since emphasis in the latter is placed on the independent action of many small units, whereas in the former the immediate manipulation of major variables appears to be an obvious device. In practice, economists who advocated a high degree of government regulation adopted the macro-economic approach, whereas the economists favoring a minimum of governmental interference in economic life favored the micro-economic approach. In American literature, the two approaches are represented by such works as Alvin H. Hansen's *Fiscal Policy and Business Cycles* (1941) and Henry C. Simons' *Economic Policy for a Free Society* (1948) for micro-economics.

Since the latter part of World War II, the conflict over Keynesian economics has died down to a considerable degree and has been resolved through a division of economic analysis into two related parts which are usually designated as price analysis and national income analysis. This trend had begun in England before the war and was given considerable impetus by the work of John R. Hicks, who had attempted such a relation in *Value and Capital* (1939), and whose more popular work was adapted to the American scene by Albert G. Hart in *The Social Framework of the American Economy* (1945). Although the battle over Keynesian economics was resolved by the recognition of different but equally valid and mutually related approaches to economic theory, the conflict over the degree and kind of regulatory activity in which the government should and could engage has not been resolved. But this is primarily a political rather than an economic issue.

National Differences—It has become commonplace to point to the differences between the economic literature of the U.S.S.R., on the one hand, and that of the West, on the other. It is similarly well known that the German economic literature of the Nazi period and some Italian economic literature of the Fascist period often displayed aspects that are clearly attributable to the political predilections of those countries. What is less often recognized is that the American or British economic literature is influenced by similar factors, and that the entire form of exposition, argument, and validation of propositions contained in these works is contingent upon the value structure generally acknowledged in these countries.

But apart from ideological trends, the very stage in economic growth determines to a large extent the forms and kinds of writings on economic problems in a given country. We may choose as a convenient example the Latin-American countries. Up to the middle 1930's, the economic literature of Latin America was both sparse and poor in quality. Of course, not all works about economic questions published in Latin America were worthless; there was a thin trickle of factual government reports and a few valuable works of economic history. But a profound change occurred after 1940. The chief locus of this change was Mexico, but other Latin-American countries, notably Argentina, Chile, and Uruguay, followed suit. The first step was a wave of translations. The best and most useful economic works, many of which had earned international acclaim, were translated into Spanish and made available to Latin-American students of economics. Some of the good texts used in American, British, German, and French universities thus became the basis for the training of graduate students in economics in Mexico and in the other more highly developed Latin-American countries. This development was followed by the inauguration of several economic journals and the publication of modernized texts and monographs by Latin-American scholars. An example of a series of very competent studies in economics is an as yet unfinished set of some forty works on various aspects of the Mexican economy, sponsored by the Nacional Financiera.

El Trimestre Económico (1934-), an economic quarterly published at Mexico City, is one of the best regularly appearing economic journals in the Spanish language.

What caused this remarkable development in Latin-American, and most notably Mexican, economics? It cannot be related to the purely intellectual interests of Latin-American scholars, since to many of these a large part of the foreign literature had been accessible in the originals, and yet little of these influences was reflected in their own writings. Moreover, for the early translations of economic classics to be commercially successful, a market had to exist which was able to absorb these works in some quantity. The best explanation is that in the more advanced Latin-American countries economic development had progressed to a stage where in government and business a sizeable number of persons with good advanced training in economics began to be needed. Adequate literature in Spanish became imperative: hence the flood of translations. But in the course of training these new recruits to economics, some of their teachers and several of the very best students began to develop new ideas or to apply old and well established theories to new problems. Inspection of the 1936 volume and of the most recent volume of the *Handbook of Latin American Studies* (1936-) will give some idea of the progress in economics that has been made by Latin Americans in the past two decades.

Similar observations can be made about the economic literature of other less advanced countries. An important variable determining the scope and peculiarities of the economic literature of such countries as India, Egypt, Turkey, and even Japan and the U.S.S.R. is the stage of the country's economic development, which determines the most pressing economic problems. These problems are the chief preoccupation of each country's economists. The *Index Translationum,* published from 1932 to 1940 by the International Institute of Intellectual Cooperation and, since 1949, continued under the auspices of UNESCO, gives some idea of the extent and kinds of translations now being produced and of the countries affected.

Although the degree of economic development may be considered the main key to national peculiarities in the economic literature in less advanced countries, this criterion is not applicable in the countries of Western and Central Europe, English-speaking North America, and Australia. The degree of economic development, if measured by the level of per capita income, varies greatly between the United States and, for example, Italy; but this variation is reflected only to a minute degree in the economic literature of these two countries. Both countries have for a considerable time been within the capitalistic orbit; both trace their intellectual traditions back to the Christian Middle Ages; both represent sub-cultures of that great cultural complex which is usually designated as "the West." The peculiarities of economic writings in these countries are therefore not so much the result of stages in their economic development as of peculiarities of their political development and their traditions of scholarship.

This last factor can perhaps best be exhibited by a comparison of the economic literature of the last fifty years in the English, German, French, and Italian languages. Englishmen have always exhibited a practical sense in their scholarly work. To them the elaborate conceptualization common in German social science is foreign. They prefer a rough but adequate empiricism; and, as often as not, their approach and their propositions are justified by appeal to pragmatic value. Alfred Marshall's definition of economics as "the study of men in the ordinary business of life" is typical of this attitude of Englishmen. Although American social science has been strongly affected by German scholarship, notably in history and sociology, American economics displays the same pragmatic and common-sense features as British economics. This may be explained chiefly by the profound influence exercised on American economic writing by classical English economics.

French and also Italian economics is colored by the tradition, common in Romance countries, of rigorous abstract logical reasoning. Although other countries have had their share of outstanding mathematicians and logicians, in France the cult of pure mathematics is more generally practiced and enjoys more prestige than anywhere else. It is more than coincidence that the "big names" in the history of mathematical economics, at any rate before 1914, are predominantly those of Frenchmen, Italians, or Romance Swiss: Christoph Bernouilli, Jules Dupuit, Antoine A. Cournot, Léon Walras, Vilfredo Pareto, Maffeo Pantaleoni, Enrico Barone, and Luigi Amoroso, to name but a few. It is perhaps typical of the French and Italian approach to economics that the epoch-making work of Léon Walras remained almost unknown outside a limited circle of mathematical economists until well into the period between the two World Wars. Although the work itself founded its author's fame and although many people knew of it (largely because Pareto had drawn attention to it), few economists had ever read it. It was more than seventy-five years before an English translation, *Elements of Pure Economics* (1954), appeared.

In contrast to both the Anglo-Saxon and the Romance approaches to economics, the German is "philosophical." This word is used in a special sense, designating the fact that the ultimate validity and appropriateness of any piece of economic writing is judged by the test of whether or not it fits into a larger system embracing, often, not only all social science but law and parts of philosophy as well. In addition to this property of being part of a wider system, German economic works are also distinguished by the elaborate erudition they usually display. Many works are copiously documented with numerous references, often to obscure and scarce sources. This tendency to present exhaustive and elaborate documentation was furthered by the bias in favor of historical and descriptive rather than analytical economics prevailing in Germany for a large part of the nineteenth century. The characteristics of German works on economics were therefore threefold: (1) they tended to throw light on the development of economic institutions and relations; (2) they succeeded in establishing elaborate categorizations of economic institutions and in this fashion contributed significantly to the greater clarity of concepts, and indeed, drew attention to several neglected factors whose presence became obvious when classification and sub-classification were carried to extremes; and (3) because of the emphasis on economic institutions rather than economic variables, German work has focused clearly on the social nature of economic processes. This last emphasis has resulted in an economic literature of a wider generality and more profound applicability than the work of analytical economics predominant in Anglo-Saxon countries or in France and Italy. Max Weber's *The Protestant Ethic and the Spirit of Capitalism* (1930), or his *Wirtschaft und Gesellschaft* (1922), Werner Sombart's *Der moderne Kapitalismus* (1902), and Karl Bücher's *Industrial Evolution* (1901) are examples of this breadth of German economics and of the fact that economic processes are seen and interpreted within their wider social context.

But to preclude an exaggerated impression of the differences between economic studies as carried on in various countries, it should be pointed out that in recent decades the national peculiarities in economic research have tended to become less pronounced. In part this has been due to the emergence of pressing economic problems of world-wide impact, such as the economic consequences of the two World Wars and the great depression of the 1930's. In part it has been due to improved international collaboration and the impact of economic research carried on by international agencies, such as the United Nations, UNESCO, the International Labour Office, the World Bank, and others, and the exchange of views of scholars from many countries at international conferences dealing with topics in the social sciences.

The impact of these international agencies on the diminution in international differences in the approach and study of economics, at least in the non-Communist countries, has been threefold. In the first place they have published, as already mentioned, factual data and research reports which were distributed all over the world and which are regarded as authoritative source materials. Second, they have set up international associations, as, for example, the International Economic Association, which have held international conferences attended by persons from all countries, and which have also sponsored the publication of translations of economic works of importance, especially those appearing in the less widely known languages. A periodical publication, *International Economic Papers,* was inaugurated in 1951 and has brought to the attention of the English-speaking economists articles and essays in various languages, notably Italian, Dutch, the Scandinavian languages, and the Slavic languages. Third, the United Nations and the World Bank have undertaken studies of the economies of various underdeveloped countries. Although these studies were made primarily as a service for the economic development policies and plans of these less advanced countries, they were carried out by teams of economists—and other social scientists—coming from different countries and hence reflecting different approaches to economics. The concentration upon a common problem has forced these economists with often varying viewpoints to find ways and means of adjusting their approaches to one another. Some examples of such studies, especially those of the International Bank for Reconstruction and Development, have been published and present valuable evidence not only of how well international teams of social scientists can work together, but also of the economic conditions or problems of particular underdeveloped countries. Among its studies, the works on *The Economic Development of Ceylon* (1953) or *The Economic Development of Nigeria* (1955) are representative examples.

A final word must be said about the relation between economics in the West and economic writings in the Soviet orbit. Among the various countries in the Communist portion of the world, Russia and China have long traditions of economic thought and practice. The Chinese traditions, in particular, go back some 2500 years; and although one of the earliest economic works on China, the *Kuan-Tzu,* has given rise to a good deal of controversy as to authorship and date of composition, there exist in English translation two economic works which date back to the first century B.C. and the first century A.D. The former, of which part was published in a translation by Esson M. Gale under the title *Discourses on Salt and Iron* by Huan K'uan (1931), as well as the latter, which was translated in its entirety by Nancy Lee Swann under the title *Food and Money in Ancient China* by Pan Ku (1950), contain numerous passages which appear remarkably "modern" in character. The later pre-Communist economic literature of China is based on treatises such as these, and only in the last thirty years has Western economics made any inroads into Chinese economic thinking. Contemporary Chinese economic scholarship has taken on most of the characteristics of Soviet Russian scholarship and employs most of the methods and techniques practiced in contemporary Russian economics.

In Russia itself, the indigenous tradition of economic speculation goes back much less far than in China. Although a few Russian mercantilist writers have been discovered, economics as a field of interest was introduced in Russia during the nineteenth century. Even then, Russian writers were under the influence of Western thought but adapted the lessons they learned to their own problems. In the late nineteenth century Russia produced a number of outstanding economic historians, as well as some very competent economic theorists. Some basic work was done in Russia in quantitative and mathematical economics and economic statistics. The economic historians Maksim M. Kovalevskii and Paul Vinogradoff, the statistician Aleksandr A. Chuprov, and the economic theorist Ladislaus von Bortkiewicz gained international fame.

At the same time, however, Marxism began to take firm root in Russian economics. By the turn of the century a large part of Russian economic writings were produced by men with more or less socialist persuasion.

Writers like Peter Struve or Mikhail Tugan-Baranovsky, who were both Marxists, though opposed to Lenin, also attained an international reputation. With the Revolution, the "orthodox" theories of Marxist economics attained a victory. In the first years after the Revolution there had not yet been elaborated a line from which deviations were not tolerated. Thus the early issues of the main Russian economic periodicals contain lively discussions of a number of economic problems. But this was changed with the consolidation of the power of Joseph Stalin.

Hence, as concerns more recent economic works, those published since about 1930, two types must be distinguished. One group comprise the major official compendia on economic history and structure, programmatic statements, and textbooks. These works are all characterized by their strict adherence to Marxian language and ideas, although the latter are modified from time to time so as to suit the official line of the Communist Party at any one time. These works abound in quotations from Marx, Engels, Lenin, and, since about 1932, Stalin. On the whole, these works are of little value, since the doctrine is laid down in the speeches and other declarations of the Soviet leaders, and the texts are essentially compendia supplying the supporting evidence and historical justification.

The second group of economic writings are essentially on a technical level. In conformity with the dominant patter of publications in the U.S.S.R., these works also begin with references to the Marxian classics, notably to the opinions of Stalin. But this is a mere formality. Russian economic planning requires the publication and distribution of technical works on such problems as industrial economics, production policies, accounting systems, money management, and the like. Hence this kind of literature is little different in its general aspects from the corresponding literature in the West. Unfortunately, most of the technical writings are available only in Russian. They consist chiefly of articles in learned journals and occasional monographs. Since the old saying *Russica non leguntur* is still largely true, only a small part of the output of Russian economic scholarship is accessible to most western students, although translations of such economic works as the *History of the National Economy of Russia to the 1917 Revolution* (1949) by Petr I. Liashchenko have been made available through the cooperation of the American Council of Learned Societies.

In the last few years, other services have been opened up which supply Russian and other East European materials in English. For example, the National Committee for a Free Europe publishes a monthly magazine, *News from behind the Iron Curtain* (1952-), which contains occasional articles of the Eastern European press in translation and which also publishes digests of laws and newspaper articles from these countries. Another similar service on the Russian press is published weekly by the Joint Committee on Slavic Studies of the American Council of Learned Societies and the Social Science Research Council, entitled *Current Digest of the Soviet Press* (1949-).

This has been imitated for the Indian press by the Bureau of International Relations of the Department of Political Science at the University of California at Berkeley, which publishes a quarterly magazine entitled *Indian Press Digests*. These digests are, of course, highly selective in their coverage, but they present very adequate summaries of the main political and economic developments as reported in the press of countries whose languages are understood and read by only a few Americans. Since the selection and digesting is very well done, they have great value, even for scholars who read these languages, in providing a quick over-view of the most important developments in the public opinion forming organs of these countries.

On the whole, scholars who do not read Russian can obtain more exact and better information from the writings of non-Russian scholars who have devoted themselves to a study of Russian economics than from the available translations of Russian works. More specifically, the writings of Eugene Varga, or even of Joseph Stalin, are less revealing than such studies as Gregory Bienstock, Solomon M. Schwarz, and Aaron Yugow, *Management in Russian Industry and Agriculture* (1944); Abram Bergson, ed., *Soviet Economic Growth* (1953); and Aaron Yugow, *Russia's Economic Front for War and Peace* (1942).

Levels of Economic Writing—In the past twenty years, doubtless as a consequence of the impact of the great depression and the economic complexities resulting from the war, the general public has become more aware of and more interested in the effects of major economic changes upon daily life and activities. But not only has popular interest in economics increased; activities of central and local governments requiring the services of economists have been greatly extended, and as a consequence of these developments more people have been motivated to acquaint themselves with the rudiments and foundations of economics. In other words, economics as a discipline in colleges and universities has gained in popularity; more students are enrolled in courses; more and more varied curricula are being offered. Many high schools now offer courses in elementary economics, and even elementary schools with well-rounded social studies programs incorporate some economic topics. The past twenty years, therefore, have brought considerable growth to one form of popularization, the issuing of more and more varied textbooks.

Not all textbooks are popularizations. For example, Alfred Marshall's *Principles of Economics* has been used often as a text, yet no one would regard this work as a popularization. Marshall's book is written not with the purpose of providing the beginning or even the more advanced student with a foundation in economics, but rather with the aim of providing a summary of economics in its most advanced stage at the time the book was written. Thus the book contains a large amount of original material, and by its nature is more a treatise than a text.

The college text, although a popularization in the widest sense of the term, usually has several distinguishing marks which other forms of popularization do not have. For the most part, texts are written by competent scholars, sometimes even by men who have made pioneering contributions to their field. Second, texts are organized so as to be systematic and comprehensive accounts of the fields they deal with. Third, texts are often, though not always, theoretical in tenor; and even when they deal with practical or policy problems, they base the exposition upon underlying theoretical propositions. Fourth, texts usually contain, explicitly or implicitly, an exposition of the methods by which the propositions set forth are attained.

This discussion is not meant to imply that there are no qualitative differences among textbooks. On the contrary, they vary greatly in quality, so much so that one is constantly surprised that several of the poorer texts apparently compete successfully with the better ones. But whatever their quality, even the poorest texts display some of the characteristics indicated, and this fact justifies a separate consideration of them.

A few words should be said concerning the authorship of texts and of popular economic literature in general. The fact that the author of a popular work is a competent scholar is, of course, no guarantee of its success. But if a text or other popular work is written by a scholar of high repute, it has certainly the quality of exhibiting the thinking of an original and fertile mind and usually also of making a significant contribution accessible to a public wider than the narrow circle of scholars. Examples of successful texts that have been written by men of high competence are Kenneth Boulding's *The Economics of Peace* (1945), Paul Samuelson's *Economics* (1948), and Dennis H. Robertson's *Money* (1922).

Apart from textbooks, one can distinguish three kinds of popularizations of scholarly works: digests, popular accounts in the narrow sense, and vulgarizations. The author of a digest uses his skill not primarily to present his own thought, but to interpret in a more generally accessible form the work of another. It goes without saying that digests, like any other form of literary production, may vary greatly in quality. Often the staunch adherence to an original produces a less useful digest than a freer treatment. An excellent example of how a very difficult technical book was digested in a form understandable to the average reader is A. P. Lerner's article, "Mr. Keynes' 'General Theory of Employment, Interest, and Money,' " which was published in the October 1936 issue of the *International Labour Review*.

Digests of scholarly books are rare, however. Most scholarly books do not lend themselves readily to digesting, and it is usually easier to write an independent account incorporating the views of an author or of a school. Hence much of the popular economic literature consists of independently written works rather than digests. Thus, while the article mentioned above may be considered a digest of the volume by Keynes, a small book by Joan Robinson, *Introduction to the Theory of Employment* (1937), which came out a little later, is designed to be "a simplified account of the main principles of the Theory of Employment for students who find that they require some help in assimilating Mr. Keynes'

General Theory." Books of this kind are closely akin to textbooks, the chief difference being that they are not written specifically for use in a classroom but are destined rather for the average non-specialized reader who wants to gain a fuller understanding of the most recent advances in economic thinking. With the increasing technicality of scientific economic writing and the growing number of high school and college graduates who have had some elementary training in economics, the audience for this type of simplification is growing.

More important from the standpoint of the general reader are, however, books which deal not with the popularization of a particular theoretical advance, but rather with the exposition and analysis of current economic problems and policies for the purpose of informing and perhaps influencing the layman. The greater significance of these works consists in their advocating or defending some currently discussed measure of wide significance. Sometimes the immediate urgency of the policy discussed in such a book is obvious. An example is Seymour Harris' *The European Recovery Program* (1948). Sometimes it is more remote, as in Sir William Beveridge's *Full Employment in a Free Society* (1944) or in Friedrich A. von Hayek's *The Road to Serfdom* (1944). The mere fact that such a book is concerned with problems of policy means that the author takes sides and that he is advocating measures that he regards as steps toward certain implicit or explicit values or goals. Works of this kind are the primary concern of the general reader, for here competent people discuss policies in terms comprehensible to him, yet on a basis of sound scholarship.

All the contributions in economics which have relevance for the general reader are in some applied field. But numerous writings in applied fields are produced primarily for specialists and are not even of interest to general economists or economists in other specialties. In economics, as in other fields of knowledge, specialization has been driven to a rather high degree, and for this reason a considerable portion of the literature which is commonly included among economic writings and is reviewed and discussed in economic journals and magazines is of interest to only a small proportion of the subscribers of these journals. For this reason many economic works written "for the general public" also become one of the main sources of information of a special field for economists in other specialties. For example, the field of agricultural economics is one in which there exists a rather specialized literature which has its own clientele. In the United States, a special quarterly journal, the *Journal of Farm Economics* (1919-), is published which numbers among its subscribers few individuals whose research and teaching interests are not in the field of agricultural economics. In addition, there are being published by the United States Department of Agriculture and by many state agricultural departments numerous specialized reports on various aspects of agricultural economics which also have appeal for the same body of readers. However, at various times, agricultural economists publish more general works, which then become writings of a much wider appeal and which are read by economists in other special fields—and sometimes even by persons who do not specialize in economics at all. Examples of such works are Theodore W. Schultz's *Agriculture in an Unstable Economy* (1945), or a book edited by him under the title, *Food for the World* (1945).

Other specialized fields in economics present the same features, and it is only books like the ones listed by Schultz, or corresponding ones in other fields, which circulate among economists in general. By far the larger percentage of specialized publications have, therefore, a rather well-defined and rigorously circumscribed readership. This also holds for periodical publications. In the United States there are three scholarly journals in economics which contain contributions in all specialized sub-fields of economics and which, therefore, appeal to economists regardless of their field of special interest. Chief among them is the *American Economic Review* (1911-), the official journal of the professional association of American economists. The other two are distinguished both by their long history and their skillful editorship over many years. These two journals are published by the economics departments at Harvard University and the University of Chicago and, like the official journal of the American Economic Association, the *Quarterly Journal of Economics* (1886-) and the *Journal of Political Economy* (1892-) are read by economists in all fields of special interest and also circulate over the whole world. Among more specialized journals there are some with specially regional interests, such as, for example, the *Southern Economic Journal* (1933-) or, in Britain, the *Scottish Journal of Political Economy* (1954-); but the greatest number of periodical publications with less than general appeal are in specialized fields. Corresponding to the *Journal of Farm Economics,* there are published, for example, *Land Economics* (1925-), specializing in the fields of planning, housing and public utilities; the *Journal of Finance* (1946-), which as its title indicates specializes in publishing essays on problems of private finance. Some specialized journals are published by governmental or international agencies, as, for example, the *Monthly Labor Review* (1915-), published by the United States Bureau of Labor Statistics, or the *International Labour Review,* published by the International Labour Organization. Some journals contain contributions which often tend to go beyond economics or to discuss the interrelations between economics and other social science. For example, the *Canadian Journal of Economics and Political Science* (1935-) contains essays in economics as well as other social sciences. This is considered preferable to publishing separate journals in the various fields which would have difficulty maintaining a sufficient circulation. Since Canadian economists usually have easy access to American or British journals, this may be regarded as a wise policy. *Social Research* (1934-) also publishes articles in the various social sciences, but here a special viewpoint, i.e., the desire to present materials more on an interdisciplinary level, seems to be the prevailing reason for the inclusion of essays in various social science fields. Finally, a publication like *Economic Development and Cultural Change* (1952-) publishes essays in the various social sciences, primarily because its editorial policy is based on the assumption that a thorough investigation and analysis of the problems of economic growth, to which it is devoted, requires a careful study not only of economic factors, but also of those customarily falling into other social disciplines.

In addition to these journals, which are all concerned with the needs and requirements of the scholar or the student, there exists of course a large mass of periodical publications which are of social appeal, such as *Fortune* (1930-). They range to highly specialized periodicals, like *Time Sales Financing* (1936-), which deals exclusively with problems of installment credit to consumers. Although many of the periodicals have usually little interest to the economist, and above all to the general economist, it should not be forgotten that some very important contributions to economics have sometimes been published first in journals or magazines which were specially oriented toward the needs of a particular group of businessmen or administrators. For example, a most important contribution to the economic theory of value, Jules Dupuit's "De la mesure de l'utilite des travaux publics," appeared for the first time in 1844 in the *Annales des ponts et chausées,* a periodical concerned primarily with the engineering and administrative aspects of roadbuilding and transportation facilities in general. Although only a few examples of this kind could be cited, it is nevertheless possible that ideas which, at a given time, do not find entrance in the more "orthodox" economic journals may appear first in specialized business publications, either because they are considered too limited or one-sided in approach. Sometimes such contributions are "rediscovered," and their full importance for general economics is recognized.

CHAPTER VI

Sociology

Sociology is often called the study of society or of social life. But such a simple definition in terms of subject matter does not distinguish it from the other social sciences. For they all study social life or, to put it more precisely, patterns of conduct that are common to groups of people. It is not their subject matter but their approach to it that differentiates the various social sciences. They ask different questions about social conduct, focus upon different regularities in it, and hence arrive at different explanatory principles for it. The economist, for example, is concerned with those patterns in a society that are produced by men's attempts to allocate means to ends rationally. And the psychologist analyzes how characteristics of the human personality or organism develop and give rise to patterns of behavior. In contrast, the sociologist is interested in the regularities in social conduct that are due neither to psychological traits of individuals nor to their rational economic decisions, but that are produced by the social conditions in which they find themselves.

There is, of course, an almost infinite number of social conditions that may influence the way people act, interact, and think, such as marital status, rural or urban residence, prestige, membership in a certain religious group, being an outcast who is discriminated against, sharing one cultural tradition rather than another, or living in a totalitarian or a democratic society, to name but a few. To bring order into this great variety of social factors, sociologists subsume them under two broad categories: the social relationships between people and their common value orientations.

Every group of people is characterized by a complex network of social relationships. Strong attractions may develop between some members, whereas others do not particularly care for one another. Some members may be generally respected and others looked down upon or ignored. In one group, co-operative practices may prevail; in another, competitiveness. A leader whose suggestions are followed emerges in one group, while status relations remain egalitarian in a different one. Social relationships, then, define the individual's status in the group, and they distinguish groups from each other. In larger collectivities, moreover, group membership helps to define social status, and there are also patterns of relationships between groups. The social status of professionals differs from that of factory workers. One community may be little stratified; in a second, differentiation between social classes exists, but there is little conflict; whereas in a third, class conflict is acute. All these aspects of social relationships and their influence on patterns of conduct comprise the first type of factor with which the sociologist is concerned.

Differences in social status tend to become associated with differential role expectations. Once one member of the group has assumed the role of leadership, the rest will expect him to take the initiative and act like a leader and expect the others not to act like a leader. In addition to these different role expectations, normative expectations applying to all members usually develop in groups. Among factory workers, for example, there often exist informal standards of what constitutes a fair day's work, and the individual who exceeds these output standards will be penalized by his fellow workers. Other normative beliefs are shared by most members of an entire society or one of its major segments, such as the conviction that stealing is wrong, that one does not walk barefoot on the street, or that it is not proper to wipe one's mouth with the back of one's hand. Common beliefs not only define what is right and what is wrong but also which objectives are most valued. Thus, our society places a higher value on becoming an outstanding baseball player than on becoming an expert cook. In essence, the cultural tradition of a society consists of nothing but such shared beliefs that have been transmitted from one generation to the next. To be sure, these beliefs exist only in the minds of individuals: there is no group mind. But the crucial fact is that as far as any individual is concerned social values and norms constitute the shared basic convictions of the other members of the community in which he is born and socialized and among whom he must live and find social acceptance. Hence, common values and norms are social forces that exert a constraining influence upon the conduct of individuals; they are the second type of social factor with which the sociologist is concerned.

But what accounts for the differences in social relationships and common normative expectations between groups or societies? Although there is no simple answer to this question, it calls attention to the important problem of social change, since it is possible to explain why social structures differ by investigating their historical development. At any one time, the common orientations and social relationships in a community affect the way people act and interact. But in the course of social interaction, the beliefs and relationships of people change. Thus, when prejudiced white soldiers were compelled to fight shoulder to shoulder with Negroes, the need for co-operative interaction in combat produced changes in their relationships with Negroes and their beliefs about them. Only by taking social processes of change into account can an unrealistically static concept of social structure be avoided. Hence, sociology involves the scientific study of how social relationships and common normative orientations influence patterns of conduct, and how social conduct under various conditions in turn leads to modifications in the social structure.

This conception of sociology as a distinct science has gradually emerged only during the last century. The most conspicuous difference between earlier social philosophy and modern sociology is a methodological one. Earlier scholars primarily used historical sources to illustrate their theoretical conceptions. Contemporary sociologists, on the other hand, are much more prone to use systematic procedures of interviewing and observation to obtain data with which general hypotheses can be tested. Underlying this difference in method, however, are fundamental differences in objectives and in the formulation of problems to be investigated. It is in terms of these changes in focus and approach that we shall look at the historical development of sociology.

THE DEVELOPMENT OF SOCIOLOGY

Early Social Philosophy—Men have thought about social life and society and tried to explain them since ancient times. Two kinds of ancient thought about social life have been preserved—folk sayings and religious maxims, which often contain perceptive notions about the relationships between human beings, and the works of systematic philosophers, most of whom dealt extensively with society and its historical development.

Folklore and proverbs typically pertained to practical problems of everyday life. In general, the social thought of ancient philosophers was similarly concerned with finding solutions to the practical problems of society and not with a detached scientific analysis of social phenomena. In the *Ethics,* Aristotle made the classic statement of the distinction between "scientific knowledge" and the kinds of knowledge we can have of "things human." Since "things human" are variable, it is not possible to derive general principles about them but only to deliberate about them to arrive at a "true and reasoned opinion." This meant for Aristotle the attainment of practical and political wisdom, which enables a man to run his own life well, manage his household, and govern wisely and virtuously.

The Greek philosophers did not approach the study of society with a disinterested scientific attitude but with an interest in helping to create an ideal society. Plato, for example, developed his conception of an ideal society governed by philosophers in *The Republic,* and then he encouraged his pupils to institute such a political system in Syracuse. Aristotle's *Politics* is essentially a manual for statesmen to guide them in governing wisely and establishing a good society. These two works illustrate not only the utopian character of Greek social thought, but also that it did not distinguish the study of society and social institutions from the study of governments and political institutions.

These conceptions of an ideal state were related to theories of the origin and history of governments. Both Plato and Aristotle, although quite different in their approach, advanced evolutionary theories of historical development, and still another evolutionary theory was proposed by the Epicureans, whereas Polybius developed a cyclical theory of political change. In these theories, which suggest principles of social development and attempt to support them with historical data, the ancient philosophers came closest to what was later to become social science. But even here the approach was that of the philosophy of history rather than that of an analytical social science.

Three characteristics of ancient social thought are particularly pertinent for an understanding of the development of sociology. First, it failed to differentiate between the study of political systems and that of social structures. Second, interest in creating a utopian society discouraged a disinterested, objective approach to the study of social phenomena. Third, concern with explaining the origins of social or political institutions and the course of history focused attention upon unique historical occurrences rather than upon recurrent social patterns. To consider these three characteristic limitations is not to deny that some of the ancient social philosophers dealt very imaginatively with important problems of social life. Indeed, their profound insights were resurrected many times in succeeding centuries; social thought followed closely in the footsteps of the great ancient philosophers until quite recently. Nevertheless, the development of sociology as we know it today was contingent on a change in orientation to the study of social life in these three respects.

The Separation of State and Society—Perhaps the earliest major break with traditional social philosophy was made by the social-contract theorists. The doctrine of social contract, first clearly set forth by Thomas Hooker in the sixteenth century, dominated social and political thought during the seventeenth and eighteenth centuries. Its two outstanding proponents, Thomas Hobbes and John Locke, used it in fundamentally different theories. Hobbes assumed that the state of nature is one of "war of all men against all men." To escape from this state, men enter into an irrevocable contract. Governments, Hobbes argued, are legitimated by this original contract and therefore do not require the consent of the governed. Locke, in sharp contrast, held that men are by nature sociable and that the state of nature is peaceful. Men enter into a social contract primarily to protect their rights, notably the right of private property. The consent of the governed is essential for legitimate governments, and if a government violates the social contract the people have not only the right but the moral duty to overthrow it. Jean Jacques Rousseau, who is best known for his glorification of the state of nature, also emphasized that the social contract is an expression of the consensus and common purpose of the people—"the general will" of the community.

In most respects, these theories are polemical arguments rather than scientific investigations. Their major objective is not to advance a detached analysis of society but to advocate a political philosophy, and their primary significance and influence have been political and ethical, not scientific. In attempts to bolster their political positions, these authors based their moral philosophies on theories of social origins. Their use of empirical material in support of these theories, however, indicates the limitations of this approach from a scientific standpoint. Since no direct evidence on social origins exists, concern with them encourages a tendency to use source materials to justify *a priori* assumptions rather than to test theoretical hypotheses. This tendency is strongly reinforced by an interest in defending a political position. Thus, both Hobbes and Locke cited the American Indians as examples of pre-political society, but Hobbes claimed that they "live at this day in [a] brutish manner," while Locke saw in their social life an illustration of the virtues of the state of nature.

Although the main concern of the social-contract philosophers was political, they did make an important contribution to the future development of sociology by stressing the distinction between society and its government. This distinction is implicit in Hobbes's argument that the foundation of political society is the social union of men in a country, not any particular form of government. It clearly underlies Locke's thesis that the preservation of organized society, without which "natural" rights cannot prevail, may even justify a revolution against the existing government. And Rousseau's concept of the general will, which he considered the root of the people's sovereign power and which he juxtaposed to the political government, anticipates the sociological concept of common value orientation.

It was not until the nineteenth century, however, that the difference between the political study of government and the sociological study of society was explicitly defined and became widely accepted. In a controversy with Heinrich von Treitschke, Robert von Mohl stated early in this century, "only quite lately have we arrived at a definite recognition that the life which men lead in common by no means has its existence in the state alone." Claude Henri de Saint-Simon proposed the establishment of a new science, devoted to the systematic study of the changes in social and economic conditions that have resulted from the industrial revolution and scientific advancements and aimed at discovering the general laws of the movement toward "social happiness." He also advocated that society should be ruled scientifically by social scientists. These ideas were elaborated, and the new science was given the name "sociology" by Saint-Simon's disciple, Auguste Comte.

Comte's *philosophie positive (Cours de Philosophie Positive,* 1830-42) rests on a conception of the organic nature of society and its progressive development. The social organism, just like that of the individual, consists of differentiated interdependent elements working together for common ends, but, in contrast to the biological organism, it is not immutable. Elaborating the formulations of Marie Jean de Condorcet, Saint-Simon, and others, Comte conceived of historical progress as advancing through three stages—the theological, the metaphysical, and the scientific or positive era. Each of the three basic parts of the human mind–feeling, action, and intellect–undergoes parallel development in three stages. Feelings also provide the motivating force for social progress, and intellect the guiding principle.

Methodologically, Comte set forth a hierarchy of the sciences, with mathematics at the base, followed in order by astronomy, physics, chemistry, and biology, and culminating in the new science of sociology. Since each science is a prerequisite for the higher ones, Comte held that sociology is the most complex. He differentiated it from the prevalent political philosophy by insisting that sociological investigations must use the objective or positive methods of observation, experimentation, and comparison characteristic of the natural sciences. The application of scientific knowledge about society would bring about the most advanced stage of human progress. Comte explicated in great detail the characteristics of this positivistic state, ruled by a sociological priesthood of positivism. It is, however, not this utopian vision, which was so dear to him, for which Comte has been remembered. His major contribution is methodological. Although he did not practice what he preached and did not conduct social research by scientific procedures, he was the first who explicitly defined sociology as the systematic empirical study of social phenomena rather than the abstract analysis of political principles and who delineated roughly the boundaries of this new discipline as encompassing investigations of social order and social progress or, as we would say today in less value-laden terms, social structure and social change.

Inevitable Evolutionary Forces–Opposing Comte's notion that the application of scientific knowledge can hasten social progress were the increasingly influential Social Darwinists. They shared his assumption that social change is an evolutionary process but added the postulate that it is governed by unrelenting forces that cannot be modified by human action. Attempts to influence the inevitable course of evolutionary development, however well meant, only disturb the inherent social equilibrium and have necessarily ill effects. The aim of social science was held to be the discovery of the inevitable stages of social evolution, analogous to Charles Darwin's tracing of the evolution of animal species.

The most influential proponent of the evolutionary doctrine was undoubtedly Herbert Spencer. It was he (and not Darwin) who originated the phrase "survival of the fittest," to describe the basic force underlying evolutionary progress, a conception influenced by Thomas R. Malthus' work on population pressure, *An Essay on the Principle of Population* (1798). The struggle for survival within and between societies produces a social equilibrium as it transforms incoherent homogeneity into coherent heterogeneity. Societies evolve from a state where all do the same kinds of things in disregard of one another into a state where specialization and mutual co-operation prevail. Early in the struggle for existence, militarism emerges. Organized warfare forces small isolated groups to combine into increasingly larger societies, and within these peace reigns. In time, "equilibration" between societies makes long periods of peace possible, and this gives rise to the industrial stage. Evolutionary processes continue to operate within industrial societies, but criteria other than primitive force now govern the survival of the fittest. Spencer believed that "Evolution can end only in the establishment of the greatest perfection and the most complete happiness." But a prerequisite for the emergence of this utopia is that the natural processes of selection are not interfered with in any way. Spencer carried his laissez-faire position to the extreme of denying that the state has a right to assume responsibility for coining money, postal services, education, or sanitary measures. *First Principles* (6th ed., 1928) and *The Principles of Sociology* (3d ed., 1892) are representative works of Spencer.

Another interpretation of Social Darwinism focuses upon the conflicts between races and nationalities as the most fundamental processes of social life. It may well not be fortuitous that the two major proponents of this viewpoint—Ludwig Gumplowicz and Gustav Ratzenhofer—were both Austrians, that is, lived in a polyglot empire that was continually torn by strife between various nationality groups. This illustrates that the social conditions in which a scholar finds himself may influence the theories he advances (a thesis which was developed in detail much later by Karl Mannheim in his *Ideology and Utopia,* 1936). Similarly, the tremendous vogue that Social Darwinism and particularly the Spencerian evolutionary doctrine enjoyed in England and the United States at the end of the last century was probably partly due to their compatibility with existing social conditions. Evolutionary principles provided "scientific" sanction and justification for the cut-throat competition, the growing monopolies, the imperialistic wars, and other characteristics of this period of expanding capitalism.

The use of Social Darwinism to defend the capitalistic system is, perhaps, nowhere as evident as in the writings of William Graham Sumner, the outstanding follower of Spencer in the United States. Today, Sumner is best remembered among sociologists for his concepts of mores and folkways, the normative orientations, and social usages that he analyzed and illustrated in his book *Folkways* (1906). In his lifetime, however, he was probably better known for his espousal of evolutionist and laissez-faire doctrines. The titles of his works are indicative of his orientation, for instance, "The Absurd Effort to Make the World Over," (in his *War, and other Essays,* 1933) or *What Social Classes Owe to Each Other* (1883).

Not all Social Darwinists, however, subscribed to its laissez-faire implications. Lester F. Ward, a contemporary of Sumner, was one who did not *(Dynamic Sociology,* 1883). He accepted the principle that conflicts between individuals and groups give rise to social evolution, although emphasizing that it is governed not so much by a struggle for sheer existence as by one for developing the optimum social structure. But he argued that once social evolution reaches the stage where man can scientifically understand social phenomena, intelligent social action is possible. After this stage, sociological knowledge can and should be applied through legislation to accelerate social progress.

Most informed people today would tend to agree with Ward's position that the welfare of the community can be improved by deliberate social action and reject Sumner's thesis that legislation cannot be used as an instrument to guide social change. But even if in error, the notion that the social forces that govern society and its development are entirely beyond human control can be considered to have been, from the standpoint of the development of sociology, a "fruitful error." It helped to direct the efforts of sociologists away from constructing social utopias and toward the study of existing social conditions and the objective social forces that produced them. Although the writings of many Social Darwinists were far from detached in their defense of the *status quo,* the deterministic assumption underlying the evolutionary approach invites a detached orientation toward the study of social life. By inadvertence, as it were, Social Darwinism seems to have been instrumental in bringing about the kind of detached orientation toward social research without which a science of social life is not possible.

Concern with Social Reform—Reformism was a current of thought that antedated Social Darwinism and continued parallel with it throughout the nineteenth century. In England, the misery-making potential of the new industrial system became glaringly evident at the beginning of the century. As early as 1802, advocates of reform raised their voices in Parliament, and their efforts were finally successful in the 1830's. The famous Factory Acts, regulating employment of children and correcting other abuses, were partly a response to the fact-finding endeavors of the reformers. Extensive inquiries into the state of affairs in the industries and cities of England were made during the first few years of the Reform Parliament. This survey movement was championed by Jeremy Bentham, who felt strongly that "scientific" legislation must be based on adequate knowledge about the actual conditions of social life. By the end of the century, not only government-sponsored surveys but also others not immediately concerned with policy had been conducted on a wide scale in England and on the Continent. Among the most famous are Pierre Frédéric Le Play's theoretically oriented *Les Ouvriers Européens* (1855) and Charles Booth's (ed.) monumental *Life and Labour of the People in London* (1892-97), which is a landmark in the development of empirical techniques of research.

The earliest large-scale empirical investigation of social conditions in the United States was Paul U. Kellogg's *Pittsburgh Survey* (1909-1914). But the pioneering empirical studies of important theoretical as well as social problems were carried out at the University of Chicago shortly after World War I. William I. Thomas and Florian Znaniecki's *The Polish Peasant in Europe and America* (1918-20) is a five-volume investigation of immigrants and their counterparts in the old country. By deriving a variety of theoretical conceptions from a detailed analysis of letters, life histories, and interviews, the authors gave considerable impetus to the growing conviction that sociological generalizations based on data collected specifically for this purpose can be as interesting as and are apt to be much more trustworthy than generalizations supported only with illustrative material from second-hand historical or ethnographic sources.

Robert E. Park, a journalist turned sociologist, stimulated research on a large variety of social problems, such as crime and minority groups. His interest in the problems of urban life led him, together with Ernest W. Burgess and Roderick D. McKenzie, to formulate a method for the systematic study of the social diversity and growth of cities, thereby creating a new branch of sociology–human ecology (Park, Burgess and McKenzie, *The City,* 1925; Burgess [ed.], *The Urban Community,* 1926). Park and Burgess also published what was for years the most influential text and source book in the field, *Introduction to the Science of Sociology* (1921).

Concern with social problems is not incompatible with an interest in fundamental theoretical questions. William F. Ogburn's *Social Change* (1923) is essentially a theory to account for the persistence of social problems. Ogburn suggested that value orientations, as well as social and political institutions, necessarily change more slowly than do technological and economic conditions; the resulting "cultural lag" is responsible for social problems.

In contrast to utopian visions, which encourage preoccupation with abstract conceptions of the ideal society, the reformer's zeal to improve existing social conditions motivated him to obtain more accurate knowledge about these conditions and the social forces that have produced them. Reform movements, therefore, helped to promote an interest in empirical social research and in the methodological problems of obtaining reliable information about social phenomena. Moreover, whereas the evolutionist's concern with social origins directed attention to unique historical data, the reformer's concern with prevailing problems indirectly had the effect of directing the attention of sociologists to recurrent social patterns, and it is only if data are conceptualized as recurrent phenomena that scientific generalizations can be derived from them.

History and Sociology–The principle that analytical social science conceptualizes historical conditions not as unique events but as recurrent phenomena became clarified in Germany in the course of theoretical and methodological controversies, notably that between the idealistic and the materialistic conception of social life, on the one hand, and the so-called *Methodenstreit,* centering on the difference between the historical and the analytical scientific approaches, on the other.

Karl Marx, accepting Georg Hegel's dialectic conception, juxtaposed his dialectical materialism to Hegel's idealistic interpretation of history. It is not spiritual forces but material conditions that underlie historical developments from thesis through antithesis to synthesis, and these material conditions can be scientifically studied. With technological advances, there arises a conflict between the state of technological knowledge and the traditional social organization of the economy. The reason for this conflict, and the form in which it finds expression, is the basic conflict of interest between social classes. The ruling class, in control of the means of production, is able to exploit the other classes for its own benefits and is, therefore, interested in preserving the *status quo*. The exploited classes are interested in fundamental changes in the social order that will bring an end to their exploitation. Once they recognize their interest, a revolution is inevitable, and this revolution permits further technological advances, heretofore prevented by the outmoded socio-economic organization. For example, the productive potential of the Industrial Revolution could not be fully realized until the feudal order had been overthrown, and the fact that the other classes found themselves disadvantaged by the feudal aristocracy provided the motivating force for overthrowing it. Further technological progress makes the capitalistic system obsolete, and once the exploited working class becomes class conscious and realizes that their interests conflict with those of the capitalistic ruling class, the proletarian revolution will occur.

Three elements in Marx's writings are of particular sociological significance. First, by concentrating on objective "material" conditions instead of spiritual forces, he defines social phenomena in a way that makes their scientific study possible. Second, his emphasis on the relationships between social groups as central for explaining historical processes is more conducive to a sociological approach than the essentially biological concept of survival of the fittest. Third, he was perhaps the first scholar to anticipate what Talcott Parsons, a contemporary theorist, calls the voluntaristic theory of social action (in *The Structure of Social Action,* 1937). Marx's conception that revolution, although in an ultimate sense inevitable, occurs only when people are motivated to carry it out (when they have become "class conscious") implies that deterministic social forces exist, but that they become operative only through affecting voluntary action—an important insight made explicit and elaborated by Max Weber.

The haphazard use of historical material as evidence for "laws" of evolutionary progress evoked protests from many historians at the end of the nineteenth century. In the midst of this controversy, a number of German scholars, such as Wilhelm Windelband, Wilhelm Dilthey, and Heinrich Rickert, sought to clarify the nature of history by distinguishing it from the natural sciences. History, they held, is concerned with ideographic knowledge, that is, with understanding unique historical events and the particular conditions under which they occur. Science, on the other hand, is concerned with nomothetic knowledge, which means that it subsumes specific facts under general categories and derives generalizations about them. Many historians, such as Eduard Meyer, argued on the basis of this distinction that it is impossible to make generalizations about society and its development, since every historical event is unique. But other scholars used this distinction to formulate a new conception of sociology as an analytical science and to differentiate it from history.

Max Weber, the outstanding German social theorist and one of the fathers of modern sociology, was profoundly influenced in his thinking by these two controversies, the materialism-idealism and the history-science issue. His attempts to resolve them are illustrated in his most famous work, *The Protestant Ethic and the Spirit of Capitalism* (1930). Opposing a Marxist interpretation of historical change in terms of rational economic interests, he advanced the thesis that the ethic of Calvinism was a prerequisite for the development of modern capitalism. He showed how the various tenets of this religious dogma gave rise to "worldly asceticism," a moral devotion to disciplined hard work in one's own vocation. The Calvinist's religious duty is not to adjust to this world, which he considered corrupted by man's sinfulness, nor to withdraw from it into a monastery, but to help transform it *ad majorem Dei gloriam* through unceasing effort in his secular job. The doctrine of double predestination, according to which good works cannot affect whether a man will be saved or damned, encourages an orientation to disciplined conduct and hard work, not as means to an ultimate end, but as intrinsic moral values. By elevating ceaseless effort and disciplined work in the mundane affairs of economic life into man's religious obligation, Calvinism produced a value orientation without which capitalism could not have come into existence. In support of this argument, Weber tried to show in his *Gesammelte Aufsaetze zur Religionssoziologie* (1920-21), partly translated as *The Religion of China* (1951) and *Ancient Judaism* (1952) and in Hans Gerth and Wright Mills (eds. and trs.), *From Max Weber: Essays in Sociology* (1946), that socio-economic conditions in other countries, such as China, were at least as favorable for the development of capitalism as those in Western Europe at the time of the Reformation, but that the modern form of capitalism did not emerge there because the religious system did not engender an orientation of worldly asceticism.

Weber's two most important methodological contributions to sociology are illustrated in this theory of the rise of capitalism. First, he held that it is not "material" economic conditions that are the major driving force in social life, but rather the spirit of a community. In contrast to the idealistic philosophers, however, he conceived of this spirit, not as a supernatural force, but as the common value orientation that prevails among the members of the community which can be objectively ascertained and studied. The distinctive characteristic of sociological explanations is that they provide an understanding of how common value orientations motivate people's conduct. (Weber discusses this principle of *Verstehen* in *The Theory of Social and Economic Organization,* 1947.) It is not enough to show that social conditions produce, say, a certain economic organization; it is also necessary to demonstrate how these conditions give rise to a value orientation that motivates people's conduct in ways that find expression in that economic organization. Whereas in this respect sociology is different from the natural sciences, in another it is like the natural sciences and unlike history. That is the second methodological principle Weber emphasized—namely, that sociology is a generalizing science *(On the Methodology of the Social Sciences,* 1949). To be sure, every historical event is unique, but the sociologist ignores the unique aspects of events and treats them as social types in order to generalize about them. Even if there is only one modern capitalism, it is not conceptualized as a unique historical phenomenon, but as an "ideal type" that can be compared with other types of economic systems.

This methodological principle, which is related to the distinction between nomothetic and ideographic knowledge, is so important that it should be spelled out in some detail. Essentially, a scientific explanation involves reference to a generalization that can be empirically verified. To derive such explanatory generalizations, the scientist advances a hypothesis about what happened in a specific situation, and he tests this hypothesis by determining whether it holds true in other cases of the same kind. But this procedure is possible only if we arbitrarily decide to disregard the unique characteristics of each specific case and subsume it under a general category. Evidently, each relationship between two individuals is unique; but it is impossible to derive a scientific generalization about how this unique relationship influences the conduct of these two people. Only if we are willing to classify all kinds of otherwise different relationships into co-operative and competitive ones (or in some other way) can we derive a generalization about the effects of co-operation on, say, productive efficiency of workers. But what if there is only a single instance of a certain social structure, as in the case of modern capitalism? Then, in our opinion, you cannot derive scientific generalizations about it. In short, commitment to sociology as an analytical science requires a willingness to give up the study of all those very interesting historical phenomena that are unique, because no empirically verifiable generalizations about them are possible. Weber, although advancing the position that sociology is an analytical science, was not quite willing to pay the price such a commitment demands. He was too interested in the unprecedented characteristics of Western capitalism to forego studying them, and by defining his problem as explaining a unique historical occurrence, he made it inherently impossible, it seems to us, to find a scientific solution for it.

The Scientific Study of Social Facts—A few contemporaries of Weber arrived by quite different routes at a fundamentally similar methodological position. One of these was the German sociologist Simmel (Kurt H. Wolff [ed. and tr.], *The Sociology of Georg Simmel,* 1950). He stressed that sociology is not concerned with the substantive or psychological content of social life, but with the general form assumed by social associations. This means that the sociologist analyzes observed patterns of conduct in terms of the recurrent processes of social interaction that give human conduct its social form, such as competition, superordination and subordination, or conflict. He is not interested primarily in whether these observed patterns of conduct are part of the economic or political organization, nor in what kinds of psychological states motivate them.

Guided by this methodological conception, Simmel does not hesitate to tear social phenomena from their historical or situational context to use them in support of a general sociological principle. Thus, the role of the consumer in a competitive economy, the influence exerted by small third parties in German politics, and what happens in a group of three individuals if two of them struggle for leadership—all of these different social situations serve Simmel to illustrate his principle of *tertius gaudens*. It may be objected that he sometimes ignored important analytical distinctions, such as that between relations among groups and relations among individuals. In principle, however, the complete disregard of the unique features of the historical situation, of which Simmel's writings offer an extreme example, is a prerequisite for deriving testable generalizations about recurrent social phenomena, and thus for a science of sociology.

Emile Durkheim, a French contemporary of Simmel and Weber, has probably exerted a more profound influence in shaping modern sociology than any other man. Avowedly a positivist in the tradition of Comte, he conceived of sociology as the scientific study of the relationships between social facts. Social facts, he explained in *The Rules of Sociological Method* (8th ed., 1950), are general phenomena characterizing an entire community, such as laws; they exercise external constraint upon individuals; and they must be treated as objective "things," no less objective than the facts of any other science. Indeed, as a social realist Durkheim considered social facts to be more basic and objective phenomena than the variable psychological states of individuals. Later, however, he modified his position, claiming no longer that social facts are necessarily external to the individual, but that they are internalized as the *"conscience collective,"* the common value-orientation of the community.

Durkheim was perhaps the first to draw the full implication of the conception of sociology as a generalizing social science and to translate it into systematic empirical research on recurrent social phenomena in support of theoretical principles. In his first major work, *De la Division du Travail Social* (1893), he tried to demonstrate that social facts must be explained in terms of other social facts, rather than in terms of psychological factors. He argued against the implicit psychologistic assumption of the evolutionists and utilitarians that social heterogeneity and specialization are the result of a striving for greater happiness and a higher standard of living. He suggested instead that the division of labor is generated by increasing population density—a social condition. Although he initially defined his problem as one of social origins, his major interest centered not on the origin of the division of labor, but on its significance for social solidarity. He showed that specialization destroys the homogeneity of outlook that provides the bond uniting the members of simple societies, but that it simultaneously produces a new basis for social solidarity by making the members of the society increasingly dependent on one another. Hence, the "organic solidarity" of complex societies is largely based on mutual dependence, and the "mechanical solidarity" of simple societies on common values.

The fundamental difference between Durkheim's approach and that of the evolutionists became fully evident only in his later works. Nineteenth-century anthropology was permeated by evolutionism. Ethnographic material on preliterate societies was used primarily to illustrate theories about the origins of modern social institutions and the evolutionary stages through which they have presumably progressed. This essentially historical and taxonomic orientation made anthropologists content with classifying societies on an evolutionary ladder. There was little interest in the systematic investigation of preliterate social life in its own right. In *The Elementary Forms of the Religious Life* (1915), Durkheim used ethnographic data on Australian aborigines in an entirely different manner. No longer concerned with social origins, he analyzed the religious life of these tribes to derive generalizations about the functions that religious beliefs and rituals serve for the community, theoretical generalizations that he considered relevant for the religious institutions of any society at any time. Although his research methods were not unexceptionable and his sources were of questionable reliability, the approach he charted to the systematic study of social structures helped to stimulate the development of reliable research methods in anthropology as well as sociology. Specifically, his conception of analyzing social structure, not in terms of social origins, but in terms of functional interdependence had a profound influence in both of these social sciences.

It is, however, an earlier work of Durkheim that exemplifies theoretical sociological research at its best—*Suicide,* published in 1897. At first sight, suicide might appear to be a purely individual phenomenon, best explained in psychological terms. Durkheim, however, observed that suicide rates differ from group to group, and he addressed himself to the sociological problem of explaining these social differences in suicide rates, not to the psychological question of what motivates an individual to take his own life. His main thesis was that social integration —the strength of the social ties that unite the members of a group—affects the likelihood of suicide, and he showed that this theoretical generalization, with some refinements, can explain a great variety of known facts about suicide rates. Catholicism leads to greater social integration than the individualistic faith of the Protestant; hostility and persecution create particularly strong integrative bonds among Jews; married people have integrative ties that single individuals lack; the unity of the community is greater in periods of war than in peace times; social integration is stronger in the rural villages than in the impersonal city. All these and many other differences in social integration are reflected in corresponding differences in suicide rates.

Profound theoretical insights and incisive analyses of source materials characterize all of Durkheim's works, but only in *Suicide* were his empirical data the kind that can support the theoretical generalizations advanced. Data from one religious system are obviously not sufficient evidence to test generalizations about the functions of religion in all societies. But how many religious systems can one man systematically investigate? One answer to this dilemma is to make information about many societies easily accessible to social scientists, as has been done recently in the Human Relations Area File. Durkheim found another solution for the same dilemma by defining his problem for investigation in *Suicide* in a way that assured sufficient empirical cases to test his theoretical generalizations. Scientific social research must confine itself to problems that deal neither with unique historical situations nor with social conditions about which information is so rare that they must be considered virtually unique, such as the emergence of the division of labor. The recognition of this basic limitation of social science has profoundly affected the course of sociology during the past half-century.

Implications and Reactions—The new conception of sociology as an analytical science that emerged at the beginning of the twentieth century altered the character of sociological investigations substantively as well as methodologically. Concern with entire social systems and their historical development declined as it became increasingly apparent that finding enough cases that were reliably reported poses an almost insuperable obstacle to testing theoretical generalizations. More and more, sociologists devoted themselves to the study of recurrent social patterns that can be observed today—for example, how the power relations in a community influence its various institutions, how neighborhoods change as a city expands, how prestige is related to patterns of social association, how informal relations in work groups affect productivity, or how social status influences voting.

This change in substantive focus fostered a growing interest in quantitative methods of collecting and analyzing data. Once the sociologist turned from the study of historical materials to the investigation of patterns of conduct in contemporary society, the need for new methods of research became apparent. In response to this need, there developed a large body of methodological literature, particularly in the United States, dealing with problems of sampling, statistical techniques of analysis, reliable procedures for interviewing and questionnaire construction, systematic methods of observation, and the development of scales and other measuring devices. A variety of methodological controversies arose; for example, that between the advocates of complete life-histories—like those used in Thomas' and Znaniecki's study of immigrants previously cited—and the proponents of large-scale attitude surveys, such as Samuel A. Stouffer.

Another implication of the new focus in sociology was an increasing interest in social psychology. The study of how social conditions affect patterns of conduct raises the question of the psychological mechanisms involved in these social processes. The importance of understanding socio-psychological processes was emphasized by Max Weber, and although their significance for sociological investigations was explicitly denied by Durkheim, both he and Simmel implicitly recognized it in their psychologically perceptive analyses of social phenomena.

In the United States, a conception of social psychology peculiarly suited to the needs of sociology emerged, curiously, out of a philosophical tradition. The pragmatists Charles S. Peirce, James Baldwin, William James, and John Dewey were greatly interested in the human mind as a social product, and two of their followers, George Herbert Mead and Charles Horton Cooley, made outstanding theoretical contributions to the field of social psychology. Mead, a philosopher, advanced a theory of how the human mind and self develop in the course of social interaction, published posthumously from lecture notes as *Mind, Self and Society* (1934). The distinguishing characteristic of human beings is their ability to communicate with significant symbols, which arises in the process of social interaction. As the infant experiences that his meaningless noises elicit a social response–crying brings the mother with a bottle, he learns that crying is a sign with which he can communicate his need for food. More complex patterns of communication develop as the child advances to the stage where he can take the role of the other person and, thereby, anticipate the response his communications will elicit. By taking the role of the other, the child also learns to conform with the expectations of others. As he moves in wider social circles than his immediate family, the expectations of many different others are generalized and internalized. The "generalized other," as Mead calls it, is that part of the personality (or self) that governs human conduct in accordance with the moral precepts of the society. Without the restraints it imposes, social co-operation and, indeed, social life would not be possible. Although Mead's theory was not supported by empirical evidence, many of his insights have since been confirmed in empirical research, notably in Jean Piaget's studies of children's language, thinking, and moral standards.

Cooley was a sociologist with a special interest in social psychology. In *Human Nature and the Social Order* (1902), he argued against the twin fallacy of studying either individuals in isolation from society or social institutions as abstractions independent of human conduct. In his extensive treatment of the process of socialization, he coined the phrase, "looking-glass self," to refer to the influence a person's perception of how others view him has upon his self-conception. The social context in which the social nature of the individual is formed, Cooley elaborated in his *Social Organization* (1909), is the "primary group," a small group characterized by intimate face-to-face association and strong "we-feeling," notably the family, the play-group of children, and the close neighborhood. The concept of primary group, used somewhat more broadly than Cooley intended, has exerted much influence on recent empirical research.

Not all sociologists have accepted the scientific conception of sociology even today. In the struggle to gain acceptance for this new orientation, some extreme reactions against the older social philosophy developed. One form this reaction took has been a radical positivism, accompanied by almost total rejection of theory as a legitimate scientific concern. This extreme empiricism found expression in behaviorism in psychology, historicism in history, exclusive concern with ethnographic facts in anthropology, and operationalism in sociology. The operational approach, originated by the physicist Percy W. Bridgman, stresses that scientific concepts must be derived, not from theoretical frameworks, but from the empirical operations used in measurement. While this general position has not been widely accepted, most sociologists agree with its emphasis on using only concepts—albeit theoretically derived ones —that can be operationally defined. The operational approach is presented in George Lundberg's *Foundations of Sociology* (1939).

Another reaction against the earlier philosophy of history, especially its evolutionary version, has been an ahistorical orientation in sociology, best exemplified by functionalism, a theoretical framework derived from Durkheim and elaborated by anthropologists such as Bronislaw Malinowski *(Magic, Science and Religion,* 1948) and Alfred R. Radcliffe-Browne *(Structure and Function in Primitive Society,* 1952), who exercised considerable influence among sociologists. Their dictum that social institutions should be explained on the basis of the present functions they serve in the social structure, rather than in terms of their historical development, is fully justified in preliterate societies, since any interpretation about social developments necessarily remains speculative in the absence of historical records. But when data about different time periods are available, there is no reason to ignore them. To state that sociologists are not concerned with unique historical events does not imply, of course, that they are not concerned with patterns of social change, and change can be studied only by examining relationships between social conditions at two or more different times. Indeed, the functional approach as originally conceived cannot cope with problems of social change. Many sociologists not committed to the functional viewpoint, however, have also neglected the study of social change, in large part because the systematic collection of data at several time periods is exceedingly costly and time-consuming.

Controversies between "empiricists" and "pure theorists" as well as between "functionalists" and those favoring a historical approach to sociology continue, but they appear to be waning. Recent years have seen an increasing emphasis on the integration of theory and empirical research. And even if the pious declarations that such integration is essential are often honored in the breach today, because many sociologists have been primarily trained either as theorists or as empirical researchers, the need to make these declarations may well be indicative of the future trend. Similarly, there has been an increasing interest in the study of social change and in adapting the functional approach to make it suitable for dealing with problems of change. To both of these trends, Robert K.

Merton has made important contributions in *Social Theory and Social Structure* (1949). He was one of the first to emphasize that the only practical way to achieve an integration of theory and research in the near future is to concentrate on theories of the middle range–theories dealing with specific scientific problems rather than with the whole gamut of social life. He also reformulated the functional approach to make it applicable to the important problems of differential power and social change, particularly by emphasizing that dysfunctional as well as functional consequences of social patterns must be investigated–the disturbances they create as well as the contributions they make to stability.

CONTEMPORARY SOCIOLOGICAL LITERATURE IN SELECTED AREAS

Social Theory–As a result of the growing interest in middle-range theories, theorizing has not remained confined to purely theoretical treatises in recent years, but has penetrated into many empirical studies. Increasingly, empirical research has become theoretically oriented, and social theorists have become interested in supporting their generalizations with a systematic body of empirical facts. An outstanding illustration of this trend is *The Human Group* (1950), by George C. Homans. He re-analyzes five studies dealing with work groups and professional staffs in factories, street-corner gangs, and small communities in Polynesia and New England, and derives from them a systematic set of elemental hypotheses about social interaction in groups. In this case, a variety of empirical studies made by different researchers are subsumed under one set of theoretical generalizations. A somewhat different approach to secondary analysis is exemplified in *Continuities in Social Research* (1950), edited by Robert K. Merton and Paul F. Lazarsfeld. Here the empirical findings from one large research project (Samuel Stouffer and others, *The American Soldier* . . . , 1949, a monumental survey conducted during World War II) are reworked from different theoretical or methodological viewpoints by several sociologists.

Some contemporary sociologists continue to be interested in "pure" theory, but they are apt to be concerned with theoretical frameworks for systematic research rather than with constructing the kind of grandiose cosmology characteristic of earlier social philosophy. Thus, Talcott Parsons has developed an over-all theoretical scheme of social action, partly in collaboration with Edward A. Shils, and applied it to a variety of substantive areas (*Essays in Sociological Theory,* 1949; *The Social System,* 1950; *Toward a General Theory of Action,* 1951, with Edward A. Shils; and *Family, Socialization and Interaction Process,* 1954, with Robert F. Bales). Florian Znaniecki, another "pure" theorist, has also set forth a systematic theoretical framework that has implications for empirical investigation (*The Method of Sociology,* 1934; *Cultural Sciences,* 1952). Even Pitirim A. Sorokin, one of the few sociologists still interested in the kind of theory of historical development so typical of the nineteenth century, has paid a great deal of attention to problems of empirical evidence (*Social and Cultural Dynamics,* 1937-41). Quite a different theoretical approach, with emphasis on the socio-psychological dimension, is represented by David Riesman's *The Lonely Crowd* (1950), an insightful analysis of changes in value orientations that occur with changes in social conditions.

Interviewing Surveys—The interviewing survey is, of course, not a substantive branch of sociology, but a research procedure applicable to a variety of fields. It deserves special mention, however, not only as the most widely used method of systematic social research and the one for which reliable techniques have been most fully developed, but also because its availability has influenced the kind of substantive problems that have been most thoroughly investigated. Texts on research methods typically devote most of their space to the discussion of procedures that pertain directly or indirectly to interviewing surveys. (Well-known texts are William J. Goode and Paul K. Hatt, *Methods in Social Research,* 1952; Marie Jahoda, Morton Deutsch, and Stuart W. Cook, *Research Methods in Social Relations,* 1951; and, dealing with more advanced problems of analysis, Paul F. Lazarsfeld and Morris Rosenberg, *The Language of Social Research,* 1955.) A special text on survey methods has recently been published (Herbert Hyman, *Survey Design and Analysis,* 1955). The various techniques of measurement and index formation which have been developed are also usually based on interviewing data, such as the so-called Guttman scale and Lazarsfeld's latent attribute analysis (see Samuel Stouffer and others, *Measurement and Prediction,* 1950).

The survey approach is best suited for the study of attitudes and their relation to social background factors, and this type of socio-psychological investigation has become particularly popular in sociology. A recent illustration of such a study is Stouffer's *Communism, Conformity and Civil Liberties* (1955). One of the major criticisms that has been leveled against the survey approach is that the attitudes which a person expresses in a brief interview with a stranger, even if they reflect his honest beliefs at the moment, may not be directly related to his overt conduct. Thus, both Edward A. Shils and Seymour M. Lipset make the point that those individuals who make the most intolerant statements against a minority in an interview are not necessarily more antagonistic than others when personally confronted by a member of this minority. Uneducated people, for example, may well be particularly apt to express themselves in violent language and perhaps even say that all Communists should be electrocuted, but they may be less intolerant toward Communists in actual life than better educated people who simply are not wont to make such extreme statements. (See Richard Christie and Marie Jahoda [eds.], *Studies in the Scope and Method of "The Authoritarian Personality,"* 1954.)

In the study of voting behavior, election results furnish a check on how realistic the attitudes obtained in an interviewing survey have been. Partly as the result of this reality check, the study of political behavior has advanced from superficial public opinion polling to sophisticated investigations of attitudes and their formation. Of particular significance in this respect was the pioneering study *The People's Choice* (1944), by Paul F. Lazarsfeld, Bernard Berelson, and Hazel Gaudet, in which the panel design was developed. Repeated interviews with the same sample ("panel") of respondents throughout the political campaign of 1940 made it possible to trace the processes by which people make political decisions and change their attitudes. Few people, it was found, change their vote intention in the course of the campaign, and those that do typically have little interest in the election. A systematic national survey of a Presidential election is Angus Campbell, Gerald Gurin, and Warren E. Miller, *The Voter Decides* (1954).

Another criticism that has often been leveled against the survey method is that its focus on the attitudes and characteristics of a sample of unrelated individuals fails to provide the very information most needed for sociological analysis, namely, data on the relations between individuals and on the social structures of which they are a part. Within the last few years, however, a start has been made on adapting the survey method to meet this criticism. The way the opinions of friends and fellow workers affect a person's political attitudes is analyzed in Bernard Berelson, Paul F. Lazarsfeld, and William N. McPhee, *Voting* (1954), by the simple expedient of asking respondents what the opinions of their associates are. Other studies went one step further and obtained more reliable data by actually interviewing the associates of the original sample of respondents. Perhaps the most successful adaptation of the survey method to the study of a social organization has been made in Seymour M. Lipset, Martin Trow, and James Coleman's *Union Democracy* (1956), a very suggestive sociological investigation of membership participation in the International Typographical Union and the conditions that have sustained its unique two-party system.

Social Psychology—The study of small groups, the newest and most rapidly expanding branch of social psychology, illustrates especially well the substantive implications of the new conception of sociology discussed above. As long as sociologists were interested in explaining the "important problems" of human history or of society as a whole, it was only natural that they almost completely ignored the social structure of small groups, since its study did not seem relevant for their purposes. But once the focus shifted and the objective became to explain recurrent patterns of social conduct, the systematic study of social processes in small groups began to assume increasing significance. The very problems of social relationships and social structure that tend to be neglected in interviewing surveys can readily be studied in small groups, and experimental situations can be created to investigate how various social conditions affect patterns of conduct and the development of a social structure.

Since small groups can easily be studied under controlled conditions, some investigators have used them to derive generalizations about larger social systems. They have, in effect, assumed that the processes observable in the small group are completely analogous to those operating in larger groups, or even in whole societies. Obviously, however, the small group is not a society in miniature, and this approach is no more justifiable than that of many of the earlier experimental psychologists, who attempted to derive generalizations about how children learn to read from observation of how rats learn to run through mazes. But although small groups undoubtedly do not replicate larger social structure, they pervade them. Since all large organizations and even societies consist, in one sense, of many small groups, an understanding of small groups and the social processes that occur in them is a prerequisite for an understanding of more complex social systems.

Most of the systematic methods used in the study of small groups are relatively new. The most widely used of these methods is the sociometric technique, developed by Jacob L. Moreno (*Who Shall Survive?*, rev. ed., 1953) originally for the purpose of group therapy. In essence, it consists of asking each member of a community–in Moreno's original study it was a girls' reformatory–which others he or she would most like to be in the same group with, and which ones would be least desirable as companions. The responses to these questions make it possible to trace the network of social relationships in each group–choices, mutual choices, in-group choices, etc.–and to determine the popularity of each member on a variety of dimensions.

In the past fifteen years, increasing attention has been paid to the problem of finding objective measures of the social interaction in groups, although there were some earlier attempts at quantitative observation of interaction among nursery-school children. The first simple measure of interaction was devised by Eliot D. Chapple–a record of the amount of speaking activity and inactivity of each person in a group. This method has been elaborated and used outside the laboratory by Conrad Arensburg and by William F. Whyte, for example, in the latter's perceptive *Street Corner Society* (1943). More recently, a variety of procedures that differentiate between various types of interaction have been developed. The best known of these is Robert F. Bales's *Interaction Process Analysis* (1950), which involves classifying each sentence and some non-verbal acts in a group discussion into one of twelve categories, in addition to noting who makes the statement and to whom it is addressed. There is a growing body of research using this system, and a collection which includes representative studies has been published (Alexander Paul Hare, Edgar F. Borgatta and Robert F. Bales [eds.], *Small Groups*, 1955).

Small-group research is one of the few areas in sociology where controlled experiments are conducted frequently. A famous series of early experiments is that in which Kurt Lewin, Ronald Lippit, and Ralph White explored the effects of authoritarian, laissez-faire, and democratic leadership. One of these studies, as well as many other small-group investigations carried out by followers of Lewin, has been reprinted in Dorwin Cartwright and Alvin Zander (eds.), *Group Dynamics* (1953). Another classical experiment is the one by Muzafer Sherif dealing with the effects of group norms on perception, *The Psychology of Social Norms* (1936).

The study of small groups is, of course, only a small sector of social psychology. Indeed, social psychology is such a broad and pervasive branch of sociology that Amos Hawley and other sociologists have complained that the dominant socio-psychological orientation threatens to lead to the utter neglect of the systematic study of social structure itself. The wide range of socio-psychological concerns is exemplified in the *Handbook of Social Psychology* (1954), edited by Gardner Lindzey, as well as in Guy E. Swanson, Theodore M. Newcomb, and Eugene L. Hartley (eds.), *Readings in Social Psychology* (2d ed., 1952). Of central concern to the sociologist is the psychological aspect of the process of social interaction–in short, the study of communication with significant symbols, to which George Herbert Mead made such great contributions. This so-called symbolic-interactionist approach is presented by Alfred Lindesmith and Anselm Strauss in their recently revised text, *Social Psychology* (1956). Probably the most important empirical studies on the development of language and moral values in the course of social interaction are Jean Piaget's *The Language and Thought of the Child* (1926) and *The Moral Judgment of the Child* (1932).

With the development and increasing acceptance of Freudian theories of personality development, a number of social scientists began to use psychoanalytic insights to reconceptualize their own fields. One psychiatrist, Harry S. Sullivan, has attempted a broad theoretical synthesis of the contributions of Sigmund Freud and George Herbert Mead (*The Interpersonal Theory of Psychiatry,* 1953). In sociology, his and Freud's direct influence have been particularly important in the study of socialization–the study of how personality develops in the course of interaction with others.

About a quarter of a century ago, anthropologists became interested in investigating the ways in which cultural differences in family structure and child-rearing tend to produce different "normal" personalities in different cultures. Ruth Benedict used data from several cultures to show how relative is the concept of a normal person in *Patterns of Culture* (1934), and Margaret Mead demonstrated how much cultural variation there is in the definitions of age and sex roles and in the practices of child-rearing in *From the South Seas* (1939). The most systematic elaboration of this insight that the institutional system affects the personality structure was made by two psychiatrists. Abram Kardiner, employing the concept of basic personality structure to refer to that aspect of personality common to all members of a culture, stresses that the primary institutions, notably the economic ones, govern the basic personality structure, which, in turn, affects the secondary institutions, such as the mythology *(The Individual and His Society,* 1939; *The Psy-*

chological Frontiers of Society, 1945). Erich Fromm, in his *Escape from Freedom* (1941), does not assume that all members of a society are equally affected in their personality development by the institutional structure. The socio-economic conditions in which a group of individuals find themselves will shape their social character, which is similar for all members of a social class but different for members of various classes in the same society. These conceptions of anthropologists and psychiatrists have influenced a variety of sociological investigations, particularly studies on the ways class and ethnic differences affect family structure, child-rearing, and, therefore, personality development (Allison Davis and Robert J. Havighurst, *Father of the Man,* 1947). It should be noted, however, that many criticisms have been made of these conceptions in general and of their specific application to American class differences.

In the study of mass communication, the focus is not upon the process of communication *per se,* nor upon the development of the capacity to communicate, but upon the effects of various media of mass communication on attitudes and conduct. The extensive systematic research into the effects of Army orientation films and other media, reported by Carl I. Hovland, Arthur A. Lumsdaine, and Fred D. Sheffield in *Experiments on Mass Communication* (1949), showed that, while subjects learned new facts from these propaganda films, their attitudes were usually little affected by seeing them. Recent work has indicated that the group context in which communications are received exerts much influence on the meanings attributed to them and the effect they produce. Direct social contacts influence opinions and attitudes more than do mass media, but the latter do have some indirect effects. Elihu Katz and Paul F. Lazarsfeld demonstrate, in *Personal Influence* (1955), that opinion leaders help to transmit the influence of the mass media; that is, the individuals most influential in shaping the opinions of others are in their own thinking considerably affected by the mass media. These authors also show that there are types of opinion leaders, and that political news, movie gossip, and home-making information travel by different social routes to their ultimate audiences.

An important task of the communications researcher is the analysis of the contents of messages in order to find out which specific elements actually produce changes in opinion. A thorough summary of the uses and difficulties of such content analysis was made by Bernard Berelson in *Content Analysis in Communication Research* (1952). Robert K. Merton combined content analysis with a focused interview of listeners to explain the success of the Kate Smith radio marathon to sell war bonds in *Mass Persuasion* (1946).

Demography and Human Ecology*—Whereas the covert and subjective aspects of social conduct are at the focus of social psychology, its overt and objective aspects are at the focus of demography and human ecology. Demography is the study of population—its size, distribution,

*We gratefully acknowledge Donald J. Bogue's helpful comments on this section.

and composition. Traditionally, the emphasis has been upon developing precise quantitative methods for describing and analyzing population trends, such as changes in birth and death rates and migration patterns. Demographers have usually approached their research with an empirical orientation, and they have shown little concern with underlying socio-psychological processes. More recently, however, a number of studies have been undertaken that combine interviewing surveys with demographic analysis in order to investigate these socio-psychological processes associated with various overt characteristics of population (for example, Pascal K. Whelpton and Clyde V. Kiser [eds.], *Social and Psychological Factors Affecting Fertility,* 1946-). Interest in developing theoretical generalizations from demographic findings has also become more pronounced (Joseph J. Spengler and Otis D. Duncan [eds.], *Population Theory and Policy,* 1956, a companion volume to their *Demographic Analysis,* 1956). Excellent overviews of the field are provided by the summary of demographic findings in the United Nations, Department of Social Affairs, Population Study No. 17: *The Determinants and Consequences of Population Trends* (1953); and by the collection of articles just published by Philip M. Hauser and Otis D. Duncan, *The Study of Population.* Notable examples of demographic research are Dudley Kirk's *Europe's Population in the Interwar Years* (1946), and Kingsley Davis' *The Population of India and Pakistan* (1951).

As originally conceived by Robert E. Park, human ecology has been primarily concerned with the ways in which cities grow and change. It has been defined as the "study of the spatial and temporal relations of human beings as affected by the selective, distributive, and accommodative forces of the environment." (See Robert E. Park, Ernest W. Burgess, and Roderick D. McKenzie, *The City,* 1925.) The procedure of urban ecology has been, fundamentally, to distinguish geographical areas in the city that are relatively homogeneous in economic or demographic respects and then compare the social characteristics of these areas, as illustrated by Harvey Zorbaugh's *Gold Coast and Slum* (1929). An early interest of ecologists in social problems was encouraged when researchers found that the incidence of a wide variety of "pathological" phenomena–such as juvenile delinquency, crime, divorce, mental illness, and suicide–is systematically distributed throughout the city, being highest in the so-called "area of transition" right around the central business district and diminishing gradually as one goes out toward the suburbs (Clifford R. Shaw and Henry McKay, *Juvenile Delinquency and Urban Areas,* 1942, and Robert E. L. Faris and Henry Warren Dunham, *Mental Disorders in Urban Areas,* 1939.)

The greatest contribution of urban ecology to sociology is that it constituted one of the earliest attempts at systematic study of social structures rather than individual behavior. On the other hand, the ecological approach has been criticized for providing a basically economic interpretation of city growth which ignores other important social factors that affect it, such as the traditions that develop in a neighborhood and the common values that attach people to it (Walter Firey, *Land Use in Central Boston,* 1947, and Milla Alihan, *Social Ecology,* 1938). Recently, however, the field had broadened to encompass interests far wider than those of the original urban ecologists, and ecological research has taken into account some of the criticisms that have been made. New problems have been incorporated into ecology, such as that of the relations between cities, or that of the relations between a metropolis and its hinterland (Donald J. Bogue, *The Structure of the Metropolitan Community,* 1949). Indeed, Amos Hawley developed the framework for a general sociological theory based on the ecological approach, and he conceived of ecology very broadly as the study of "the nature of community structure in general, the types of communities that appear in different habitats, and the specific sequence of change in community development" *(Human Ecology,* 1950).

Social Differentiation in Community and Nation—A totally different approach to research on communities is that of the social anthropologists, many of whom became interested in the study of contemporary society and started to conduct community studies around 1930. Their approach is to take the community as a whole and not to attempt to break it down into segments for analysis, as do the ecologists. Furthermore, in contrast to the ecological focus on material economic and geographical conditions, anthropologists place primary emphasis on the cultural values of the community. Finally, they are not as committed to the use of quantitative methods as the ecologists are. A good example of an anthropological community study is Conrad Arensberg and Solon Kimball's *Family and Community in Ireland* (1940).

The central concern of many anthropologically-oriented studies of modern American communities, including the two best-known series, is the social stratification of the community. Robert S. and Helen M. Lynd, in *Middletown* (1929), and particularly in their follow-up of the same Midwestern community during the depression, *Middletown in Transition* (1937), are primarily interested in differences in economic power and their implications for the life chances of individuals and for the institutional structure of the community as a whole. William Lloyd Warner's Yankee City series, taking quite a different view of stratification, analyzes class differences in style of life and patterns of associations in an old New England community (Vol. I, *The Social Life of a Modern Community,* with Paul S. Lunt, 1941). A number of later community studies concentrated on specific aspects of stratification; thus, August Hollingshead's *Elmtown's Youth* (1949) deals with class differences among adolescents and their significance for education, and Floyd Hunter's *Community Power Structure* (1953) is an investigation of institutional leadership in a Southern metropolis.

Another major interest of community studies is the investigation of the relations among ethnic groups and the emerging patterns of ethnic differentiation. The third volume of the Yankee City series (William

Lloyd Warner and Leo Srole, *The Social Systems of American Ethnic Groups,* 1945) exemplifies this, as do Elin Anderson's study of another New England city, *We Americans,* and Everett C. Hughes's research on a Canadian town, *French Canada in Transition* (1943). Particular attention has been paid to the semi-caste relations between Negroes and whites in Southern communities (see Allison Davis, B. Burleigh and Mary R. Gardner, *Deep South,* 1941; John Dollard, *Caste and Class in a Southern Town,* 1937; Hortense Powdermaker, *After Freedom,* 1939). Research into the social structure of ethnic sub-communities is illustrated by Louis Wirth's *The Ghetto* (1928), and St. Clair Drake and Horace R. Cayton's *Black Metropolis* (1946). The effects on prejudice of social contacts between Negroes and whites in more and less integrated housing communities is analyzed by Morton Deutsch and Mary E. Collins in *Interracial Housing* (1951), and research on the effects of school desegregation in various Southern communities.

Ethnic and race relations have also been studied outside the community setting. Gunnar Myrdal's *An American Dilemma* (1944), a collaborative work of great scope, and Edward Franklin Frazier's *The Negro in the United States* (1949) are comprehensive investigations of the social situation in which the American Negro finds himself. A great deal of research has been devoted to the problems of prejudice and discrimination. One approach has been to study the personality and social background of prejudiced people (Theodor W. Adorno, and others, *The Authoritarian Personality,* 1950; Bruno Bettelheim and Morris Janowitz, *Dynamics of Prejudice,* 1950). Another approach has been to analyze intergroup relations (Everett C. and Helen M. Hughes, *Where Peoples Meet,* 1952). Robert M. Williams, Jr. made an inventory of existing knowledge on prejudice and discrimination in *The Reduction of Intergroup Tensions* (1947). Sophisticated research on the effects of environmental differences on racial differences in intelligence is exemplified by Otto Klineberg, *Negro Intelligence and Selective Migration* (1935). A collection of studies in this area was made by Arnold Rose, *Race Prejudice and Discrimination* (1951), and there exists an *Inventory of Research in Racial and Cultural Relations* (1948), compiled by the University of Chicago Committee on Education, Training and Research in Race Relations.

Class differentiation is to an even greater extent than ethnic differentiation, a society-wide phenomenon. Generalizations about stratification based on studies of single communities have been criticized not only for using an inadequate sample, but also because the aspects of stratification most relevant in the study of the status system of a community are different from those most pertinent for the analysis of the class structure of the society. In particular, it has been emphasized that prestige and social associations, conspicuous as they may be in differentiating the members of a local community, are not as important as power relationships in the investigation of a society's stratification system.

Despite widespread awareness of the significance of examining stratification on a nation-wide scale, no comprehensive systematic study of this kind has been carried out in the United States. There are, however, a number of investigations that are concerned with specific problems of the American stratification system rather than that of a single community. Thus, Cecil C. North and Paul K. Hatt conducted a national survey of the prestige associated with different occupations, which is reprinted in Reinhard Bendix and Seymour M. Lipset's collection of studies on stratification, *Class, Status and Power* (1953). Several studies have explored the extent of "class consciousness" in America, such as Alfred W. Jones's *Life, Liberty and Property* (1941) and Richard Centers' *The Psychology of Social Classes* (1949), a national survey which shows that political attitudes and class identification are related to occupational position. Charles Wright Mills in *White Collar* (1951) and in *The Power Elite* (1956) presents intensive studies of single strata.

One of the earliest works on the important subject of social mobility was Pitirim A. Sorokin's *Social Mobility* (1927). Currently, studies of the changes in occupation from father to son are being carried out in a number of countries (for example, David V. Glass [ed.], *Social Mobility in Britain,* 1954). There have been a variety of inquiries into possible changes in the opportunities for advancement in this country over the past few decades. Natalie Rogoff reports in *Recent Trends in Occupational Mobility* (1953) that, except for the effects of the expansion of white-collar occupations, the chances for upward mobility in Indianapolis were the same in 1940 as they had been in 1910, although in 1932 Frank W. Taussig and Carl S. Joslyn, in *American Business Leaders,* predicted that mobility from lower levels into top business brackets would decline in the United States. William Lloyd Warner and James Abegglen found in their recent study that there is more mobility into the business elite today than there was at the time when Taussig and Joslyn made their investigation (*Occupational Mobility in American Business and Industry, 1928-1952,* 1955; and *Big Business Leaders in America,* 1955).

Formal and Informal Organization—Since sociology can be considered the study of the social processes by which the activities and interactions of people become organized into an integrated whole, the formal organization provides a particularly good "natural laboratory" for social research. In the army or factory, the government office or hospital, we find a clearly circumscribed social situation that has the special advantage of being, unlike the controlled conditions in the experimental laboratory, a natural social product rather than the artificial creation of the investigator.

Early students of formal organization tended to focus on the requirements any organization must meet to persist and to operate efficiently, and on the social implications of these requirements. Thus, Weber, in his classic essay on bureaucracy (in Gerth and Mills [eds. and trs.], *From Max Weber: Essays in Sociology,* 1946) systematically analyzed the characteristics of the bureucracy and its personnel that are associated with maximum efficiency in the administration of large-scale tasks. Robert Michels in *Political Parties* (1915) suggested that the inevitable bureaucratization of large democratic political parties or unions, because of the need for administrative efficiency, perverts their original egalitarian principles of organization; and he argues that, therefore, oligarchy is inevitable, and no democratic organization can survive for long periods. Adolf A. Berle, Jr. and Gardiner C. Means, *The Modern Corporation and Private Property* (1933), show that the bureaucratic organization of the giant business corporation, in effect, contradicts the American values of private property and profit as an incentive.

In the thirties, empirical research in industry led to the concept of the "informal organization" that exists within the formal organization—the networks of social relationships and the common norms that arise in work groups. For example, factory workers often develop informal production standards of what constitutes a "fair day's work," and most individuals conform to this group norm, pay-incentive systems notwithstanding. Since these social norms and the interpersonal relations that develop in work groups affect the operating practices and patterns of social interaction of workers, their social conduct cannot be explained in terms of the formal organization alone; it is also shaped by their informal organization. Operating efficiency as well as morale suffer if the latter is ignored by management. (Elton Mayo, *The Social Problems of an Industrial Civilization,* 1945; Fritz J. Roethlisberger and William J. Dickson, *Management and the Worker,* 1939; Chester I. Barnard, *The Functions of the Executive,* 1938.)

The effects of the informal organization on productivity, performance quality, work satisfactions, absenteeism, and turnover made the investigation of it important for management and stimulated the development of the so-called "human relations" approach in industry. Daniel Katz, Robert L. Kahn, and others of the Survey Research Center at the University of Michigan published a number of studies exploring the significance of informal relations for supervision. Along similar lines, Charles R. Walker and Robert Guest investigated the social conditions and special problems created by the assembly line in *The Man on the Assembly Line* (1952) and, with Arthur N. Turner, *The Foreman on the Assembly Line* (1956).

There have been several studies of how emergent informal patterns mold and even transform the formal organization. One of these examines the social structure of a hospital (Alfred H. Stanton and Morris S. Schwartz, *The Mental Hospital,* 1954). Another deals with the repercussions of a change in management on the organization of a factory (Alvin W. Gouldner, *Patterns of Industrial Bureaucracy,* 1954). William F. Whyte analyzes the cross-pressures created by conflicts between authority relations and the flow of work in a service industry *(Human Relations in the Restaurant Industry,* 1948). Several investigators have been concerned with the sources and processes of change in government agencies (Philip Selznick, *TVA and the Grass Roots,* 1949; Peter M. Blau, *The Dynamics of Bureaucracy,* 1955).

Most of these are case studies of a single organization, and this fact calls attention to a fundamental methodological problem in organizational research. The more rigorous an empirical investigation is in its methods, the less it tends to deal with questions of organizational life. Samuel A. Stouffer's *The American Soldier* (1949), for example, is based on reliable quantitative data on a large scale, namely, interviews with samples of thousands of soldiers. This approach, however, permits him to make only socio-psychological generalizations about soldiers, not to generalize about the social organization of the army. Interviews with a sample of isolated individuals cannot furnish reliable information about the organizational context. But even if many members of an organization are not only interviewed but also systematically observed in their organizational setting where they interact with one another, the data obtained pertain only to one organization, and scientific generalizations cannot be based on a single case.

This is not a new dilemma. It is the same one that faced sociologists at the end of the last century when they attempted to make scientific generalizations about the development of modern capitalism or the origin of the division of labor. And sociologists resolved the dilemma, as we have pointed out, by resigning themselves to the fact that social phenomena that are so rare as to be virtually unique are simply outside the realm of a generalizing science. But formal organizations are not quite that rare—surely not in our age of bureaucratization. As case studies of single organizations accumulate, sufficient systematic data for testing generalizations about organizational life will become available. Moreover, some recent empirical studies of one formal organization have made comparative analyses of various organizational segments within it, and this, too, makes it possible to derive tentative generalizations about social organization. On the one hand, then, formal organizations are neither as rare nor as complex as entire societies, and this facilitates their systematic investigation. On the other hand, research on formal organizations deals with complex social structures, not merely with small groups or with individuals in isolation from their social relations and structural context, as attitude surveys, as well as demographic analyses, tend to do. It is for these reasons that the systematic study of formal organizations appears to us to be a particularly fruitful field in which to advance scientific knowledge about the ways in which human conduct becomes socially organized.

This preference for a specific field is, of course, based on a value judgment in which not all sociologists would concur. The conception of sociology as outlined in this chapter has been as an analytical science. Although it has only recently emerged out of divergent traditions and continues to be refined and modified, it is a conception that most sociologists today share, however different their specific interpretations and emphases might be. The persistence of conflicting theoretical viewpoints combined with the growing agreement on fundamental methodological issues promises to stimulate research that will increase the body of scientific generalizations in sociology.

*

* *

Three types of general references which have not been discussed should be briefly illustrated—introductory texts, histories of sociology, and periodicals.

Two popular simple texts are John F. Cuber's *Sociology* (3d ed., 1955), and William F. Ogburn and Meyer F. Nimkoff, *Sociology* (1940). Introductory texts on a somewhat more advanced level are illustrated by Robert M. MacIver and Charles H. Page, *Society* (1949); Kingsley Davis, *Human Society* (1949); and Robin M. Williams Jr., *American Society* (1951), which is focused on a discussion of American institutions. The integration of selected readings into an introductory text, made famous by Robert E. Park and Ernest W. Burgess, *Introduction to the Science of Sociology* (1921), has recently been revived in Leonard Broom and Philip Selznick, *Sociology* (1955). Another source book of introductory readings has been prepared by Logan Wilson and William L. Kolb, *Sociological Analysis* (1949).

Histories of the development of sociology include the following: Harry E. Barnes (ed.), *An Introduction to the History of Sociology* (1948); Harry E. Barnes and Howard Becker, *Social Thought from Lore to Science* (2d ed., 1952); Floyd N. House, *The Development of Sociology* (1936); Pitirim A. Sorokin, *Contemporary Sociological Theories* (1928). An excellent over-view and assessment of American sociology during the first half of this century is provided by Edward A. Shils, *The Present State of American Sociology* (1948), and developments in the various branches of sociology during the last decade are covered in two volumes, one sponsored by UNESCO and edited by Hans Zetterberg, *Sociology in the United States of America* (1956), and the other edited by Joseph B. Gittler, *Review of Sociology* (1957).

The two major sociological journals are the *American Sociological Review* (1936-), the official publication of the American Sociological Society, and the *American Journal of Sociology* (1895-). Other important journals in sociology are *Social Forces* (1922-), *Sociometry* (1937-), the *British Journal of Sociology* (1950-), *Sociological Abstracts* (1952-), *Sociology and Social Research* (1916-), *Rural Sociology* (1936-), and *Social Problems* (1953-). Periodicals in related fields that often contain sociological studies include *Human Relations* (1947-), the *Public Opinion Quarterly* (1937-), and *Human Organization* (1941-).

C H A P T E R VII

Anthropology

Introduction—For the non-specialist, the subject-matters of general anthropology hold a fascination which is, perhaps, unique among the social sciences. For instance, interest in the "exotic" is always strong, and accounts of travels among strange peoples with strange customs have had a continuous popular audience. The field of anthropology, by embracing such studies, has acquired this "ready-made" public. An interest in some aspect of anthropology frequently develops without knowledge of the general field. Thus, the amateur will pursue his interest in Indians or primitive technology without being aware that it is part of something called "anthropology."

Anthropology has several kinds of interested publics. Perhaps the most consistently enthusiastic is the body of amateurs which has cultivated an interest in one or more aspects of aboriginal life somewhere in the world—e.g., native Africa or native North America—and which reads traditional historical and ethnographic literature of the area. In the past, such amateurs have frequently contributed to the pool of ethnographic materials by their own researches. A more recent trend in non-specialist interest in anthropology is in the field of cultural comparison. The concern with contemporary social problems has led many people to the popular accounts which describe the ways in which non-Western peoples handle similar situations—child-rearing and adolescence, for example. The relatively large number of works of general anthropological interest to be found in paper-backed editions, as well as the popularity of anthropology courses in various adult education programs, attests to the widespread interest in anthropological subjects.

Another sort of public is formed by specialists in the humanities and the social sciences who sometimes turn to anthropological data. To the humanists, much of this anthropological material is of immediate importance. In the routine description of primitive cultures, the traditional ethnographer commonly records myths, folk tales, music, art forms, and the like, which may be the subjects of analysis by humanists. When there is extensive interest in some aspect of primitive culture, it may become a relatively autonomous field of study or be partially incorporated by one of the humanities—thus, primitive plastic art has increasingly become the concern of art historians. Anthropologists have rarely been interested in the exclusively esthetic aspects of primitive artistic productions. However, these materials continue to be of interest to anthropologists for illustrating aspects of a total culture.

Other social scientists frequently use specifically anthropological materials. They come to cultural anthropology for information concerning primitive peoples which may add a comparative dimension to the study of some social or cultural process. Anthropological literature has had a new importance in the past decade. Economists, sociologists, historians, and political scientists have shown an increasing interest in problems of contemporary non-Western societies. Though they are concerned with the study of more complex units than was the traditional ethnographer, they find many uses for this material. The anthropological literature is sometimes the only serious, detailed social scientific work available for a given area, and those non-anthropological specialists who are preparing to do field work themselves will become familiar with this literature.

Anthropology is that discipline which claims an interest in "man and his works" at all times and in all places. Though no single investigator may be expected to be familiar with all of the sub-fields of anthropology, it is assumed that the professionally trained anthropologist will have had at least some exposure to the full variety of interests encompassed by the discipline—physical anthropology, linguistics, archaeology, social anthropology, and ethnology.

As might be expected of a discipline which claims an interest in all of the aspects of human life at all times, anthropology includes among its students persons of widely varying backgrounds and of divergent interests, brought together by their common orientation toward this very general perspective on human activities. Much anthropological literature, not only in its early years, but continuingly, has been the work of people professionally affiliated with disciplines outside anthropology to whom this broad perspective has seemed attractive. In order to continue to encompass these sweeping interests, anthropology has been dependent upon its receptivity to a diversity of methods and approaches. This flexibility has attracted specialists to anthropology and sensitized anthropologists to advances in special fields. Thus anthropology, which already covers an exceedingly broad area, continues expanding through this ability and readiness to incorporate ideas from allied fields. If it cannot demonstrate that it does, in fact, successfully encompass the study of man in all aspects of his existence, anthropology can at least claim that it offers a greater variety of knowledge and approaches to this study than does any other field. The volumes *Anthropology Today* (1953) and *Current Anthropology* (1956) survey the current knowledge in the various fields which comprise contemporary anthropology and provide substantial bibliographies for the sub-fields.

Anthropological research has historically emphasized peoples and cultures outside the province of other academic specialties; no other nineteenth-century discipline formulated its hypotheses and did its research in terms of all societies and cultures. This research has concentrated on those societies which have been variously called "preliterate," "non-literate," "primitive," or "savage," and anthropology has thus attempted to perfect its methods and approaches for the study of relatively non-complex societies.

Despite significant changes in problem orientation and research methods, anthropologists have continued, though not exclusively, to concentrate on primitive peoples. When they have shifted their attention to contemporary Western society, anthropologists have tended to approach it as much as possible as they would approach a primitive group. American anthropologists have frequently attempted to study sub-groupings within Western society. *Plainville, USA* (1945), by J. West (pseudonym for Carl Withers), Hortense Powdermaker's *Hollywood, the Dream Factory* (1950) and Evon Vogt's *Modern Homesteaders* (1955) alike employ anthropological method for the study of contemporary subcultures in the United States. Anthropologists have continued to be attracted to the study of peoples either isolated from, or on the margins of, the great civilizations. A significant recent trend has been toward the investigation of more complex groupings, both Western and non-Western, particularly toward the study of villages and peasant communities. These are sometimes studied as isolates, in the tradition of older ethnography, or as part of a larger civilizational complex.

All the social and cultural sub-fields of anthropology are referred to as "cultural anthropology." The division of cultural anthropology on the basis of objectives gives rise to two major categories—the so-called "descriptive-historical" fields, and the "social-analytic" fields. The first class includes ethnology (the theoretical and comparative study of human custom), ethnography (the description of individual cultures), and archaeology (the description of the remains of past cultures). The second class, social anthropology, is sometimes called "comparative sociology." It is concerned primarily with the study of social organization, rather than custom. It is characteristic of twentieth-century anthropology that its practitioners are at some time in the course of research engaged in each of these pursuits—data-gathering and interpretation, both historical and non-historical.

Each of the major divisions has contact with and is oriented toward other social sciences. The descriptive-historical fields particularly are intimate with history proper and, to a lesser degree, historical and cultural geography. Social anthropology shares joint interests with these fields, but perhaps more with other social sciences, particularly sociology and social psychology. These relationships are complex, and no attempt can be made here to chart them.

Archaeology is one of the descriptive-historical fields. The branch of archaeology which was stimulated by the ideas of social evolution and by those who have been concerned with early man is considered anthropological archaeology. Its practitioners have been concerned with the study of the cultural origins of early man and with peoples outside of the Western tradition. To the extent that material remains permit, archeologists provide descriptions of extinct cultures and societies. These descriptions serve, like those of ethnographers, to illustrate the variety of human cultural productions, range of adaptation, etc. Archaeology differs, however, in that it is concerned with cultural processes over enormous spans of time. The descriptive work of archaelogy appears in monographs which describe and order the materials discovered in digging at a site, the relationships between these finds, and some interpretation of their significance. Increasingly, archaeologists, particularly American archeologists, have come to value broader investigations of archaeological cultures which are more nearly comparable to the results of ethnology. These investigators recognize the desirability of functional interpretation of materials found in the same archaeological context and, further, go beyond a mere description of these artifacts and their relation to consider problems of the relationship of the archaeological cultures to their environmental setting, e.g., settlement patterns and their interpretation are examined in Gordon R. Willey (ed.), *Prehistoric Settlement Patterns in the New World* (1956). Though the techniques for accumulation of this data are unique to archaeology, the interpretations put upon them are derived from theoretical and interpretive frameworks which are a part of general anthropology. Some of the problems of the relationship of archaeology to anthropology and summary statements of principles and methods representative of modern American archaeology are to be found in Gordon R. Willey and Philip Phillips, *Method and Theory in American Archaeology* (1958), and many of the same problems are approached in an evolutionary perspective by Vere Gordon Childe in *Piecing Together the Past: The Interpretation of Archaeological Data* (1956).

ETHNOLOGY

Ethnographic studies, though not labeled as such, go back very far in time. A concern with the explanation of customs, mores, etc., marks the antecedents of contemporary ethnography. The account by Herodotus of the customs of the people he visited is the first ethnographic description of which we have record. Subsequent, particularly post-sixteenth-century, accounts of travelers, mercantile explorers, and missionaries, as well as accounts of voyages of discovery, constitute basic source materials for social anthropological and ethnological studies. Occasionally observers were sent by governments to accompany parties for the purpose of gathering ethnographic materials to aid in conquest or administration. For the most part, however, such ethnographic material is incidental to the reports of other aspects of expeditions. These reports appear separately, or in some notable collections. Of particular interest are the works issued by the Hakluyt Society, founded in 1846 for the purpose of publishing such accounts. The series of publications following James Cook's famous voyages is also of interest to anthropologists. Such works usually provide only brief, sketchy accounts of any one tribe or group of tribes.

(An exception is provided by the *Jesuit Relations* [73 vols., 1896-1901], an invaluable collection of ethnographic materials, covering the period from 1610 to 1791 in the northeasern United States, which is an account of extended contact with the aborigines of one area.) Another source for these accounts is Edward Godfrey Cox's *A Reference Guide to the Literature of Travel, Including Voyages, Geographical Descriptions, Adventures, Shipwrecks, and Expeditions,* published in three volumes—*The Old World, The New World,* and *England*—by the University of Washington (1935-49). These accounts by travelers, discoverers, and conquistadors, however, were not systematic expositions of cultures; their authors were more interested in recounting daring feats or describing quaint and exotic customs than in furthering the knowledge of the varieties and similarities of human culture.

Anthropological works of greater theoretical importance began to appear in the middle of the nineteenth century. Prior to that time, there had been various attempts to schematize the history of man in universal developmental frameworks, or to study single institutions for the purpose of reconstructing their origins. Some of these were of a high order of scholarship and provided arguments (for example, Grotius' defense of the comparative method) still considered valid. More frequently, they were simply speculative accounts of origins or stages of development which have ceased to have importance for anthropological thought. The data available were used in support of *a priori* developmental schemes, and, where data were not available, rational conjecture filled the lacunae.

Sir Henry Maine, John F. McLennan, and Edward B. Tylor in Britain; Johann Bachofen in Switzerland; Lewis H. Morgan and John W. Powell in the United States; Philipp W. A. Bastian, Gustav F. Klemm, and Friedrich Ratzel in Germany; and Emile Durkheim in France may be regarded as the founders of contemporary social and cultural anthropology. The distinctiveness of the new approach which characterizes the work of these "founders" of the discipline, as compared with earlier writers on anthropological or ethnographic topics, is their search for generalizations about the evolution and growth of human culture or some part of it, in the manner of natural scientific investigation. The belief that man could be studied scientifically was basic to the development of ideas of social evolution. Maine, who dealt chiefly with legal and political institutions, attempted to explain the changes in social relations from simple to complex societies, in terms of the gradual replacement of status by contract relationships. Morgan developed a theory to describe various stages of cultural evolution from savagery to barbarism and, further, to civilization. Bachofen attempted to show the historical primacy of matriarchy over patriarchy, and McLennan's work centered on an attempt to formulate a natural history of the family.

Generalizations to be found in earlier writings were based chiefly on common sense rather than on reliable empirical data, or they were static associations between certain given traits and given conditions, rather than attempts to explain why and in what manner cultural traits or institutions changed under the impact of external or internal factors. But in the course of the nineteenth century, some empirical confirmation was provided for the theory of progress, which had dominated much of the thinking of social scientists during the eighteenth and nineteenth centuries. This was accomplished by the final destruction of the belief in the history of creation related in Genesis, and the gradual development of evolutionary ideas in biology, which found empirical verification in paleontological and geological data. The result of these developments was to induce social scientists to turn to the development of theories of social change and social evolution, similar to biological and geological theories.

The impact of the idea of biological evolution, therefore, was of the greatest importance to the development of anthropology; and although modern cultural anthropologists view the theories of such writers as Lewis H. Morgan (*Ancient Society,* 1877, and *Primitive Marriage,* 1865), and Johann Bachofen *(Das Mutterrecht,* 1861) as antiquated, they acknowledge the profound value which the work of these men had in furthering the study of social anthropology. At the same time, there are many parts of the work of Sir Henry Maine *(Ancient Law,* 1861), or Edward B. Tylor *(Researches into the Early History of Mankind and the Development of Civilization,* 1865, and *Primitive Culture,* 1871), and particularly Emile Durkheim and Friedrich Ratzel *(Völkerkunde,* 1885), which are considered largely valid by many modern students of social anthropology. With the exception of Morgan, these were "armchair" theorists who collated data from various sources. Much of the criticism directed toward these students has pointed out the relatively uncritical use of available source materials. The critical approach to data has largely been characteristic of twentieth-century anthropology, particularly American anthropology.

In its early years, in the 1840's and '50's, anthropological interests were carried on by associations of amateurs. These displayed the same variety of interests and approaches to the study of man which has characterized later anthropology. Anthropology continued primarily as an avocational pursuit until late in the century. However, by the early 1900's, much of the present structure of the academic discipline of anthropology had come into being–chairs of anthropology and anthropology departments were created. Museums, government agencies (interested in colonial or aboriginal peoples), and universities were all contributing to anthropological researches.

A great many schools of anthropological thought have existed since the 1850's. Some of these have ceased to be significant, but a surprising number have survived in only slightly modified form to the present day. A critical analysis of these will not be presented, but rather the major divisions of cultural anthropology and trends in ethnological thought which have had continuing importance will be summarized–evolutionism, the concept of culture, American historical anthropology, and social anthropology. Anthropologists have been little concerned with exploring intensively the history of ethnological theory; however, Alfred C.

Haddon's *History of Anthropology* (1910), Robert H. Lowie's *The History of Ethnological Theory* (1937), and Thomas K. Penniman's *A Hundred Years of Anthropology* (1935) all present adequate summaries of major figures and orientations of nineteenth- and twentieth-century anthropology and sketches of earlier developments, concentrating primarily on English and American schools.

Evolutionism—It was seen above that some variety of evolutionistic thought seemed to pervade the anthropological theorizing of the nineteenth century. The intellectual biases and predispositions toward evolutionistic theory antedated Charles Darwin, but notions of biological evolution did change the view of social evolutionists somewhat. The radical rationalist view gave way to the notion that man might have little to do with influencing the shape of some kinds of institutions which evolve independently, according to laws of social evolution.

In general, the theory of early evolution was focused on gross developments in the succession of particular types of institutions by other types, all of them being categorized according to their presumed central function. Herbert Spencer's list is typical: domestic, ceremonial, political, ecclesiastical, professional, industrial. Evolutionists at the end of the century placed a high value on ethnographic fact. The difficulty with the earlier theories, so they thought, was that they were much too speculative. They, on the other hand, could make use of accumulated data furnished by an assortment of reporters. In the sense that they took these statements of fact and arranged them in huge compendia, according to some classification or other, they were more empirical than their eighteenth-century prototypes.

In addition to the idea of progress and the assumption of an inevitable, determined development, most anthropologists assumed the "psychic unity" of mankind. In simplest terms, this theory is that all men, other than the pathological, have the same general instincts or drives, and all are capable of the same processes of cognition. In both cases, the assumption has to do with capabilities, not with cultural modifications and the content of cognition under specific circumstances. If, however, the specific societies are taken to be the essential or typical aspects, then the working assumption may lead one astray. Similarly, if capabilities are taken as actualities, then one is bound to misinterpret. The latter situation led to the interpretation of primitive religion in purely intellectualistic terms by Edward B. Tylor *(Primitive Culture,* 1871), and of magic by James G. Frazer *(The Golden Bough,* 1894). Some of these concepts have been found useful in modified form. The latter work has had tremendous influence in creating interest in anthropology among educated laymen.

All Victorian anthropologists were not equally evolutionistic in orientation. Some assumed the evolutionist framework, but without explicit concern for its major outlines. Edward A. Westermarck *(The History of Human Marriage,* 1889) and Henry Maine *(Ancient Law,* 1861) both questioned the unilineal scheme of the evolution of the family which postulated primitive promiscuity as the first and monogamy as the final stage of development of that institution.

Although contemporary students of culture are not averse to considering historical reconstructions, they are, on the whole, opposed to one set of theories of culture which has made elaborate reconstructions and which is generally designated as "evolutionism." The formulation of stages of culture through which societies must inevitably pass in the evolutionary process has been rejected. The most famous of these schemes was Lewis H. Morgan's *Ancient Society* (1877), in which he outlined an evolutionary scheme which was derived both from his study of kinship relations among primitive people and "from his presumptions on" the environmental influences and economic pursuits of people in different levels of "advancement towards civilization." Unilineal evolution has few serious adherents in archaeology at present, though both Leslie A. White *(The Science of Culture,* 1949) and Vere Gordon Childe *(What Happened in History,* 1942) have championed somewhat modified versions of Morgan's views. They differ from their nineteenth-century predecessors in postulating general sequences of the development of the culture of mankind which are abstracted from specific historical examples. They demonstrate that the general trend of human history has been toward increasing complexity and differentiation and, in world-wide perspective, that the nineteenth-century hypothesis of the development from "savagery" to "barbarism" to "civilization" is confirmed. These are very general formulations, referring to human culture as a whole and not to the development of single societies.

Recently there has been a revival of interest in cultural evolution. This interest is seen in the work of Julian Steward *(Theory of Culture Change,* 1955) and his students, and is largely independent of earlier evolutionist theories. The current evolutionism is multilineal rather than unilineal. It admits the possibility of various lines of cultural development, positing no necessary stages of cultural achievement through which all societies must pass. Multilineal evolution postulates, rather, that similar social forms having like functions have developed through similar, though independent, adaptational processes and sequences. Steward believes that through a detailed analysis of such instances we may be able eventually to formulate universal laws of cultural development. The data used in the formulation and testing of these hypotheses of multilineal evolution concerning cross-cultural regularities are taken both from ethnological and archaeological sources. In *Irrigation Civilizations: a Comparative Study* (1955), edited by Steward, an interesting attempt is made to bring together both New and Old World archaelogical materials in an attempt to test one of the hypotheses relating to the conditions of the development of civilization.

The Concept of Culture—From a consideration of stages of societal development, the focus in anthropology shifted to culture. "Culture" is the central concept of anthropology. It helps to give some kind of unity to the diversified activities of anthropology. The concept of culture (in the sense of a cumulative non-biological heritage and the products of man) and the concept of *a* culture (in the sense of the heritage and products of a given society at a given slice of time) have helped to order the phenomena which interest anthropologists and to orient these anthropologists toward possible goals.

The history of the use of these concepts is a history, on the one hand, of definitions sharpening and refocusing observations and statements of problems and, on the other hand, of observations and immediate problems demanding the redefinition of concepts. Therefore, it is not surprising to find that anthropologists seem to mean different things when talking either of *a* culture or of culture in general, or that they use these concepts in different ways. Clyde Kluckhohn and Alfred L. Kroeber have compiled and ordered anthropological and other definitions of culture and have discussed culture theory in their excellent monograph, *Culture; A Critical Review of Concepts and Definitions* (1952).

Edward B. Tylor was the first to emphasize the concept of culture in English *(Primitive Culture,* 1871) as the central concept around which a new branch of knowledge was to form. (Klemm had used it much in the same fashion in German thirty years earlier.) For Tylor, culture is "that complex whole which includes knowledge, belief, art, law, morals, custom, and other capabilities and habits acquired by man as a member of society." Culture has been thought to consist of traits and institutions which can be subjected to historical (evolutionistic) investigation. In consequence of this view, several important studies were written which made comparative analyses of particular culture traits in several societies or tried to trace the evolution and changes of a single culture trait through time. One of the most famous comparative studies of a set of culture traits is Sir James G. Frazer's *The Golden Bough* (1894), which deals with certain aspects of religious belief. Later, such comparative studies were challenged on the grounds that the things compared were out of meaningful context. Whether or not such studies are methodologically admissible depends, of course, upon whether culture traits are considered sufficiently separable from one another to make possible the full examination of each in isolation from others.

Questions of the place of origin of various aspects of culture were of particular concern to ethnological theorists in the early part of the twentieth century. The so-called diffusionist schools assumed the non-inventiveness of man, which meant that aspects of human culture either have a common origin or have been invented only a small number of times and were then transmitted from culture to culture. The proof which representatives of the diffusionist school provide for their view is that certain culture traits are common to several societies, or that certain ornamental forms, or tools, or other aspects of culture are found in otherwise unrelated societies. The chief representatives of the view (heliocentricism) that the common origin for human cultural traits is to be found in ancient Egypt have been William J. Perry *(The Children of the Sun,* 1923) and Grafton Elliott Smith *(The Migrations of Early*

Culture, 1915). A less one-sided, but still essentially diffusionist, theory is held by the culture-historical school, the main representative of which is Father Wilhelm Schmidt *(The Culture Historical Method of Ethnology,* 1939). This school sees its intellectual ancestor in Friedrich Ratzel, whose *Anthropogeographie* (1882-91) had a tremendous influence not only on anthropology but also on the development of human geography in Germany. The main adaptation to anthropology of Ratzel's ideas was undertaken by Fritz Graebner, who, in his *Methode der Ethnologie* (1911), outlined the program of the school which is called *Kulturkreise.* It is named for the *Kulturkreise* (culture circles) process–i.e., geographically deployed complexes of culture are identified and converted into culture strata, which gives a chronology of events. The main object of this school was clearly anti-evolutionary. Many of its chief adherents were Roman Catholics, whose efforts, in essence, may be viewed as an attempt to reconcile ethnographic findings with the history of humanity outlined in the Scriptures. In contrast to some other anthropological schools, notably the functionalists, who were either non-historical or anti-historical in orientation, the cultural historical school and the diffusionists emphasize historical relationships and developments.

American Historical Anthropology–American anthropology has diverse origins. Though Lewis H. Morgan is one of the acknowledged great figures of early theoretical anthropology, his influence was probably greater in England than in his own country, the United States. The early American anthropologists were not as much interested, on the whole, in ethnology as in ethnography, particularly in the study of American Indians. By the latter part of the nineteenth century, the Indians no longer posed a threat to the whites. Many persons were beginning to romanticize the "vanishing Americans," and were eager for detailed information about their pre-contact mode of life. There was, in general, a growing interest in ethnographic subjects; new museums were founded, and, in 1879, largely through the work of Major John Wesley Powell, the Bureau of American Ethnology was established. This bureau has continued to publish a sizeable proportion of the available ethnographic materials dealing with aboriginal American subjects.

The school of anthropology developed under the guidance of Franz Boas, called the American Historical School, has been most significant in shaping American anthropological thinking. It has been viewed as primarily a reaction against ideas of social and cultural evolution, though it bears no resemblance to the cultural diffusionist schools discussed above (which were also reacting against evolutionism). Boas contended that it was essential to control knowledge of the specific historical past of the peoples studied; that primitive peoples as well as great civilizations had histories which were important to the understanding of present cultural situations. This led Boas and some of his followers to seek increasingly refined techniques for reconstructing the histories of non-literate cultures.

Boas' influence on the development of American anthropology has been immense, though he did not himself write a major work. Some of his articles and essays have been collected in *Race, Language, and Culture* (1940). An earlier collection of technical papers, *The Mind of Primitive Man* (1911), is a slightly more popular presentation of Boas' views. These views are not amenable to concise presentation. The influence of Boas is felt mostly through his students. He is not identified with a single "cause" in anthropology, unless his emphasis on the importance of field work would be so considered. Boas' own field work was done with the Central Eskimo and with the Kwakiutl Indians of Vancouver Island. His work is highly regarded for the accuracy and thoroughness with which he studied those aspects of culture which he thought relevant for anthropological inquiry. Boas is most frequently criticized for the choices of subject matter—i.e., for omissions from field study—and, more importantly, for his reluctance to generalize on the basis of his work.

Historical reconstruction has been a continuing concern of some American anthropologists. It is the field of cultural anthropology which is most closely allied with archaeology. Some anthropologists have contended that anthropology is basically a historical discipline whose business it is to test laws formulated by those who are "foolish" enough to present them; it is not the business of anthropology to formulate such laws. There seems to be an increase of interest in recent years in historical problems concerning American Indians. This is indicated by the establishment of a new journal, *Ethnohistory* (1954-), which publishes work done by anthropologists with historical sources covering the period of early contact with aboriginal Americans.

It is easily seen how reconstructing the history of non-literate peoples should have become such an important part of anthropology. Sociologists dealing with the Western world, or with other societies (though this is infrequent) that had writing, could take advantage of a variety of records available for these societies and of the research of historians. For the most part, they did not have to do sociological and historical analysis (in the sense both of depictive integration and chronological work) at the same time, and pre-historical research was not a part of their training or interest.

Techniques and literature of both linguistics and archaeology are available to the anthropologist in his attempts at reconstruction. Following Edward Sapir, American anthropologists have been particularly sensitized to the potential value for cultural reconstruction of linguistic techniques. Linguistic reconstruction, which is part of linguistics proper, is based on comparative techniques and provides formulations of the degree of relationship between languages, and thus of the relationship between peoples speaking related languages. Linguistic analysis, particularly comparison of lexical items, has been used as a basis for the reconstruction of earlier features of a culture, i.e., by comparing vocabulary the cultures share, it is possible to make inferences about the character of the culture at the time the languages diverged. Recently there has been an added refinement in the field of linguistic reconstruction which is of considerable importance to anthropologists. Morris Swadesh has devised a lexico-statistical technique (glottochronology), based on empirically observed rates of linguistic change, for estimating not only the probable familial relationships, but also the actual dates when branches of language became separated.

Archaeology has been the primary anthropological sub-field concerned with the problems of reconstruction of the cultural past. Archaeologists have, of course, devised techniques for dating their findings, both in relative terms, e.g., stratigraphy, and absolute, e.g., dendrochronology and carbon 14. The reconstruction work of the archaeologist and the ethnologist have ordinarily been carried on as independent researches. Very recently, in line with the general trend toward interdisciplinary area work, there have been attempts to integrate archaeological and historical researches with ethnography and cultural geography, in an effort to provide a more comprehensive picture of man to the environment within a given area.

SOCIAL ANTHROPOLOGY

Social anthropology may be seen to stem from attempts during the 1860's and 1870's to develop general theories of social evolution, or the evolution of kinship organization, and its relation with legal or economic institutions. Religion and the family were institutions of particular interest to the major figures of nineteenth-century theoretical anthropology, many of whom were lawyers or, if professional scholars, comparative religionists. Social anthropology stems primarily from this concern with the nature and evolution of the family and kinship. Recording of kinship terminologies and descriptions of family life were necessary adjuncts to traditional ethnographic works. Lewis H. Morgan's *Systems of Consanguinity and Affinity of the Human Family* (1870) stands as the first important attempt to systematize and compare knowledge of kinship systems found in various parts of the world. But there were few conscious attempts to subject the internal structure of family and kinship relations to intensive study. It is this study of internal relationships which characterizes the field of social anthropology. Shortly before the turn of the century, social anthropology blossomed in France, mainly under the aegis of Emile Durkheim. Durkheim, his followers, and those who were influenced by him, are theoretical sociologists who from the beginning have worked with ethnographic data, not as an afterthought, but as the basis of their investigations. Few of them have been field workers, but their theoretical influence on English and American anthropologists, as well as sociologists (see the previous chapter), has been of considerable importance. There has been virtually no gap between sociology and anthropology in France since Durkheim's time, and those who have been inspired by him to any extent, no matter what their official label, are likely to see no major difference between sociology and social anthropology.

Through his analysis of values and beliefs, Durkheim was concerned with the problem of how a social system achieves stability and conformity. In several of his works, but notably in *The Elementary Forms of the Religious Life* (1915), he stipulates as the unit of culture the "collective representation" or "shared idea" which arises unconsciously in the minds of the members of a society and forms the vehicle by which they develop their thought. Our ideas of space, time, and logical order are examples of such representations. According to Durkheim, they function to maintain the solidarity of the group, although he admitted that they might survive when their original function was no longer apparent.

Durkheim and his followers saw the significance of comparative research for their problem areas, and most of his students did comparative studies of institutions. Pre-occupation with the persistence of social groups tended to emphasize social statics rather than dynamics; problems of social change, with social change viewed as the common phenomenon, were not the focus of Durkheim's work nor that of his followers.

For contemporary anthropology, the primary impact of Durkheim's theories on the study of the cohesiveness of the social system has been on the development of structural-functional theory, particularly through the work of the British anthropologist, Alfred R. Radcliffe-Brown. Radcliffe-Brown's reputation was established by the publication of a study of a small tribe on an island in the Indian Ocean, *The Andaman Islanders* (1922). What is of importance in this context, however, is Radcliffe-Brown's contribution not to ethnology but to social theory, which is presented in a series of essays written over a period of many years, collected and published in 1952 under the title *Structure and Function in Primitive Society*. He accepted from Durkheim the interpretation that cultural (though he preferred the term "social") phenomena may be accounted for by their contribution to the solidarity of the group, and that cultural institutions may be looked at as primarily functioning to hold together a given social group.

The influence of Durkheim and Radcliffe-Brown, each in his own way, has been considerable. Radcliffe-Brown's stress on the functional relations of the structural elements of a social group has led, among British anthropologists, to an exhaustive study of the social structure of various primitive cultures. An outstanding example is Edward E. Evans-Pritchard's *The Nuer* (1940), but many more could be cited, e.g., Raymond Firth's *We, the Tikopia* (1936), Meyer Fortes' *The Dynamics of Clanship Among the Tallensi,* (1945), and Fred Eggan's *Social Organization of the Western Pueblos* (1950). Bronislaw Malinowski's functionalism, though different from Radcliffe-Brown's, converged with his in its emphasis on detailed descriptions of the organization of single cultures. Another development of which Radcliffe-Brown may be regarded as the initiator is the intensification of the study of kinship among different societies, one of the foundations of social structural relations.

A general account of the work done along these lines, discussing past theories and achievements as well as presenting Radcliffe-Brown's own views, is the "Introduction" to *African Systems of Kinship and Marriage* (1950), a volume he edited with Cyril D. Forde. A compendium of social structural principles and findings, stemming from the work of Radcliffe-Brown and other students of social structure, is George P. Murdock's *Social Structure* (1949).

The work of Bronislaw Malinowski must be included also as part of "social anthropology." Like Radcliffe-Brown, Malinowski stressed a "functionalist" approach to the study of primitive society, though his focus was cultural rather than social. All parts of a culture were, in his view, functionally related to one another. Malinowski's conception of function stressed the manner in which the culture takes account of motivations of the individual and manages to mold and provide for his needs. Radcliffe-Brown's was a more purely sociological approach, analyzing the contribution of institutions and beliefs to the maintenance of the social system. Malinowski's views of culture are summed up in his article, "Culture," in the *Encyclopaedia of the Social Sciences* (1930-35), and in a collection of his essays, *Magic, Science, and Religion* (1948). Malinowski and Radcliffe-Brown stressed many of the same aspects of anthropological investigation, particularly the need for detailed intensive field study and theoretical analysis by the same investigator and the focusing of theoretical attention on the internal processes of a society. Malinowski's own field work was done with the Trobriand Islanders, and led to a series of notable monographs—e.g., *Argonauts of the Western Pacific* (1922). Malinowski's contributions to anthropology are examined in a series of critical essays written by former students, *Man and Culture* (1957), edited by Raymond W. Firth.

ETHNOGRAPHY

Anthropological material for the study of culture, society, and the individual is derived from ethnographies which describe data gathered by the anthropologist in the field.

Ethnography occupies a central position in anthropological research. Adequate cultural descriptions are a prerequisite for historical or sociological interpretation. Adequacy, for these purposes, is determined by the completeness of the coverage and the quality of the data for the problem at hand. Obviously, the ethnographer cannot anticipate in advance the variety of uses to which his description may be put. Sometimes descriptions are made without explicit problem frameworks; others focus on specific theoretical problems or on gathering information to fill gaps in data previously acquired. Recent ethnography, on the whole, has been more concerned with this kind of problem orientation. It includes a much narrower range of materials, usually dealt with more intensively, than did the early general monographs.

A major consideration in the late nineteenth and early twentieth century was to gather the necessary descriptive materials before the indigenous culture (and its bearers) died out. This is still a problem for the anthropologist, and it is still thought desirable to obtain information from and about those persons who have been least contaminated by contact with Western civilization, though this consideration has ceased to have the priority it once had. Related to this is the aim of reconstructing the cultures of people who have been changed through contact with other cultures, especially Western culture. The social anthropologists, though largely non-historical in orientation, have increasingly felt the need of taking historical materials into account in various phases of their work. Contemporary anthropologists usually approach field work with a series of questions to be answered, and they publish monographs, when possible, which attempt to answer these questions. Since there is some prior ethnographic knowledge of the people available to him, he will not ordinarily feel compelled to describe all the aspects of the culture which were thought essential by earlier workers. The monograph which deals in greater or lesser detail with the whole cultural and social life of a people, from their gods to their pots and pans, is a thing of the past.

The tradition of field work by trained anthropological investigators is a product of the late nineteenth century, further developed in the twentieth. We have seen that, with few exceptions, ethnologists up to that time had been content to rely on data gathered by all varieties of collectors, but had not themselves worked with non-Western peoples. There was a sudden florescence in the final decades of the nineteenth century which produced a number of what are now deemed classic ethnographic accounts. These reflect the increasing interest and proficiency in techniques of data-gathering and introduced a flood of new concepts (native words) which constitute the core of the present anthropological vocabulary. Some of these monographs have had influence far beyond anthropological circles. Baldwin Spencer and F. J. Gillen's *The Native Tribes of Central Australia* (1899) is particularly notable in this respect, since these data figured importantly in the formulations of Frazer, Durkheim, and Sigmund Freud. The field work that an anthropologist must do today is almost always preceded by a detailed examination of the materials already available on the peoples and cultures which he is to study. He may consult documents in the district officer's records or the minutes of the tribal council, but ordinarily he will still be primarily dependent on the work of his anthropological predecessors. Though anthropologists were not traditionally much concerned with providing guides to the available materials, a number of excellent bibliographic works have appeared recently, and reference sources in general seem to be improving.

North American Indians—The study of American Indians has been the principal, though not the exclusive, concern of American ethnography. The aboriginal peoples of North America are, perhaps, the best known in the world. Boas' students worked mostly on this continent. Independent ethnographers also have contributed an enormous amount of data to the pool. The government publications of the Bureau of American Ethnology and of the Smithsonian Institution are a particularly rich source of descriptive materials on the American Indian. Ordering the great mass of available data was the significant anthropological task which has occupied many of the most talented workers. Clark Wissler's *The American Indian* (1917) is a pioneering attempt to codify the culture areas of North American aborigines.

There are few works attempting to summarize our knowledge of American Indian culture. Ruth Underhill's *Red Man's America* (1953) is an introduction; Alfred L. Kroeber, *Cultural and Natural Areas of Native North America* (1939), and Fred Eggan (ed.), *Social Anthropology of North American Tribes* (2d ed., 1955) are more detailed summaries of aspects of American aboriginal culture. George P. Murdock's *Ethnographic Bibliography of North America* (2d ed., 1953) classifies many of the available sources according to tribal groupings.

Students of American Indians have produced a large number of monographic studies of the tribes of native North America dealing both with the pre-European contact and with the post-contact periods. Many of these studies were aimed at recording what is remembered of aboriginal culture and at reconstructing the culture of the pre-contact period; others were attempts to trace the distribution of certain culture traits. Such studies are to be found in the publications of university departments of anthropology (Yale, Washington, California, Columbia) and in the publications of learned societies (American Philosophical Society, American Ethnological Society, American Anthropological Association), as well as in government and museum publications.

Africa—The ethnography of Africa has been the combined province of anthropologists representing several national traditions. The African continent was an object of interest to Europeans for centuries. From the 1700's on, there are detailed accounts of contact with the native peoples. Some of the early ethnographic material has been compiled in topic outline by Emil Torday in *African Races* (1930). Charles G. Seligman's *Races of Africa* (1930) is a good introduction to native Africa and has recently been republished. The *Ethnographic Survey of Africa,* published by the International African Institute, Cyril D. Forde (ed.), (1950-), provides detailed summaries of the ethnographic data for six African cultural areas. There are two bibliographies for general African materials: Cyril D. Forde's *Select Annotated Bibliography of Tropical Africa* (1956) and Heinrich A. Wieschhoff's *Anthropological Bibliography of Negro Africa* (1948). Wilfrid D. Hambly's *Source Book for African Anthropology* (1937) presents summary accounts of aspects of native African life and also an excellent bibliography. It is supplemented by his selected *Bibliography of African Anthropology 1927-1949* (1952), which includes materials of interest to anthropologists through 1949. There are, additionally, several periodicals devoted exclusively to Africa.

Asia—Only sporadic ethnographic coverage is available for Asia, the largest continent with the greatest population and greatest variety and range of cultures. During recent decades, anthropologists have directed more attention to Asia than in the past, and surveys and summaries are now being made available, though much of the area is not, at present, accessible for direct field study. Northern and Central Asia, the homes of pastoral peoples and reindeer breeding, are among the best known areas of the continent. They were a primary area of ethnological interest during the first part of this century. Much of this material is included in the Human Relations Area File. The remainder of Asia can be divided into three cultural regions—Southwest Asia, India, and Southeast Asia. In these areas, anthropological interests sometimes converge with those of other fields of research—e.g., with Indic studies or with Sinology. For the most part, anthropologists have concentrated their attention on the relatively isolated or marginal peoples. They have become increasingly interested in the relationship between these peoples and the great civilizational complexes. An example is *Village India* (1955), edited by McKim Marriott. David Mandelbaum has compiled a *Bibliography of Indian Ethnology* (1949), and John F. Embree and Lillian Dotson's *Bibliography of the Peoples and Cultures of Mainland Southeast Asia* (1950) is a guide to materials of anthropological significance.

Oceania—There is relatively extensive ethnographic coverage of much of Oceania, the area which includes Australia, Malaysia, Melanesia, Micronesia, and Polynesia. Melanesia and Polynesia were well-known prior to World War II, partly because of the importance for anthropological theory of some of the field work done in the area—e.g., the work in Melanesia of Bronislaw Malinowski and Margaret Mead. With the publication of the work of the Coordinated Investigations of Micronesia Anthropology, a series of excellent monographs is now available for that area. Anthropologists, particularly Australian anthropologists, have been filling in the coverage of New Guinea as well as of the aborigines of their own continent. Clyde R. H. Taylor's *A Pacific Bibliography* (1951) covers the entire area and provides a detailed bibliography of Micronesia, Melanesia, and Polynesia.

South America—For the size of the geographical area, South America is probably the least well-known of the major ethnological areas of the world. American, German, French, and English anthropologists have done field work there, but large areas still remain almost completely unknown. South America has, however, been the subject of some comprehensive survey work; most notable is the *Handbook of South American Indians* (1946-), edited by Julian Steward.

Europe—The ethnology of Europe has not attracted many students of anthropology in the present century, while the emphasis of ethnography has been on the non-literate peoples of the world. Many of the major figures of anthropology's formative period were concerned with European folk culture—Maine, Bachofen, and Frazer, for example. Recently, consistent with the new interest in peasant and village studies in other parts of the world, there has been some important work done with small European communities—e.g., Julian Pitt-Rivers' *The People of the Sierra* (1954). Around 1950, Raymond Kennedy compiled a bibliography of European materials of interest to anthropologists—*General Bibliography on Europe.*

General Works—There are not many syntheses or comparative descriptions of primitive cultures which make ethnographic materials comprehensible or meaningful for introductory study, though an acquaintance with a variety of the world's cultures is essential for learning anthropology. There are, however, books which do present "thumbnail" sketches of a cross-section of the primitive world which are valuable for this kind of introduction: George P. Murdock's *Our Primitive Contemporaries* (1934), Cyril D. Forde's *Habitat, Economy and Society* (1934), and Margaret Mead's (ed.) *Cooperation and Competition Among Primitive Peoples* (1937).

For more specialized interests, the Human Relations Area File is attempting to make available, in topical outline, equivalent descriptive coverage for cultures throughout the world, derived from ethnographic sources. These files are available in several major university libraries.

CONTEMPORARY TRENDS IN ANTHROPOLOGY

Culture Theory—The general result of the work in which almost all American students participated in some fashion during the last fifty years was the development of a particular set of theories, perhaps most conveniently summed up in Ralph Linton's *The Study of Man* (1936) and in Alfred Louis Kroeber's essays, *The Nature of Culture* (1952). The theory is somewhat eclectic, and there is not complete unanimity among all the students. It is neither evolutionist nor rigidly functionalist. Culture elements or factors are considered, in the main, to be independent of each other, but it is freely acknowledged that for the participants in any culture the cultural elements have meaning and internal consistency. This view is summed up by Robert Redfield in a passage in his work, *The Folk Culture of Yucatan* (1941):

> In speaking of "culture" we have reference to the conventional understandings, manifest in act and artifact, that characterize societies. The understandings are the meanings attached to acts and objects. The meanings are conventional and therefore cultural insofar as they have become typical for the members of that society by reason of intercommunication among the members.

This definition clearly establishes the relationship between the reality of culture elements and the values and beliefs of the human group. Thus, even if two cultures have similar or identical institutions or artifacts, if different meanings are attached to these elements the cultures are clearly different. The distinction among cultures chiefly consists of sets of culturally determined values and beliefs, rather than of the objects and acts of man.

This conception of culture fits very well into the wider framework of "social relations" (including cultural anthropology, sociology, and social psychology) as it is presented by, for instance, Talcott Parsons and Edward A. Shils, editors of *Toward a General Theory of Action* (1951). It should be noted that the main stress is on interaction and mutual communication. Moreover, the emphasis on the meaning of the various cultural elements and their integration in a value system clearly implies that whatever independence is postulated for the elements is due chiefly to the method of investigation. We may analyze any one element by itself, assuming the others remain unchanged. If, however, the existence of a reasonably integrated system of values which is necessary for a tolerable degree of social stability is assumed, then the mutual interdependence of the various culture elements must be postulated. This mutual interdependence of the components of a culture arises from their subordination to a common system of values.

The acceptance of this conception has promoted the mutuality of interest between sociologists of the structural-functional persuasion and social anthropologists of this stamp. Additionally, it has focused anthropological interest on the crucial position of the concept of value in anthropological research. Clyde Kluckhohn and Alfred L. Kroeber (*Culture*, 1952) make a detailed theoretical statement of the relationship of values to culture theory. Some notable values monographs are the products of the Harvard Values Project, under the direction of Clyde Kluckhohn: John Ladd's *The Structure of a Moral Code* (1957) and Evon Vogt's *Modern Homesteaders* (1955) and *Navaho Veterans* (1951) are representative.

"Language and culture" is a name given to the various studies which have attempted to examine the relationship between language and other cultural systems. Primarily, these Language and (or in) Culture studies consist of attempts to refine and/or to test the hypotheses of Edward Sapir and Benjamin Lee Whorf concerning the relationship between the structure of a language and the world-view of its speakers. These formulations range from those which assert that linguistic categories determine thought processes to those which contend only that the language, to some extent, reflects the thought-world of the speaker. Impetus to the consideration of these ideas has come from work done on American Indian languages. The conception that the language and Weltanschauung of a people are interrelated is not new, but descriptions of languages having structures so markedly different from those of Indo-European languages has provided much richer evidence for the examination of these possible interrelationships. The papers in which Whorf presents his ideas regarding the role of language in organizing human experience, with numerous examples from his work with the language of the Hopi Indians, are to be found in his selected writings, *Language, Thought and Reality* (1956), edited by John B. Carrol. Some of the criticisms and discussions, as well as a resume of the researches stimulated by the Sapir-Whorf hypothesis, are available in Harry Hoijer (ed.), *Language in Culture* (1954).

Culture and Personality—The field of culture-personality has occupied the attention of many of the most able theoretically oriented American anthropologists. These investigators have examined various phases of the relationship between the two orders. In this research, anthropologists have been chiefly influenced by psychoanalytic thinking. As long as the concepts of psychoanalysis were employed mainly by scholars primarily interested in psychiatry who saw in the application of these concepts and doctrines to problems of social relations primarily a means of testing their theories, the most significant problems of social psychology remained unexplored. Only when sociologists and social anthropologists themselves began to use some of the theories of psychoanalysis, often in severely modified form, did really promising vistas appear. The application of psychoanalytic and related psychological theories to the explanation of behavior in relatively uncomplex groups promised to be particularly useful. Edward Sapir, in a series of programmatic papers reprinted in his *Selected Writings in Language, Culture and Personality* (1949), edited by David Mandelbaum, brought the possibilities of the attention of cultural anthropology. Several attempts were made to explain behavior patterns in a given culture by appeal to psychological types which were directly or indirectly derived from Freud's psychoanalytic concepts and theories. For example, one of the early works in this field, Ruth Benedict's *Patterns of Culture* (1934), uses the terminology of Carl G. Jung. Abram Kardiner, in *The Psychological Frontiers of Society* (1945), attempts to provide a general outline of the procedure and potential results of this method for studies of personality development. These are pioneer contributions to the field. There have been a number of subsequent contributions which attempt to evaluate and measure the actual contribution made by psychological and psychiatric theories to anthropological and social relations research, and to restate the theoretical assumptions of this work afresh. Examples of these efforts can be found in a number of summary accounts, readers, and texts. For the total area, perhaps the most complete summary and bibliography are to be found in Clyde Kluckhohn's "Culture and Behavior" in Gardner Lindzey (ed.), *Handbook of Social Psychology* (1954).

The field of culture-personality covers a wide variety of types of work, including the analysis of the process of socialization and enculturation of children in different environments, the consequences of socialization for adult behavior and its extension into standard behavior patterns (sometimes also called "national character"), as well as attempts to describe an entire culture in terms of the personality patterns of the individuals embraced by it. Since the earliest of these studies in the early 1930's, methods and theories in the field of culture and personality have been much refined. Projective tests have been tried; a notable early experiment is to be found in Cora DuBois' *The People of Alor* (1944), and a survey of the work with projective tests used up to 1953 is available in Jules Henry and Melford E. Spiro, "Psychological Techniques: Projective Tests in Field Work," in *Anthropology Today* (1953).

Anthropologists formed the vanguard in the field of national character studies (Ruth Benedict, Margaret Mead, Geoffrey Gorer), but this interest is now shared by social psychologists and sociologists. Work in this field is summarized by Alex Inkeles and Daniel Levinson, "National Character: The Study of Modal Personality and Sociocultural Systems," in Gardner Lindzey (ed.), *Handbook of Social Psychology* (1954).

Social and Cultural Change—Concern with social and cultural change is quite possibly older than the intensive study of any other set of problems in social relations. The early founders of sociological and anthropological theories, the evolutionists, the organicists, and scholars attempting to treat sociology as an aspect of history, were all interested, predominantly, in social change. The questions which these scholars wanted to answer were: (1) What are the main indicators of change in a social system? (2) Must we look primarily to internal or to external factors to account for change within a social system? (3) Can we ascertain any general sequence of changing variables for all or for certain classes of social systems which account for the transformation of the systems in their entirety?

Many scholars have written about these problems, and many others have made special studies of particular instances of social change which were intended to throw light on all or some of these general questions. In view of the great bulk of the literature and its considerable variety, and perhaps also because a consistent, generally accepted body of theory is, as yet, still unavailable, a classification and ordering of this literature is extremely difficult.

The problem of whether social change originates within the culture or is imposed upon it from the outside is usually discussed under the heading of "invention versus diffusion." By "invention" in this context is understood the internal development of new cultural forms within a closed system; by "diffusion," their introduction from abroad. All contacts between peoples may lead to diffusion of traits, regardless of the nature of contact.

As was seen before, the problem of diffusion versus invention has given rise to a group of theories which considered that the process of invention is generally freakish and that it occurs only once, or at least very rarely, in human history, and that the main process by means of which new procedures and even beliefs are learned is diffusion. This is the position of the cultural diffusionist (Heliocentric) school and, to a large extent, of the cultural historical school (Kulturkreis). Modern American anthropologists tend to believe that diffusion and invention are processes occurring simultaneously. Even the strictest functionalists do not deny that diffusion occurs, and that it may occur often. But the mere transfer of an artifact from one culture to another is not a complete process of adaptation, and this adaptation is the chief functionalist interest. What is necessary, in addition, is the development of some meaning of the use and function of the new artifact which has been accepted from outside; and this second process must have its origin in the adopting culture.

The problem of acculturation, or culture contact (both synonyms for diffusion-in-process), has received extensive treatment by anthropologists. At various intervals this knowledge has been summarized, and among the studies containing most adequate presentations of such knowledge are Melville J. Herskovits, *Acculturation* (1938), and Sol Tax (ed.), *Acculturation in the Americas* (1952). The forms of culture contact are manifold; they vary from the most tenuous contacts of occasional travelers to the closest intimacy between two previously unconnected groups which may be thrown together in a factory, plantation, or newly formed political unit. Moreover, the two groups which come into contact with one another may be coordinated as equals, or one may dominate the other. Acculturation involves, therefore, not merely the acceptance and adaptation of culture traits imported from the outside, but it may involve, in many instances, the complete change of life patterns of one or both societies which come into contact.

CHAPTER VIII

Psychology*

Introduction—Psychology may not be the oldest profession, but surely it was the earliest hobby. Most men turn amateur psychologist, pure or applied, at some time in their lives, and the best of these amateurs have made contributions whose importance may not be discounted even in our own very much more organized day and age. Curiously enough, however, the pressures for technological progress which elsewhere seem to be replacing the ranks of amateurs with small groups of highly trained professionals have had no such effect upon the amateur psychologists; on the contrary, today circumstances and the public prints seem determined to make professionals of us all. We cannot turn our heads without reading analyses of the psychological implications of the important social, industrial, educational, and medical problems of our time, long on theory and short on fact.

Sometimes such concern reflects real societal or environmental change. The Supreme Court decisions outlawing segregation, for instance, have stimulated a great deal of interest in the psychological consequences of constrained interracial contact, much of it realistic and entirely appropriate in view of the far-reaching potential effects. Recent critiques of the very bases of professional education in the United States are equally well grounded in fact. As Harry Schwartz has pointed out in *The New York Times* (June 2, 1957), more than half of the members of the Presidium of the Soviet Communist Party under sixty-five years of age have been trained as engineers. This number includes both Nikolai A. Bulganin and Nikita S. Khrushchev himself. The U. S. S. R. is fast becoming the closest thing to a technocracy the human race has yet produced; and while the really fundamental threat implied by this development is by no means fully apparent to Americans as yet, the consequent and adequately demonstrated ability of the Soviet system to educate mounting numbers of top flight scientists and technicians is reason enough for the recent troubled re-examinations of our own educational system, and more broadly, of the fundamental social and psychological incentive systems which determine the distribution of effort in the United States.

---

*The writer gratefully acknowledges invaluable assistance from Dr. John W. Atkinson, Dr. Daniel Katz, and Dr. E. Lowell Kelly. Errors of fact or interpretation are, of course, solely the responsibility of the writer.

It is more difficult in other cases to discover situational alterations which account for increased public concern over psychological problems. There is little evidence, for example, to suggest that the marked upsurge of concern for mental health follows upon any corresponding increase in the proportional incidence of mental illness. Quite the contrary, after careful study of some of the most complete records available, Herbert Goldhamer and Andrew W. Marshall conclude in *Psychosis and Civilization* (1953) that the relative frequency of psychoses for age groups under fifty in their sample had shown no increase at all over the past 100 years. Here we may be dealing less with any specific situational alteration than with a change in the popular orientation towards mental well-being. The present-day growth of large-scale management training programs and of business support for studies of industrial psychology poses somewhat similar problems of interpretation. Big industrial organizations, presupposing a high level of functional organization, have existed in quantity for a good number of decades. Aside from a limited number of pioneering investigations conducted prior to World War II, however, the growth of interest in collaborative effort, "teamwork" and team products, and particularly in the group dynamics of management, is a recent phenomenon.

Whatever the sources of popular interest and concern for specific problems, the cumulative result has been a marked expansion of the literature of psychology. The *Psychological Abstracts* (1927-), a bimonthly journal summarizing most of the material of psychological interest published in the Western world, in 1956 alone reviewed some 500 periodic sources, and in this single twelve-month period abstracted more than 8500 articles and books.

Of these numerous periodicals, the group published by the American Psychological Association probably enjoys the widest circulation among psychologists. Besides the *Psychological Abstracts,* there are, first of all, five journals distinguished principally by the content areas they serve. These include the *Journal of Applied Psychology* (1917-), the *Journal of Comparative and Physiological Psychology* (1921-), and the *Journal of Consulting Psychology* (1937-), which contains contributions primarily on clinical psychology. The *Journal of Abnormal and Social Psychology* (1906-), publishing studies of many facets of human psychology, and the *Journal of Experimental Psychology* (1916-), reporting research on sensation, perception, learning, and other aspects of general psychology, also fall under this heading. Longer research reports appear as separate numbers of the *Psychological Monographs* (1895-). The *Psychological Bulletin* (1904-) publishes research reviews and critiques, together with papers on statistical and research methodology, while the *Psychological Review* (1894-) specializes in theoretical articles and interpretations of research in all areas of psychology.

The extent of the literature on psychology would seem to preclude a comprehensive review, and the intent of this essay is rather more limited. It attempts to outline the scope of psychology, describing in somewhat greater detail those areas presumably of more immediate interest to other social scientists. Representative classics, reference works, and surveys are cited where further detail may be desirable, and writings which seem to be instances of important trends are discussed in connection with suggestions as to the underlying orientations of academic psychology and the problems it must face in realizing its potentialities.

All selection implies bias. Efforts are made throughout, however, to note the omission of important alternate materials and points of view; in most cases, specific references for such materials also are included. Mention should be made in this connection of three highly regarded volumes providing excellent coverage of the many traditional topics of general experimental psychology not considered here. The surveys in Stanley Smith Stevens' (ed.) *Handbook of Experimental Psychology* (1951) are uniformly excellent, as is the major revision by Robert S. Woodworth and Harold Schlosberg of *Experimental Psychology* (1954), traditionally an authoritative work. Finally, Charles E. Osgood's *Method and Theory in Experimental Psychology* (1953), invaluable for its devoted attention to crucial detail, attains in its finest sections to an almost "systematic" exposition of modern experimental psychology.

Orientation—The focus of psychological concern is the individual in interaction with his environment. So bald a definition would seem to encroach upon the preserves of other specialties, and yet the overlap is less an artefact of the definition or a portent of imperialistic aspirations than an evidence of the extensive frontiers which psychology holds in common with other social sciences. In point of fact, it is just these shared boundaries which provide a firm foundation for psychological participation in the broad interdisciplinary enterprises which have waxed so popular in recent years.

But if psychology is a social science, it is also a behavioral science, and, on occasion, even a biological science. Interaction of organism and environment is observed on all three levels, and communication among them, although occasionally inaccurate or even fortuitous, insures that findings at one point regularly are taken over and reappear in rather different settings as explanatory principles. Individual function provides hypotheses for studies of groups. Elaborate expositions of the principles of complex human organization take as their source the mazes and alleys of rat psychology. The intent of this volume argues against the systematic inclusion of aspects of psychology which seem so distant from the common core of social science, but numerous critical developments are nonetheless occurring in what might seem to be unlikely places, and an adequate presentation of the direction of modern psychology must include some reference to them.

The scope of psychology has not always been so broad. As recently as 1929, Edward B. Titchener argued, in his *Systematic Psychology: Prolegomena,* that psychologists should confine themselves to the study of conscious experience as it related to the organism. To be sure,

Titchener acknowledged the legitimacy of studies of behavior, but he just as surely defined them out of psychology.

The rallying cries of thirty years ago are without current effect upon our present efforts, however; the martial triumphs of earlier generations are as little known to modern psychologists as the knightly encounters of a thousand years before. Nowadays, references even to such acknowledged masterpieces as William James's two-volume *Principles of Psychology* (1890) are rare. And if we today are indifferent to our immediate antecedents, we must be accounted quite ignorant of relevant but not explicitly psychological writings of earlier periods, even though many of the basic concepts of modern psychologists are direct if unwitting descendants of such earlier pre-psychological ideas.

Psychologists are therefore most fortunate in having available a number of valuable histories of psychological thought and of the development of their specialty as a separate entity. Gardner Murphy's recently revised *Historical Introduction to Modern Psychology* (1949) nicely details the descent of our modern concepts and displays the interconnections between psychological speculation and the more general history of ideas. Edwin G. Boring, well-known for his insistent attempts to broaden the temporal and geographic range of the discipline, has contributed not only *Sensation and Perception in the History of Experimental Psychology* (1942), but also a second edition of his *A History of Experimental Psychology* (1950). Both volumes are scholarly and exciting delineations of the men and the times which advanced the field, with constant reference to the movements of the intellectual climate over the years.

Sensation, Perception, Cognition, and Thought–Lack of food will kill an organism, but so will lack of information. Adaptation to environment is impossible without information about it, and the limits of access to such information are defined by the organism's capacity to sense energy changes about him. The organism also is sensitive to many stimuli arising from internal adjustments and alterations, but these modalities have been studied less extensively than the externally oriented apparatus. The latter, particularly vision, has been the object of more than 100 years of systematic investigation. Current sensory psychology is carefully analyzed in the three general references on experimental psychology mentioned above, and further and more detailed information may be obtained from texts such as Frank A. Geldard's *The Human Senses* (1953).

It is misleading, however, to think of sensations as entirely within sensory organs. On the contrary, the peripheral alterations are simply one of several components of a continuous chain of excitation proceeding stepwise centrally to the cortex; the changes initiated within the sensory organs interact with the ongoing activity of the intermediate elements of the neuronal net; the resultant pattern of cortical activity is the product of all of these combinations and transpositions and bears an extremely complex and indirect relation to the initial sensory input from which it is so many steps removed. And as the attention of the psychologist turns from the original stimulation, the partial and indirect cause of the subsequent activity, to events that occur further and further along the neuronal network, the psychological problem gradually changes from a concern for the organism's capacity to obtain information to an analysis of the organization and patterning of the complex sequences of neural activity; at this point, the poorly defined boundary dividing sensation from perception has been crossed.

Such a conceptualization of perceptual processes, in terms of sequences of discrete ongoings and events, is in fact somewhat similar to the theory of event structure presented by Floyd H. Allport, in his *Theories of Perception and the Concept of Structure* (1955). At least as valuable as the author's theory, however, are his scholarly reviews of all the important theoretical positions on perception; there is no comparable work in the psychological literature. Allport's use of his own viewpoint as an underlying frame of reference undoubtedly contributes considerably to the unity of the critique, although on occasion the framework becomes unfortunately restrictive, limiting rather severely the specific details selected for critical discussion.

No psychological theory arising from the study of perception can compare in the scope and importance of its influence with Gestalt theory, which has provoked invaluable research upon everything from the electrophysiology of the cerebral cortex to the dynamics of social groups. Prior to Max Wertheimer's memorable demonstration in his "Experimentelle Studien über das Sehen von Bewegung" in the *Zeitschrift für Psychologie* (1912) that under proper conditions, apparent motion might be perceived even though there was absolutely no stimulus movement to which it corresponded, psychologists tended to believe that careful analysis would prove all percepts to be composed of elemental sensations, each of which corresponded to some specific physical energy. Complex percepts were explained in accordance with "laws of association" as aggregates of simpler percepts bonded together through association due to similarity, contrast, or contiguity. Wertheimer's experiments demonstrated conclusively that a theory dealing with mere aggregates of associated elements could not account for phenomena of perceptual patterning and organization, and the principles of Gestalt psychology were shortly thereafter applied to problems in every area of psychology, pre-eminently by Kurt Koffka in his *Principles of Gestalt Psychology* (1935). Although the Gestalt position not infrequently appeared to American environmentalists as a kind of nativistic crusade, this evidently was not the crucial point for at least some of the pioneers of the movement; Wolfgang Köhler's *Gestalt Psychology: an Introduction to New Concepts in Modern Psychology* (1947), a far more accessible if less comprehensive volume than Koffka's, seems mostly intent upon demonstrating that the empiricist, associationist, "bricks and mortar" theories of psychological organization are "quite unable to do justice to the nature of sensory experience." And it is one of the oddities of psychological history that the Gestaltists, who began with a "field" theory of psychological organization which seemed almost aphysiological in its neglect of the then accepted principles of neurological function, have actually forced a predominantly associationist American psychology into critical debate over the adequacy of the basic innate apparatus it postulates. No current theory of psychology which attempts to include a discussion of underlying neurophysiology can avoid acknowledging a tremendous debt to the Gestalt psychologists for having made explicit the complex patternings and interactions of psychological processes that are implied by our simplest perceptions.

Köhler has observed that relatively greater familiarity with the raw materials of psychology frequently makes new psychological findings seem less exciting and important than comparable advances in the physical sciences. Outstanding exceptions to this rule, however, are the discoveries of unsuspected effects due to monotonous environmental stimulation recently reported by Woodburn Heron and his associates in the *Canadian Journal of Psychology,* and summarized by Heron in an article on "The Pathology of Boredom" in the *Scientific American* (1957). Marked reduction in sensory variation produced not only motivational and emotional disturbances, but also pronounced alterations in perceptual and intellectual functioning, as well as hallucinatory experiences and alterations in brain-wave patterns. While attempts made by others to utilize these findings as explanations for the effectiveness of "brainwashing" remain speculative, they undoubtedly demonstrate, as Heron concludes, that "a changing sensory environment seems essential for human beings."

The Gestaltists' preference for working with complex whole processes rather than with parts early led them to analyses of the higher mental processes, and they left a decided mark upon the psychology of cognition and thought. If John Dewey's *How We Think* (1910) is considered a classic instance of associationistic theories, then Max Wertheimer's equally short and cogent volume on *Productive Thinking* (1945) must be acknowledged its Gestalt analogue, and certainly the extensive impact of Gestalt emphases on field forces and their effects upon cognitive organization and thought is evident in Martin Scheerer's stimulating discussion of "Cognitive Theory" in the two volume *Handbook of Social Psychology* (1954), edited by Gardner Lindzey, and in several of the best chapters in David Rapaport's (ed.) *Organization and Pathology of Thought* (1951).

If, as Plato believed, cognition is one of the three primary faculties of the human mind, then the modern psychological edifice surely would seem to be as shaky as a two-legged stool. Although there are occasional investigations of cognitive variables, such as the brilliant study of the stimulus determinants of apparent causality reported by Albert Michotte in his paper on "The Emotions Regarded as Functional Connections" in Martin L. Reymert's (ed.) *Feelings and Emotions* (1950), explicit studies of cognition are rare. In part, this comes of a preference of many American psychologists for investigations dealing with peripheral rather than central variables, since the latter seem less accessible and amenable to control. The lacuna is also partly more apparent than real, due to the overlap between cognition and perception on the one hand and cognition and thought on the other; much that might seem to involve "knowing" is analyzed in these other terms.

Thought, too, receives relatively little experimental attention, but here the difficulty is still more clearly terminological. The behaviorist who oft-times seems almost ill at ease at the idea of thought most always appears willing and able to deal with instances of "problem-solving behavior." The extensive experimental literature on problem-solving is most readily accessible in William Edgar Vinacke's *The Psychology of Thinking* (1952) and in Donald M. Johnson's survey of *The Psychology of Thought and Judgment* (1955). *Thinking; an Introduction to its Experimental Psychology* (1951) by George Humphrey, contains a sustained and scholarly analysis of the issues and experiments which gradually evolved into our modern psychology of thought. It is certainly the best general volume on the subject.

The use of probability and strategy concepts like those of information theory and the mathematical theory of games make *A Study of Thinking* (1956), by Jerome S. Bruner, Jacqueline J. Goodnow, and George A. Austin, an unusually intriguing essay on the conception and experimental investigation of thought. The volume also includes a useful "Appendix", by Roger W. Brown, which makes available an unusually adequate survey of current trends in linguistics, which may also be of some value in analyzing thought processes. The concept of a "program," essentially very similar to that of "strategy," also appears in Allen Newell, James C. Shaw, and Herbert A. Simon's intriguing discussion of computer analogues for thought, "Elements of a Theory of Human Problem Solving," to be published in the *Psychological Review*.

Recent investigations by learning theorists of the discrimination of stimulus dimensions and of the growth of differential attention to these dimensions also contain new and important implications for research on cognitive variables. Perhaps even more important, such investigations, and those of other stimulus attributes mentioned in the subsequent discussion of motivation, may well lead to an invaluable *rapprochment* between the study of perception, cognition, and thought, on the one hand, and the hitherto more narrowly peripheralist psychology of learning, with its impressive methodological techniques and its rapidly growing corpus of systematic research.

Learning—Whatever we may think of it, we live in an age which has reified conviviality and institutionalized the coffee break. Even if we did not, however, one somehow doubts that many students of learning, having tired for the moment of the innumerable condensed and detailed journal articles which are their daily fare, would turn for their respite to Burrhus F. Skinner's little novel of life, *Walden Two* (1948). Yet this slim volume by a respected learning theorist convincingly portrays a near future when a powerful and comprehensive science of learning will both educate efficiently the utopian social man and also make possible his complete and totalitarian control. *Walden Two* is hardly a subtle book, but its compelling speculations brilliantly evoke the latent potentialities which make the psychology of learning so fascinating and fundamental a subject.

The amazing development and pre-eminence in America of learning psychology, particularly compared with its insignificant position abroad, has been ascribed to the peculiar importance which the dominant values of the American culture attribute to adaptability to change. Ours, we are told, was an open, expanding society, with trails to break, foreigners to integrate. Great yeas were to be heard for progress and change, and little attention was given to the stable things handed down from generation to generation. It was William James who popularized pragmatism, an American philosophy of the *usefulness* of truth, in which the truth of a belief was judged by its results. Certainly the disinclination to accord a significant role to nativistic factors, characteristic of behaviorist learning theory, also was evident throughout American psychology as a whole, and it is easy to see why the first empirical and environmentalist formulations of the sources of behavior and behavior change took firm root here and grew rapidly.

It was a German, Hermann Ebbinghaus, who took the first important step towards an empirical science of learning, reporting in his *Uber das Gedächtnis* (1885) the first use of nonsense syllables to study without reference to meaning the formation of associations. In 1898, Edward L. Thorndike published *Animal Intelligence,* and in it he set forth an early formulation of a systematic but empirical theory of learning which was to maintain its pre-eminence in America for more than 30 years. Deriving in large part from the intellectual tradition of the English associationist philosophers, Thorndike's system replaced the notion of associations among ideas with the concept of connections between sensory inputs and response outputs which were determined by subsequent rewards or punishments following the response in this situation. His later writings had extensive practical influence upon pedagogical practice. More recent experimentation has made necessary extensive alterations in Thorndike's position, but his experimental orientation, his associationist predilections, and his emphasis upon the consequences of behavior as determinants of learning have remained dominant characteristics of American learning theory to this day.

The concern for a psychology of *behavior* and its modifications, so evident in Thorndike's writings, was made the cornerstone of "Behaviorism," a movement determinedly promoted by John B. Watson and described in detail in his *Behavior: An Introduction to Comparative Psychology* (1914). Watson attacked the mentalistic and the introspective, but instead of discarding higher mental processes, he tried to incorporate them into his psychology of overt behavior by reconceptualizing them as potential peripheral behavioral mechanisms. Thought, for example, became "implicit speech." Attractive because they seemed to offer new means of getting at elusive psychological functions, these reconceptualizations failed to distinguish adequately between peripheral behaviors as causes and as correlates, and so in themselves were really improvements only by fiat.

Ivan P. Pavlov's *Conditioned Reflexes* appeared in English translation only in 1927, but news of his work reached America over a decade earlier, and Pavlovian principles were in several places incorporated into theories of learning. Since both the neural stimuli which were associated with natural stimuli and the responses which they came through association to elicit were amenable to observation and control, Pavlovian formulations were inherently congenial to behaviorist theories, and conditioning became a fundamental learning paradigm. According to Pavlov, however, contiguity was a sufficient condition for learning; whereas Thorndike had considered reward and punishment to be more important determinants. Despite the innumerable experimental attempts to decide this issue, there still remain wide divergences among learning psychologists as to the necessary and sufficient conditions.

Clark L. Hull's principal conceptual contribution to learning theory was a nicely integrated conceptual scheme which incorporated the findings of both Thorndike and Pavlov into a single theory of learning grounded in a principle of reinforcement not very different from Thorndike's ideas about the effects of reward and punishment. But modern learning psychology is even more deeply indebted to Hull, for in large part it was his influence which established it as a systematic postulational science striving to derive quantitative predictions of behavior change. Hull's *Principles of Behavior* (1943), *Essentials of Behavior* (1951), and *A Behavior System* (1952) have been cited probably more often than the works of any other learning theorist.

Quite apart from whatever intrinsic value Hull's theoretical notions may have possessed, his systematic approach seemed to have one basic and incontrovertible merit: it would permit the deduction of hypotheses which could be tested precisely. Furthermore, since tests of these rigorously deduced hypotheses were strict tests of the entire theory, Hull's procedure appeared to make possible the quick and efficient acceptance or rejection of the underlying postulates. And for almost a decade a major portion of the literature on learning was devoted to tests of aspects of Hullian theory.

Two considerations have prevented Hullian theory from becoming the very first formulation of principles of learning to be either strictly verified or strictly rejected. As numerous psychologists have suggested, and as Sigmund Koch exhaustively demonstrates in his chapter on "Clark L. Hull" in *Modern Learning Theory* (1954), by William K. Estes and others, the theory contains important gaps, inconsistencies, and indeterminacies that render it, in fact, untestable *in toto*. Secondly, too many theorists have worked with isolated concepts, ignoring the conditions imposed by the total theoretical context. This is hardly a reflection on the theory, of course, but it remains true nonetheless that many of the specific concepts have been employed to "explain" what are plainly contradictory results. As Harry F. Harlow protested in his survey of "Learning" in the

Annual Review of Psychology for 1952, "... the present-day rubber band theoretical systems can stretch to encompass any data regardless of how opposed they may be to the original predictions of the theorist."

Oddly enough, however, the tremendous volume of research inspired by Hullian theory, for all its failure either to confirm or invalidate its conceptual bases, has nonetheless decidedly advanced the psychology of learning. For, at a time when many learning theorists were content with programmatic definitions and gross verbal "laws," as Ernest R. Hilgard puts it in a review of *A Behavior System (Psychological Bulletin,* 1954), "This is the novelty Hull contributed: a system at once fertile in its predictions, and precise enough to be vulnerable to experimental attack."

Hull's is by no means the only behaviorism. Edwin R. Guthrie's is another, and his *The Psychology of Learning* (1935; revised, 1952) is famous for its contention that the complexities of learning phenomena reduce to a single proposition: "A combination of stimuli which has accompanied a movement will on its reoccurrence tend to be followed by that movement." The very antithesis of cumbersome hypothetico-deductive theories, Guthrie's simple principle of stimulus and response association through contiguity would seem to assert nothing more radical than that you will do again exactly what you did last time in the same situation. From the viewpoint of reinforcement theorists, however, this prosaic postulate generates some astounding hypotheses, and it has provoked a number of important experimental investigations.

While Skinner's novels are unlikely to insure immortality for him, his experimental investigations of behavior, such as those reported in *The Behavior of Organisms* (1938), rank as basic contributions to the psychology of learning. Notoriously averse to formal theories, including those of his fellow behaviorists, Skinner has sought instead to determine empirically, by manipulation of parameter values, the relationship between such important aspects of the environment as the schedule of reward and the behavior emitted by organisms existing in it.

At first blush it is difficult to imagine how any of the basic principles of Gestalt theory ever could be incorporated into a behaviorist theory of learning. Yet this is probably not an inaccurate characterization of Edward C. Tolman's position as he has set it forth in his *Purposive Behavior in Animals and Men* (1932) and in subsequent statements, such as those to be found in his *Collected Papers in Psychology* (1951). Less formally worked out than Hull's position, Tolman's cognitive constructs have proven attractive to many psychologists who prefer central to peripheral constructs but who do not wish to sacrifice the indisputable methodological superiorities of explicitly behavioristic approaches to the study of learning phenomena. Kenneth MacCorquodale and Paul E. Meehl have recently utilized Tolman's constructs as the bases for a formalized expectancy theory of learning in their chapter on "Edward C. Tolman" in *Modern Learning Theory* (1954), by William K. Estes and others; such cognitively oriented presentations are rapidly becoming acceptable alternatives to the stimulus-and-response constructions of more orthodox behaviorists.

Kurt Lewin's orientation, quite similar to that of the original Gestalt theorists, has also had some influence upon recent positions. Lewin has had relatively little effect upon experimental investigations of learning, however, and his ideas are better discussed in connection with social psychology.

The current research on learning is almost always reported in individual journal articles, and it is difficult to find really good recent evaluations of the directions in which it is going at present. *Conditioning and Learning* (1940) by Ernest R. Hilgard and Donald G. Marquis is an outstanding summary and analysis of work on this subject, but it is almost two decades old. *The Psychology of Human Learning,* by John A. McGeoch, revised by Arthur L. Irion in 1952, is another authoritative volume, but it confines itself largely to verbal learning. Perhaps the best survey of recent tendencies may be found in the last four chapters of the newly revised *Theories of Learning* (1956), by Hilgard. Although the entire volume is at a consistently high level, it is interesting to note that, in contrast to the organization of the earlier chapters about principal theorists, the last sections are oriented about relatively specific problems. Perhaps this reflects a current disenchantment with research intended as a crucial test of a formal theory and a preference instead for empirical investigations of specific problems in the light of more limited formulations. If this is the case, it may make for more confusion, but it also seems to be resulting in a veritable spate of fascinating results; the "Learning" chapters of the *Annual Review of Psychology* grow more promising each year.

The Individual–The methodological cornerstone of the science of behavior is the psychological test, the systematic sampling of an individual's behavior. The results of investigations of psychological processes such as learning, perception, or thinking are obtained either as disparities in average performance on some psychological measure between groups distinguished by some antecedent difference, or else as relationships between the scores individuals obtain on one test and the scores they make on another. Firmly established associations among test scores, or between test scores and antecedent variables, really form the bedrock of scientific psychology.

An individual's test score has other uses as well. Compared with the scores of others on the same test, it measures relative standing. Contrasted with the individual's score on the same test at some other time, it denotes the degree of change. Evaluated together with the individual's scores on other tests, it yields a profile of strengths and weaknesses in the traits or abilities presumed to underlie the obtained test scores. The utilization of test scores to provide information about individuals, or groups of individuals, rather than about psychological processes, is the basis of the psychology of individual differences.

A great many of the most important psychological tests developed as solutions for specific practical problems. Although the amazing investigations of Sir Francis Galton and the *Inquiries into Human Faculty and its*

Development (1883) are a treasure trove for test makers, the first great standardized tests—the measures of complex intellectual functions—resulted from a need to identify subnormal children in order to investigate the suitability of certain educational techniques for them. The early Binet-Simon scales prepared for this purpose subsequently were revised several times, and in 1916, with the appearance of *The Measurement of Intelligence,* Lewis M. Terman's famous revision of the Binet-Simon scales, the Stanford-Binet, became available. Despite recent advances in the analysis of intelligence into several more specific factors, the latest revision of the Stanford-Binet scales (1937) and the measure of general intelligence devised by David Wechsler, described in *The Measurement of Adult Intelligence* (3d ed., 1944), are easily the most widely employed of the individual general classification tests in current usage.

Following the wide acceptance of general classification tests, increased attention was paid to measures intended to assess particular aptitudes. The rapid proliferation of specific measures to meet the growing need for efficient selection and training of industrial specialists was accelerated still further by world war and cold war; the prompt and efficient selection of individuals who could learn the indispensable specialized military and technological skills became vital for national survival. But as the flood of new tests increasingly threatened to swell beyond all control, important new handbooks and compendia appeared to maintain order and to channel the mounting confusion. The most notable of these are the *Mental Measurements Yearbooks,* edited by Oscar K. Buros. Appearing in 1938, 1940, 1949, and 1953, successive *Yearbooks,* although they covered of necessity only tests widely used or newly appearing in the interim periods, included critical reviews and evaluations by test experts and thereby made an important contribution to the technical improvement of psychological tests. Anne Anastasi's *Psychological Testing* (1954) is a comprehensive and excellent survey of the applications of the most important kinds of measuring instruments, as is Frank S. Freeman's somewhat more critical *Theory and Practice of Psychological Testing* (rev. ed., 1955). Up-to-date information on specific tests and on test usage is available in current issues of the *Journal of Applied Psychology* (1917-), the *Journal of Consulting Psychology* (1937-), and *Educational and Psychological Measurement* (1941-).

Closely associated with differential psychology are investigations of classes or groups of individuals distinguished by particular characteristics, or by age, sex, or intelligence. Leona E. Tyler's *The Psychology of Human Differences* (2d ed., 1956) includes a good general introduction to this area, and the voluminous literature on child psychology is quite adequately represented in the *Manual of Child Psychology* (2d ed., 1954) edited by Leonard Carmichael. The latter volume also contains an excellent survey of overlapping aspects of developmental psychology, an area distinguished by the fascinating and suggestive if less quantitative studies reported by Jean Piaget in *The Language and Thought of the Child* (1926) and *The Moral Judgment of the Child* (1932). Another noteworthy study is

Lewis M. Terman's invaluable collaborative investigation of genius, described in the series *Genetic Studies of Genius* (1925-) and in articles in the thirty-ninth *Yearbook* of the National Society for the Study of Education (1940). These contributions of Piaget and Terman are also outstanding in the attention given to the social consequences of the attributes under consideration.

Personality—"Personality," writes Raymond B. Cattell in his *Personality: A Systematic, Theoretical, and Factual Study* (1950), "is that which permits a prediction of what a person will do in a given situation." So defined, the study of personality has much in common with the psychology of individual differences, and in fact differential psychologists use the term to refer to such non-intellectual attributes as temperament, emotionality, and rigidity. Investigations of these attributes form but a limited segment, however, of the parti-colored spectrum of writings on the psychology of personality.

The simplicity of Cattell's definition is deceptive and conceals a very considerable implication. It suggests that far from forming a corner of differential psychology, personality not only totally comprehends that area, but also presupposes the laws of perception, learning, and motivation; for the successful prediction of behavior presumes an adequate knowledge of all psychological principles. Despite these implications, many personality theorists would quite willingly subscribe to the substance of the definition; in the absence of broad and experimentally validated psychological principles, they postulate their own. And if, on occasion, they seem to be "talking about things which everybody knows in language which nobody understands," it seems no less difficult to prefer instead the *ad hoc* studies of *ad hoc* variables which line the opposite shore. As Dan L. Adler summarizes the situation in his review of "Some Recent Books on Personality" in the *Psychological Bulletin* (1954),

> The experimentalists' efforts are now all too often vitiated by absorption in details and specious variables . . . they seem to have narrowed rather than broadened the breadth of their conceptualization and pursuits. There is a danger that the hypothetico-deductive method will be lost to them for lack of a theoretical vehicle to carry it. The clinical group presents the problem differently. They have not forsaken scientific method—principally because they have never adopted it. Although their explanatory systems have rarely lacked breadth, they have continuously lacked evidence.

To a certain extent the uninspiring condition of the psychology of personality today is a consequence of its diverse origins. The clinic must be credited with the major continuing impetus to its development, and most of the principal personality theories developed out of intimate contact with the treatment of patients suffering from ailments which gradually were perceived to be psychological in nature. Academic psychology, however, also has made extensive contributions to the study of personality, not only through individual theorizing and experimentation, but also through university clinics that were intended as much for the exploration of personality as for therapeutic purposes. Finally, a third major source of contributions has been the increasingly frequent studies making use of entirely objective test batteries and sophisticated statistical techniques, such as factor analysis. Results from these three areas of endeavor are at the present time almost entirely isolated and unintegrated.

There is a further obvious reason for the relative lack of any real progress in this area. Whatever their theoretical persuasion, personality psychologists are primarily interested in organismic variables; they lack the relatively greater opportunities for rigor available to students of learning or perception, where important stimulus and response variables are far more amenable to measurement and control; their concepts must be derived from data which are alternately manifested, imperfectly perceived, and multiply determined.

In addition to its varied origins, the numerous close affiliations of personality psychology with social and motivation psychology, with sociology and anthropology, and most important of all, with psychoanalytic theory preclude even a superficial attempt at comprehensiveness. There is, however, a unique and invaluable set of five volumes, *The Index of Psychoanalytic Writings* (1956-) compiled by Alexander Grinstein, which is claimed to list "every book, article, monograph, abstract and review published by over 5000 psychoanalytic writers in the last 60 years." The availability of this monumental reference work makes it somewhat less difficult to omit in this survey extended references to the important psychoanalytic influences on personality theory and research.

Sigmund Freud, of course, may not be omitted; there is probably no branch of the psychological literature on personality which is not immeasurably in his debt. He is the unique exception to the otherwise accurate characterization of earlier psychological writers as men who today go honored but unread. His *Psychopathology of Everyday Life* (1914), which first appeared in German in 1901, remains a compelling introduction to the psychoanalytic orientation, while such classics as *The Interpretation of Dreams* (1913, translated from the 3d German edition) continue to appear in new editions and to enjoy wide readership among psychologists and non-psychologists alike. While all of Freud's works are now available in a recently completed *Standard Edition of the Complete Psychological Works* (1953), edited by James Strachey, it may be that the most convincing evidences of Freud's ability to patiently and carefully arrive at meaningful analyses of his patients' behavior are contained in the five volumes of his *Collected Papers* (1948-1950), works which deal with individual case histories and with specific concepts and problems. Written with characteristic clarity and felicity of expression, these papers convey both the excitement at new discoveries and the cautious reserve which Freud evinced as he mulled over tentative formulations about the genesis and organization of personality.

The works of Carl G. Jung, considered by some to be second in importance only to those of Freud, have had a relatively limited effect upon contemporary psychology. Only a few of Jung's concepts have been adopted for general use, and even in these cases the use is far less systematic than is the case with terminology borrowed from Freud. The publication of Jung's *Collected Works* (1953-) undoubtedly makes his ideas more accessible, but even if they become more familiar with it, it is doubtful that a system so distinctly different in tenor and in basic assumptions will find much acceptance among contemporary psychologists.

Continued contact with the id, ego, and superego has established a certain tolerance for the familiar tripartite model of personality structure, and the center of gravity of American psychology most surely has undergone a pronounced shift toward interest in the irrational dynamics of human behavior as a consequence of the substantive merits of Freud's work. On the other hand, the more optimistic "American" view of man as a creative organism with a potential for rational, healthy self-realization (evident in such works as Carl R. Rogers' *Client-centered Therapy; its Current Practice, Implications, and Theory,* 1951) has undoubtedly had a reciprocal influence, so that recent psychoanalytic theory shows signs of more limited concern with the forces of the id and a greater interest in the constructive aspects of the ego. The appearance of Ernest Jones's excellent three-volume biography, *The Life and Work of Sigmund Freud* (1953-1957), a measured analysis of Freud's work within the context of the intellectual influences of the day, of Calvin S. Hall and Gardner Lindzey's clear and concise expositions in their chapter on "Psychoanalytic Theory and Its Applications in the Social Sciences" in Gardner Lindzey's (ed.) *Handbook of Social Psychology* (1954), and of Hall's lucid if uncritical introductory volume, *A Primer of Freudian Psychology* (1954), have also materially contributed to the rapprochement between Freudian and academic psychologies of personality and to a general abatement of the longstanding brouhaha.

The contributions of colleagues and disciples who attempted to further develop psychoanalytic theory within the Freudian framework, as well as those of one-time associates who broke with Freud and developed theories of their own, are summarized in Gerald S. Blum's *Psychoanalytic Theories of Personality* (1953), in which the stages of psychosexual development form multiple foci for the exposition of similarities and contrasts, and in Ruth Munroe's *Schools of Psychoanalytic Thought* (1955), a volume notable for its thoughtful and well balanced presentations.

Four full decades were to pass after Freud began his investigations before contributions by academic psychologists to the study of personality appeared in any significant number. Gordon W. Allport's *Personality; A Psychological Interpretation* (1937) attracted considerable attention for its indictment of what Allport claimed was an historical or genetic bias in psychoanalytic theory and for its determined insistence upon the importance of the contemporary motivation of the unique and cardinal individual. A second important volume by a Harvard author was Henry A. Murray's collaborative *Explorations in Personality* (1938). In addition to the yeoman's service it performed by freely introducing psychoanalytic notions into academic settings, this work made popular a number of novel diagnostic techniques, among them the Thematic Apperception Test (TAT), and opened important new possibilities for the empirical assessment of personality variables. A two-volume handbook on *Personality and the Behavior Disorders* (1944), edited by Joseph McVicker Hunt, represented a serious effort to bring together the diverse theoretical and experimental contributions to the studies of personality that were then beginning to appear in increasing numbers. Although largely out of date at this writing, Hunt's handbook has hardly been supplanted by any more recent publication. Newer contributions in this general tradition include David C. McClelland's *Personality* (1951), Julian B. Rotter's *Social Learning and Clinical Psychology* (1954), and George A. Kelly's two volumes on *The Psychology of Personal Constructs* (1955).

The chief argument of advocates of an objective, factor analytic approach to personality is the great potential superiority of the method over the usual intuitive alternative as a taxonomic tool for the identification of primary personality dimensions. The point is forcefully advanced in Raymond B. Cattell's *Personality: A Systematic, Theoretical, and Factual Study* (1950), and Cattell presents considerable evidence for several personality factors which show "reasonable stability" in a report on "The Principal Replicated Factors Discovered in Objective Personality Tests," published in the *Journal of Abnormal and Social Psychology* (1955). Hans J. Eysenck, author of *The Scientific Study of Personality* (1952) and *The Structure of Human Personality* (1953), is another strong proponent of the technique, and his article on "The Logical Basis of Factor Analysis" in the *American Psychologist* (1953) is an outstanding exposition of its possibilities. On other grounds, however, some of Eysenck's published findings have provoked sharp reproaches; the *Psychological Bulletin* for 1956 contained two separate, detailed, and outspoken attacks (by Milton Rokeach and Charles Hanley, and by Richard Christie) on putatively critical failings of several recent reports.

The advent of multivariate and multidimensional statistical techniques initially seemed to hold great promise for social and clinical psychology as well as for research on personality. They appeared to afford rigor and precision to analyses of the patterns and manifolds with which investigators in these areas had to deal. At the present time, it is doubtful that these objectives have been attained. While it is difficult to find agreement on the relative merits of factor analytic contributions to the study of personality, however, they have probably had two permanent and very beneficial negative effects. In the first place, they have by contrast focused attention on the ideological rather than scientific status of most of the more popular speculations which currently are classified as personality "theory." In the second place, they have made imperative renewed efforts to come up with alternate solutions to the basic measurement problems which many would suggest are being mistakenly finessed by the assumptions required for the factor analytic model, and for the powerful but stringently demanding linear statistical models in general use at the present time.

A well-balanced and representative selection of currently focal orientations to personality is contained in *Theories of Personality* (1957), by Calvin S. Hall and Gardner Lindzey, including sympathetic presentations of several important positions which could not be considered here. The appropriate chapters of recent numbers of the *Annual Review of Psychology* are also strongly recommended, however, for their considered and detailed if distinctly less cheery analyses of current theorizing and research on personality and its assessment.

Motivation and Emotion–Many overtones resulting from the varied origins and comprehensive aspirations of personality psychology find echoes in the literature of the even more recent and less well-defined area of motivation. Best understood as a collection of theory and research drawn from several distinct areas, the literature of motivation psychology is frequently the work of men who principally were learning, physiological, social, or personality psychologists and who viewed motivation as a limited topic, each within the context of his own primary frame of reference. The generalized, interrelated problems of the intensity, direction, and maintenance of behavior, which today form the focus for a growing interest in motivation *per se,* have only recently come to be conceptualized in this unitary fashion and investigated with the integrated resources of the older areas of research. Despite increased interaction among the several approaches to motivational problems, however, there exists no generally accepted single orientation as yet, and so it may be best to eschew Procrustean methods here and to review representative contributions with reference to the original points of view.

Psychologists have generally considered emotion and motivation closely related. The two are generally associated in modern theories, but no more so than in the very much earlier *Outlines of Psychology* (1902), in which Wilhelm Wundt argued that "all feelings, even those of relatively indifferent character, contain in some degree an effort towards or away from some end." Perhaps because of their preoccupation with the description of conscious content, most early investigators were concerned primarily with feelings and emotions; relatively little attention was devoted by academic psychology to the dynamics of striving. *The Psychology of Pleasantness and Unpleasantness* (1932), by John G. Beebe-Center, and *Feeling and Emotion* (1937), by Harry N. Gardiner, Ruth C. Metcalf, and Beebe-Center summarize the generally inconclusive history of these investigations and also contain excellent accounts of pre-psychological analyses of these phenomena. David Rapaport's *Emotions and Memory* (1942) is notable for its very careful and closely reasoned examination of the extensive literature of this somewhat more delimited area of endeavor. Discouraged, perhaps, by the meager returns obtained for the effort expended on them, psychologists have turned in other directions, and experimental studies of feeling and emotion in the traditional contexts have disappeared almost completely from the current literature.

The persistent probings of physiological psychologists, on the other hand, have frequently been well rewarded, and considerable importance is now quite generally attached to investigations of the biological bases of emotion and motivation. Knowledge of the physiological changes accompanying motivational states such as hunger and thirst has advanced considerably, and its significance is well recognized. To a somewhat lesser extent, psychologists also are now aware of the extent to which the primary motivational mechanisms can be conceptualized almost entirely at the physiological level; Eliot Stellar, in an article on "The Physiology of Motivation" in the *Psychological Review* (1954), actually goes so far as to theorize that the amount of motivated behavior can be viewed as in large part an immediate function "of the amount of activity in certain excitatory centers of the hypothalamus." Finally, some of the most provocative and exciting attempts to analyze the complexities of psychological organization and behavior, as for instance, Karl S. Lashley's chapter on "The Problem of Serial Order in Behavior" in Lloyd A. Jeffress' (ed.) *Cerebral Mechanisms in Behavior; The Hixon Symposium* (1951), or Donald O. Hebb's recent discussion of "Drives and the C. N. S. (Conceptual Nervous System)" in the *Psychological Review* for 1955, have been based to a considerable extent upon thoughtful extrapolations from recent neurophysiological discoveries. Physiological psychology necessarily must receive relatively short shrift in an essay such as this, but the broad importance of a number of recent physiological developments for any general behavioral science cannot be overemphasized, and social scientists of whatever persuasion who are watching for new breakthroughs could do worse than to keep an occasional eye cocked in this direction.

Walter B. Cannon's *Bodily Changes in Pain, Hunger, Fear and Rage* (2d ed., 1929) must be counted among the classical contributions to the physiological psychology of emotional states. Cannon also has contributed to the basic concepts of modern motivational theory. His concept of homeostasis, postulating the maintenance of bodily equilibria at optimal levels as a principal basis for behavior, is set forth in *The Wisdom of the Body* (1932), and has since been elaborated by some more recent authors who argue for the utility of regarding all motivated behavior as homeostatic in a broader sense. Donald B. Lindsley's chapter on "Emotion" in S. Smith Stevens' (ed.) *Handbook of Experimental Psychology* (1951) also makes excellent use of physiological findings as bases for some far-reaching propositions about motivation and emotion. An outstanding analysis of a wide range of physiological data, together with a number of promising hypotheses about the physiological concomitants of an equally wide range of important psychological processes, is to be found in Ernst Gellhorn's *Physiological Foundations of Neurology and Psychiatry* (1953). This volume also provides considerable support for the increasing tendency to accept physiological mechanisms as possible alternative sources of many motivational and emotional pathologies which quite recently were to be interpreted only in developmental, dynamic, or interpersonal terms. None of the recent neurological discoveries are of greater potential importance to the progressive improvement of the understanding of the brain mechanisms underlying emotion and motivation, however, than the striking behavioral results of direct electrical stimulation obtained by James Olds and reported in his description of "A Physiological Study of Reward" in David C. McClelland's (ed.) *Studies in Motivation* (1955), and in his chapter on "Physiological Mechanisms of Reward" in Marshall R. Jones' (ed.) *Nebraska Symposium on Motivation* (1955), which is the second volume of *Current Theory and Research in Motivation, A Symposium* (1953-) issued by the Psychology Department of the University of Nebraska.

With relatively little detailed attention to the concurrent developments in physiological psychology, learning psychologists on the one hand and social psychologists on the other also have gradually produced extensive literatures on motivation.

Learning theorists have varied considerably among themselves for several decades on the relative utilities of several plausible conceptualizations of motivational variables, but these differences have provoked an impressive body of experimental studies which have increasingly served to refine and sharpen recent formulations. Many of these studies are discussed in Leo J. Postman's scholarly critique of "The History and Present Status of the Law of Effect" in the *Psychological Bulletin* (1947). Much of the most recent material relevant to the motivational assumptions inherent in current views on learning is analyzed with comparable care and discernment in *Modern Learning Theory* (1954), by William K. Estes and others.

Anxiety as a basic motivational variable has a history of close association with theory and research from a predominantly psychoanalytic point of view. Anxiety operationally defined in animals has also been the object of a number of interesting investigations by psychologists primarily associated with the study of learning. For a time, these two uses of the term seemed to suggest it as a bridge concept between the two areas, as in Orval Hobart Mowrer's *Learning Theory and Personality Dynamics* (1950). The latest discussions of the concept, however, such as the excellent paper on "Traumatic Avoidance Learning: the Principles of Anxiety Conservation and Partial Irreversibility," by Richard L. Solomon and Lyman C. Wynne in the *Psychological Review* (1954), by and large have been somewhat more restricted to the context of animal studies.

A number of learning psychologists have become quite interested in certain classes of environmental parameters as important determinants of behavior. A series of stimulating papers from the laboratories of Harry F. Harlow, Kay C. Montgomery, Edward L. Walker, and others have proven conclusively that such factors as environmental novelty, variability, and complexity can account for major portions of behavioral variance. Further investigations in these directions seem destined to make important new additions to our understanding of motivation and may well force extensive reformulation of many current conceptions.

Several European ethologists, studying comparative behavior as a function of habitat, agree on the importance of environmental stimuli for the maintenance and direction of behavior, but nonetheless accord them a radically different role, that of releasers for innate patterns of activity. Although these scientists have been reporting their findings for some two decades, the body of work came to the general attention of American psychologists only with the publication in English of Nikolaas Tinbergen's *The Study of Instinct* (1951) and of a slender and charmingly written if scarcely less provocative volume, *King Solomon's Ring* (1952), by Konrad Z. Lorenz. For a short time thereafter, the ethologists' findings created a series of obvious disturbances in American thinking about motivation and learning which were given voice by papers such as William S. Verplanck's "Since Learned Behavior is Innate, and Vice Versa, What Now?" in the *Pychological Review* (1955).

The ethologists' investigations have no doubt resulted in a more general awareness of the elaborate possibilities for innate patterning of behavior in lower species. They also very likely have contributed, together with the work of Donald O. Hebb and his associates, to a renewed interest in studies of environmental interaction with early learning and development, such as those discussed by Frank A. Beach and Julian Jaynes in their review of "Effects of Early Experience upon the Behavior of Animals," in the *Psychological Bulletin* (1954), and by William R. Thompson's paper on "Early Environment—Its Importance for Later Behavior," in Paul H. Hoch and Joseph Zubin's (eds.) *Psychopathology of Childhood* (1955). There has, however, been no marked increase in psychological investigations of the implications of the ethological position to date, perhaps because of a lack of shared underlying orientations, and it would be premature to conclude that the ethologists' studies additionally have had anything but a very restricted effect upon the fundamental concepts of American motivation psychology.

Emphasis on the major importance of environmental determinants of motivation, a recent tendency in learning theory, has traditionally been a central feature of social psychological formulations, where present and past situational cues, their perception, and their communication are principal antecedents of behavioral direction. Learning theorists, ethologists, and social psychologists all have been concerned with somewhat different aspects of the environment, of course, and it is particularly difficult to deal with current social psychological concepts relevant to motivation apart from the context of group dynamics and interaction. While consideration of these concepts will therefore be deferred until the general consideration of social psychological literature, their influence upon much current motivation theory must be emphasized at this point; Gardner Lindzey's (ed.) *Handbook of Social Psychology* (1954) contains a wealth of material relevant to motivational problems, particularly in Gordon W. Allport's excellent introductory chapter on "The Historical Background of Modern Social Psychology," the chapters on "Field Theory in Social Psychology" by Morton Deutsch and on "Role Theory" by Theodore R. Sarbin, and in practically all of the chapters of the second volume.

Donald O. Hebb's examination of the various capacities in which environmental stimuli may determine behavior is but one of the outstanding features of his remarkable investigation of *The Organization of Behavior* (1949). Hebb's thoughtful integration of fundamental components of Gestalt theory into an associationist framework which itself incorporates many of the most important neurophysiological discoveries and speculations results in a creative theory of behavior with far-reaching implications for the study of motivation. The really unique merit of this book, however, may well be its admittedly speculative but systematic and integrated approach to the diverse and complex functions of the organism in terms of a unified and comprehensive quasi-neurological theory of behavior. Even when compared with such established orientations as the Freudian and Hullian prototypes, there is good reason to consider an expectancy formulation such as Hebb's, particularly after its modification in Hebb's recent paper on "Drives and the C. N. S. (Conceptual Nervous System)" in the *Psychological Review* (1955), as one of the most promising bases for the further development of our knowledge of human motivation and behavior.

If the literature of our time be considered *in toto,* there are many reasons to select as its most important source of motivational notions the writings of the psychoanalytic theorists, from Freud to the present time. This influence is illustrated in other chapters in this volume as well as in our previous consideration of the psychology of personality. In addition to the several psychoanalytic models and the many specific insights into personality structure and development which Freud bequeathed to posterity, he also gave wide currency to two basic assumptions which have since become fundamental tenets for many students of human motivation. First, Freud conceived of elemental motives which were in some sense inaccessible to deliberate observation, and the wide dissemination of his persuasive and convincing arguments for this position no doubt have mutually reinforced the now quite popular tendency to give up the introspective examination of conscious motivational content as a bad job. In the second place, Freud insisted that all behavior was motivated. The effects of this position have probably been at least as important. It makes the study of motivation in many ways synonymous with the operational study of behavior, much as the psychology of personality has been conceived on occasion; the position has no doubt considerably increased the importance attributed to studies of human motivation, as interest in the measurement of human motivation gradually has differentiated out of a more diffuse clinical and academic concern for the structure and dynamics of personality.

David C. McClelland, John W. Atkinson, and their many collaborators have made an interesting attempt to use a modification of the Thematic Apperception Test as a measure of basic underlying motivational tendencies, on the assumption that relatively freely associated thought content might prove a useful source for inferences about characteristic strivings of individuals. The earliest of their numerous exploratory studies and attempts to validate such measures are described in *The Achievement Motive* (1953), by McClelland and others. More recent reports are included among the papers in *Studies in Motivation* (1955), edited by McClelland.

If a Freudian interest in basic and unconscious motives is one of the dominant notes of modern motivation psychology, the recent appearance of an increasing number of investigations of rational and probabilistic choice behavior seems a promising contrapuntal theme. The interested hearing accorded this work may in part be due to the affiliation with promising new mathematical developments which is noted in *Mathematical Thinking in the Social Sciences* (1954), edited by Paul F. Lazarsfeld, and in *Decision Processes* (1954), edited by Robert M. Thrall, Clyde H. Coombs, and Robert L. Davis. Ward Edwards' "The Theory of Decision Making" in the *Psychological Bulletin* (1954) is an excellent review of the relevant psychological material.

An interesting sampling of other approaches to motivational theory and research may be found in McClelland's *Studies in Motivation* (1955), and detailed presentations of many important current lines of investigation which could not be considered here are contained in recent volumes of the annually appearing *Nebraska Symposium on Motivation,* edited by Marshall R. Jones.

Social Psychology—Although a few psychologists principally interested in perception, learning, personality, or motivation have attempted to expand their conceptual frames of reference into general theories of behavior, most typically limit their investigations to the particular aspect of the total interaction of organism and environment with which they are immediately concerned. While much the same thing is true of many social psychologists as well, social psychology as a whole really involves all aspects of this interaction, but only when it occurs among objects having some social significance. The perception of lines differing in length, for example, is hardly of concern to a social psychologist unless, as in Solomon E. Asch's investigation of the "Effects of Group Pressure upon the Modification and Distortion of Judgments," reported in Guy E. Swanson, Theodore M. Newcomb, and Eugene L. Hartley's (eds.) *Readings in Social Psychology* (2d ed., 1952), the perceptual problem is made the focus of a situation with interpersonal implications. In analogous ways, and when other socially relevant objects are concerned, the social psychologist also investigates problems in learning, cognition, motivation, development, and personality. He therefore is subject to influences in almost all other areas in psychology, as well as being more prone than most psychologists to interact with sociologists, anthropologists, and other social scientists.

The earliest works on social psychology, as far back as Gabriel Tarde's *Les Lois de l'imitation* (1890) or Gustave LeBon's *The Crowd* (2d) ed., 1897) bear more than a taste of the clinic. While Tarde ascribes social behavior to "imitation" rather than to "suggestion," which is regarded by LeBon as the critical concept, the two are largely agreed on the impulsivity and almost pathological irrationality of group behavior.

A decidedly different orientation marked William McDougall's *An Introduction to Social Psychology* (1908). Inspired by the Darwinian cosmogony, McDougall impressed the concept of instinct and founded upon it a theory of social behavior. Nativism now became the popular basis for a decade of systematic social psychology. Lists of instincts proliferated without modesty, and the term increasingly came to be applied to all supposed uniformities of human conduct, with benign disregard for the presence or absence of evidence of their innateness.

The spectacle of so massive an accord upon such slender foundations proved too tempting. "Are There Any Instincts?" Knight Dunlap asked in the *Journal of Abnormal and Social Psychology* (1919), and amidst resounding "noes!" from the new environmentalists and from anthropologically inspired adherents of cultural relativism, the idol toppled and was heard from no more. For as Edwin B. Holt, himself no mean defender of the opposite extreme, was to exclaim somewhat later in his *Animal Drive and the Learning Process* (1931),

> . . . man is impelled to action, it is said, by his instincts. If he goes with his fellows, it is the 'herd instinct' which actuates him; if he walks alone, it is the 'anti-social instinct'; if he fights, it is the instinct of 'pugnacity'; if he defers to another, it is the instinct of 'self-abasement'; if he twiddles his thumbs, it is the thumb-twiddling instinct; if he does not twiddle his thumbs, it is the thumb-not-twiddling instinct. Thus everything is explained with the facility of magic—word magic.

An associationist orientation to the objective study of behavior, increasingly becoming characteristic of the psychology of learning, made considerable headway among social psychologists with the publication in 1924 of Floyd H. Allport's *Social Psychology*, which borrowed concepts from individual learning theory and then extrapolated from them to explanations of group phenomena in terms of multi-person aggregates. In addition to many valuable hypotheses about group behavior, Allport also contributed to the growing awareness among social psychologists of the potentialities of empirical investigation. Somewhat later, Neal E. Miller and John Dollard, substituting concepts derived from Hullian learning theory for the principles used by Allport, made another interesting attempt in their *Social Learning and Imitation* (1941) to analyze such social psychological phenomena as the transmission of complex social behaviors from a somewhat similar point of view.

Although concepts from learning theory have found extensive employment in certain areas of social psychology, the field is no doubt far more indebted in its current theoretical and research orientation to the work of Gestalt psychologists and of others associated with the essentials of the Gestalt position. Muzafer Sherif's *The Psychology of Social Norms* (1936), which pointed out the influence of cultural factors upon social perception, emphasized the restructuring of cognitive organization which occurred as previously external social norms were internalized and became organizing frames of reference for behavior. Such concepts as cognitive restructuring are far more frequently invoked to explain the acquisition and manifestation of new forms of social behavior than principles of conditioning.

Like Sherif and the Gestalt psychologists, Kurt Lewin also believed that behavior was best understood in terms of the conceptualization of the total psychological situation or field. In volumes such as *A Dynamic Theory of Personality* (1935) and *Field Theory in Social Science* (1951), Lewin's arguments against theories of behavior framed with reference to historical rather than contemporary causation and acts instead of intentions were made known to American psychology. The extraordinary influence of his writings made them vehicles for what amounted to a drastic reformulation of the metatheory of much of social psychology. It was Lewin, furthermore, who made explicit and convincing the motivational propositions inherent in Gestalt and field-theoretic thinking about dynamic, self-equilibrating psychological systems, and the vectorial terminology he developed to describe such motivational processes not only incited a great deal of research on such now classic problems as the recall of interrupted tasks (the Zeigarnik effect) and the level of aspiration, but also remains a clear antecedent of many of the interactional formulations of current social psychology.

Among the most recent systematic presentations of social psychological theory and research which are sympathetic to Gestalt and field-theoretic orientations are *Theory and Problems of Social Psychology* (1948), by David Krech and Richard S. Crutchfield, and Solomon E. Asch's *Social Psychology* (1952).

Since the psychoanalytic literature typically is concerned with the history and present status of the needs of the individual in interaction with the external, primarily social, pressures affecting his development, there might seem to be little there which is not of immediate interest to social psychologists. This was the position Sigmund Freud himself took in the most explicitly pertinent of his writings, *Group Psychology and the Analysis of the Ego* (1922). Freud felt that individual and group psychology were being divided on the basis of the size of the units considered, a factor he held to be quite trivial, and he went so far as to suggest that large group phenomena which in his day were being explained by concepts such as "herd instinct" or "group mind" might be understood far more adequately and parsimoniously in terms of concepts derived from the study of the smallest and most primary group, i.e., the family.

Social psychologists apparently remained unconvinced, however. As Calvin S. Hall and Gardner Lindzey demonstrate in their analysis of "Psychoanalytic Theory and its Applications in the Social Sciences," in Gardner Lindzey's (ed.) *Handbook of Social Psychology,* the popular opinion that theory and research in social psychology owe a decided debt to psychoanalytic insemination is ill-supported by actual evidence of paternity. Although Junius F. Brown's *Psychology and the Social Order* (1936) contained not only an excellent summary of psychoanalytic theory but also an analysis of its relation to social psychology, Freudian concepts two decades later generally receive only superficial and fragmentary consideration. In the few instances where psychoanalytic thinking is incorporated in an integrated and detailed fashion, as in Theodore M. Newcomb's *Social Psychology* (1950), it typically derives from the more socially and culturally oriented analysts, such as Erich Fromm, Karen Horney, or Harry S. Sullivan, presumably because these theorists have discarded the biological bases of orthodox psychoanalytic theory and therefore are more easily translated into social psychological terms.

A good part of the major impact created by Theodor W. Adorno, Else Frenkel-Brunswik, Daniel J. Levinson, and R. Nevitt Sanford's *The Authoritarian Personality* (1950) may be traced back to its psychoanalytic orientations and to the far-reaching implications of the hypotheses they inspired. Undertaken as an investigation of anti-Semitism and prejudice, the study attempted to demonstrate the dependence of ideologies and fundamental attitudes upon specific patterns of personality structure and child rearing practices. Because of the profound social importance of the subject, the study attracted considerable attention, and a number of careful and thorough methodological critiques were made public in *Studies in the Scope and Method of "The Authoritarian Personality"* (1954), edited by Richard Christie and Marie Jahoda. Although generous to a fault in their praise of the "importance" and "impact" of the earlier work, the contributors tended to conclude after their methodological evaluations that, in the words of one, "almost nothing stands up of the original study."

Mortimer Brewster Smith, Jerome S. Bruner, and Robert W. White have studied a series of case histories for clues to the relationships between the attitudes men hold and their underlying personality dynamics and structure in *Opinions and Personality* (1956). Somewhat less inclined to strictly psychoanalytic interpretations of the antecedents of attitude than *The Authoritarian Personality,* these analyses resemble more the admirable didactic portraits of White's *Lives in Progress* (1952).

As is evident from its central position in the studies just discussed, the concept of attitude has maintained its vitality despite changes in the interests of social psychologists which have long since retired contemporaries like "instinct" and "imitation" to pasture. Although it has never attained the exclusive position implied by William I. Thomas and Florian Znaniecki, who in their classic five-volume study of *The Polish Peasant in Europe and America* (1918-20) defined social psychology as "the scientific study of attitudes," it remains, as Gordon W. Allport writes in his chapter on "The Historical Background of Modern Social Psychology" in Gardner Lindzey's (ed.) *Handbook of Social Psychology* (1954), "probably the most distinctive and indispensable concept in contemporary American social psychology."

The reasons for this popularity are easy to discern. Allport points out that the term is sufficiently flexible so as to presuppose no systematic position on the origins of attitudes, on the extent of genetic determination, or on limitations as to the kinds of objects to which they may apply. On the other hand, one wonders about the real utility of a concept which lumps together so diverse a range of phenomena. The putative similarities not only are not demonstrated thereby, but on the contrary become practically inaccessible to investigation just because they have been assumed. The cheery applicability of the term to everything from motor sets to life philosophies occasionally smacks of the successful political candidate who derives his popularity from those freely pledged commitments to every local interest which collectively make it impossible for him to satisfy any one of them.

While the numerous surveys, polls, and attitude studies of recent decades have not been distinguished for the permanent value of their contributions to the foundations of social psychology, one set of volumes, *Studies in Social Psychology in World War II*, must be accounted an outstanding exception to the general rule. Three of these volumes, *The American Soldier: Adjustment During Army Life* (1949), *The American Soldier: Combat and its Aftermath* (1949), and *Measurement and Prediction* (1950) are by Samuel A. Stouffer and his collaborators; the fourth, *Experiments on Mass Communication* (1949), is the work of Carl I. Hovland, Arthur A. Lumsdaine and Fred D. Sheffield. In addition to providing a fund of data about important practical problems of military existence, these volumes also made significant contributions to knowledge of fundamental importance about such topics as the problem of leadership in a democracy, as well as to various branches of research methodology.

A novel and rather promising recent addition to attitude methodology is Charles E. Osgood's *semantic differential.* Essentially an ingenious technique permitting assessment of the connotative meanings of concepts, the *semantic differential* also has proven useful in measuring the attitudes of individuals in terms of their idiosyncratic assessments of critical objects and symbols. A number of interesting explorations with the method are described in *The Measurement of Meaning* (1957), by Osgood, George J. Suci, and Percy H. Tannenbaum.

Social psychology, like general psychology, has analyzed its variables predominantly in terms of effects upon individuals. Studies of social perception, cognition, and attitude traditionally have found the individual a convenient unit of study. Recently, however, a number of psychologists have turned to the group, and have tried to analyze group formation, stability, communication, conflict, and change in terms of group laws, largely without reference to individual variables. The effects of Lewinian influences upon many of these investigations is evident throughout *Group Dynamics* (1953), edited by Dorwin Cartwright and Alvin Zander. Most of the relevant research is analyzed in an impressive and integrated fashion in the chapters on "Group Psychology and the Phenomena of Interaction" in the second volume of Lindzey's *Handbook of Social Psychology* (1954).

Processes of communication are of fundamental concern to most students of group dynamics, but they have been the objects of many other investigations as well. Most of these analyses, however, have not attempted to go beyond the pale of verbal communication, in part because of its greater accessibility to study, even though as clinical psychologists have long been aware, a very great deal is heard which never is put in words. And this in fact might almost be the essence of a slim but evocative study of *The Voice of Neurosis* (1954), by Paul J. Moses. Another attempt to broach the bounds of language is *Nonverbal Communication; Notes on the Visual Perception of Human Relations* (1956), by Jurgen Ruesch and Weldon Kees. Although neither of these volumes pretends to be more than suggestive, they do well in calling attention to the importance of the music which accompanies the words. Such volumes also raise the possibility that information theory may one day be able to contribute importantly to the psychology of social communication, but little has been attempted in this direction to date.

The reader who wishes a broader introduction to social psychology, including the many topics which are omitted entirely from this hardly adequate survey, is well advised to consider *Research Methods in the Behavioral Sciences* (1953), edited by Leon Festinger and Daniel Katz, and of course the many other comprehensive and authoritative chapters of *The Handbook of Social Psychology* (1954).

On the Need to Apply What You Have Not Got. It is customary to divide psychology into the "pure" and the "applied," although in truth the result is precious little light and a really uncomfortable amount of heat. There is little controversy about the very considerable experimental literature on practical problems concerning efficient design of industrial and military apparatus and the like, since the experimental manipulations are hardly different from those encountered in other laboratory investigations. But experimental manipulation is more or less impossible throughout much of clinical, counseling, industrial, and educational psychology.

It has been held that even were scientific rigor attainable in applied activities, it would be misdirected, if not positively harmful, to require that the applied psychologist adhere strictly to the usually prescribed procedures. The engineer who knows his physics still tinkers, and the corpus of knowledge which academic psychology offers as aid frequently looks rather closer to alchemy than to physics.

Several considerations weaken this analogy. In the first place, the engineer's tools are more valid and reliable than those of the applied psychologist. The best of the objective psychological measuring instruments are relatively crude, and there also is a pronounced tendency, particularly among clinical psychologists, to rely heavily on the so-called "projective tests," notably the Rorschach inkblot test and the TAT. These presume that responses to the unstructured test stimuli will be based on the attitudes and underlying feelings which the individual "projects" into them. The resulting responses are analyzed for putative insights into the dynamics of the individual, the ultimate rationale for the procedure frequently deriving from the clinician's subjective convictions about its utility. So employed, these measures are at best diagnostic aids, without scientifically demonstrated validity in the overwhelming majority of cases.

In the second place, engineers get more feedback. If the clinician plays a hunch, and utilizes a given technique at a certain point, it is he who has to decide whether the final outcome should be characterized as a success or a failure. If the engineer plays a hunch in building a bridge, it is somewhat easier to outline objective techniques to determine whether the bridge will perform to some objectively defined criterion. And published analyses of clinical predictions, such as *The Prediction of Performance in Clinical Psychology* (1951), by E. Lowell Kelly and Donald W. Fiske, and Paul E. Meehl's very fine survey and evaluation of *Clinical Versus Statistical Prediction* (1954), hardly provide any reason to believe that clinical hunches are in any way improvements over entirely objective test estimates. Presumably comparable assessment procedures in other applied areas fare no better. E. Lowell Kelly writes in his survey of "Theory and Techniques of Assessment," in the *Annual Review of Psychology* (1954):

> The curious state of affairs wherein the most widely (and confidently) used techniques are those for which there is little or no evidence of predictive validity is indeed a phenomenon appropriate for study by social psychologists. This reviewer can only assume that in the absence of evidence of their predictive validity, such techniques must serve an important function other than assessment. Is it that they serve primarily to reduce threats of anxiety for persons confronted with the necessity of making significant decisions in the lives of individual clients or patients? Lacking dependable validated techniques for making the predictions essential to wise decisions, it should not be surprising if persons responsible for professional decisions were to gravitate to the use of techniques which yield a relatively large amount of information concerning the subject, regardless of how irrelevant most of the information may be. Add to extensity of information provided by the technique a theoretical orientation sufficiently flexible to permit using the information in a manner which seems "to explain" any subject, and we have what would seem to be the necessary ingredients for an anxiety-reducing prescription!

Edward J. Shoben, Jr., points out much the same syndrome of social demand, the necessity for critical decisions in the absence of requisite knowledge, and the consequent but unfortunate result in his review of "Some Recent Books on Counseling and Adjustment" in the *Psychological Bulletin* (1955). As he puts it, the

. . . psychologist himself often is motivated to seize desperately on any idea or technique that has the appearance of usefulness. When the chips are down, as they generally are in professional practice, scepticism about one's own resources is a luxury that few can afford.

We have a paradox. How are you to apply what you have not got? The interim solution is clear, if unsatisfactory. The work must be done, and certainly there are no people better qualified, by dint of their experience and training, to accomplish whatever we currently are capable of doing than those now engaged in this work. In the long run, as has been happening in medicine, intensive research will gradually improve the situation. The primary interim consideration is well stated by Shoben. "To say that professional practice must rely on hunch and accumulations of uncontrolled experience is to say nothing derogatory *so long as one knows what is happening.*"

Recent volumes of the *Annual Review of Psychology* clearly attest to the scientific merit of a growing number of applied psychological investigations. The great portion of the applied literature does not fall in this category, however, and so rather than attempt an inadequate summary of its principal features, the present essay recommends consideration of the appropriate chapters of the *Annual Review of Psychology* volumes.

Measurement and Statistics—When in 1940 Jerome S. Bruner and Gordon W. Allport published their survey of "Fifty Years of Change in American Psychology" in the *Psychological Bulletin,* the most striking alteration they reported was the marked increase in the use of statistics as an adjunct to psychological research. At present, in fact, no major American journal of experimental psychology normally will print a research report which lacks as a bare minimum descriptive statistical summaries of the results. As Bruner and Allport suggest, this value which modern American psychologists attach to numbers undoubtedly "reflects the preoccupation with quantitative standards of excellence characteristic of most American cultural activities." But at least as important, one imagines, is the real increase in scientific efficiency which results from the rational utilization of descriptive and test statistics. All scientific knowledge is probabilistic, "best guess" knowledge. The future direction not only of the individual scientist but also of the whole scientific enterprise must be determined by best guesses from past research. In imprecise sciences such as psychology, with their large uncontrolled sources of error variance, the accurate estimation of the best guess can only be described as crucial.

The research psychologist is a gambler. He wants to maximize his chances of coming out ahead. Where the design of the next experiment hinges upon the results of the last one, the most accurate guess as to what is associated with what is most likely in the long run to lead to the most fruitful results. Since all psychologists profit from the sharpening of best guesses, it is not hard to see why attention to measurement theory and statistics has increased phenomenally; it seems a most rational and appropriate form of behavior.

The conventional uses of statistics are very well summarized in two excellent recent texts, *Statistical Inference* (1953), by Helen M. Walker and Joseph Lev, and *Design and Analysis of Experiments in Psychology and Education* (1953), by Everet F. Lindquist. The power of conventional statistics derives from the assumptions inherent in the underlying mathematical models. When these assumptions may justifiably be referred to data, the use of these statistics lends precision and generality to the conclusions drawn. The more stringent the assumptions, however, the more likely it becomes that in one or more respects the model departs from the real population parameters.

In order to avoid conventional statistical requirements in dealing with data which could not satisfy them, measurement theorists have developed a variety of "non-parametric" techniques. These forego the precision of conventional statistics in order to make possible best guesses more appropriate to the data. Keith Smith's treatment of "Distribution-free Statistical Methods and the Concept of Power Efficiency" in *Research Methods in the Behavioral Sciences* (1953), edited by Leon Festinger and Daniel Katz, is an excellent introduction to these techniques and the problems which gave rise to them. The special problems facing social psychologists, particularly when dealing with attitude data, as well as the statistical models which are applicable to such material, are briefly but cogently summarized in Bert F. Green's chapter on "Attitude Measurement" in Gardner Lindzey's (ed.) *Handbook of Social Psychology* (1954).

Factor analysis in America is intrinsically associated with Louis L. Thurstone. Thurstone's use of the technique in studies of mental abilities has yielded one of the principal collections of information in this area, and his text, *Multiple-Factor Analysis* (1947), remains one of the key volumes on the statistical bases of the method. Despite its wide acceptance as an aid to research in some areas, many applications of factor analysis continue to excite controversy. The current debate over the place of factor analytic methods in the over-all strategy of psychological investigation has, however, persuaded many psychologists to examine carefully the underlying assumptions of popular techniques of multidimensional measurement. More and more frequently we are reminded that all psychological theory about measurable variables necessarily implies a complete antecedent theory of psychological measurement, specifying in detail all assumptions and operations required in going from raw behavior to general assertions about associations among variables. Awareness of the importance of such antecedent conditions no doubt has been intensified still further by an increasingly frequent tendency in methodologically more advanced areas to make explicit the underlying mathematical bases of psychological theory, as for instance in *Stochastic Models for Learning* (1955), by Robert R. Bush and Frederick Mosteller.

A detailed exegesis of the measurement problem has been undertaken by Clyde H. Coombs in *A Theory of Psychological Scaling* (1952), and a somewhat more accessible formulation appears in his chapter on "Theory and Methods of Social Measurement" in the volume edited by Festinger and Katz. Alternate redefinitions of the aims and problems of psychological measurement in terms of information theory, decision theory, and the theory of games also have appeared; Lee J. Cronbach and Goldine C. Gleser's *Psychological Tests and Personnel Decisions* (1957) is an excellent introduction to the new insights into measurement purposes and procedures to be derived from such re-examination.

A brief consideration of current issues of *Psychometrika* (1936-) and of the statistical chapters of recent volumes of the *Annual Review of Psychology* provides convincing evidence of the present importance and real potential of these newer approaches; Lincoln E. Moses' chapter, "Statistical Theory and Research Design" (1956) actually utilizes an organization deriving from the concepts of decision theory, and it is not unreasonable to anticipate extensive reorganization of experimental methodology in the light of these developments. As Edward L. Walker observes in his survey of "Learning" in the *Annual Review of Psychology* (1957), "Psychologists, even old ones, had better accelerate their study of mathematics."

*

* *

As was suggested initially, this essay falls far short of a comprehensive or representative review of the psychological literature. A good number of areas are mentioned only in passing; others, notably the various branches of sensory psychology, applied psychology, developmental and comparative psychology, are essentially altogether omitted.

Undoubtedly few readers feel, however, that inadequate announcement of a bias against "soft" psychology should be counted among the many sins of omission. On the contrary, many no doubt believe that continual poking away at vaguely brilliant but not presently testable insights, or at highly suggestive if inconclusive experiments, has thrown out the baby with the bath. Others certainly will wonder whether a psychology foolish enough to pursue this particular primrose path would not, like the erudite major general in "The Pirates of Penzance," end up eventually with nothing more edifying than his "many cheerful facts about the square of the hypotenuse." Still others probably will wish to subscribe to the position advocated by Calvin S. Hall and Gardner Lindzey, who argue in *Theories of Personality* (1957) that by giving up inadequate theory we gain nothing, since then "we are really using implicit, personally determined, and perhaps inconsistent assumptions concerning behavior and these unidentified assumptions will determine what will be studied and how." Finally, there will be some who insist that, no matter how bad it may be from other points of view, a theory or an experiment is useful if it "provokes research."

These points of view are no straw men; it is doubtful whether they can be answered adequately. But how long, one wonders, can psychology continue to afford some of their unfortunate consequences? Consider Charles W. Eriksen's analysis of just a few of these in his review of "Personality" in the *Annual Review of Psychology* (1957).

> Research in personality as well as in psychology as a whole shows many of the characteristics of a fad. There will be a virtual flood of studies on a problem for a couple of years and then a new era or idea catches the fancy of Ph.D. candidates. . . . All too often the work is mainly demonstrational in nature. . . . And when the wave of enthusiasm moves on, there are frequently too few experimenters left to weed out and consolidate that which is theoretically useful and reproducible. . . .
>
> With some notable exceptions, research tends to be characterized by one-shot experiments rather than programmatic attacks on a problem. While this leads to suggestive hypotheses, failure to follow up in many instances leaves uncertainty as to the reproducibility of the results and unclarity as to the relevant parameters . . . there also seems to be a decrease in scholarship. Too little effort is made by many researchers to relate their findings to those of other investigators.

The net effect is a literature which in many important areas is almost totally confused, congested, and non-additive. The proverbial wheels of progress spin all right, but the gears don't mesh. And this increasingly overloaded and inefficient vehicle today faces imminent and unprecedented challenges to its limited effectiveness as a medium of communication. Today there are more psychologists than ever before; they have more money available to them for research than ever before; and with academic advancement determined by productivity, they are certain to produce more than ever before. Remember, too, the high-speed electronic computation equipment, which promises to revolutionize the kind of research we can do, also will geometrically increase our capacity to do it.

As Eriksen's critique implies, our problems are more social psychological than material; our funds, equipment, and skilled man-power are not inadequate for real advance. It would be foolish to prescribe acceptable sources of experimental hypotheses, but it is both desirable and possible to insist that research be responsible, and if possible, additive and comprehensive. Eriksen has ably analyzed many of the most serious forms of misdirected effort in current psychology. These may or may not be attributable to "soft" theory and research, as we have argued. Certainly the factors which contribute to their survival are wasteful of time and money and should be sought out and corrected, just as surely must we seek out and promote whatever will encourage efficient and really usable research. The factors cited as potential new threats to an already overloaded literature are the very same factors which if properly utilized, might lead to impressive new psychological advances. With so much potentially in our grasp, and with so very much more which needs accomplishing, every effort to make optimal use of our resources is vitally important.

Index